Blackness in Mexico

New World Diasporas

UNIVERSITY PRESS OF FLORIDA

Florida A&M University, Tallahassee
Florida Atlantic University, Boca Raton
Florida Gulf Coast University, Ft. Myers
Florida International University, Miami
Florida State University, Tallahassee
New College of Florida, Sarasota
University of Central Florida, Orlando
University of Florida, Gainesville
University of North Florida, Jacksonville
University of South Florida, Tampa
University of West Florida, Pensacola

BLACKNESS IN MEXICO

Afro-Mexican Recognition and the Production
of Citizenship in the Costa Chica

ANTHONY RUSSELL JERRY

University Press of Florida
Gainesville · Tallahassee · Tampa · Boca Raton
Pensacola · Orlando · Miami · Jacksonville · Ft. Myers · Sarasota

Publication of this work made possible by a Sustaining the Humanities through the American
Rescue Plan grant from the National Endowment for the Humanities.

28 27 26 25 24 23   6 5 4 3 2 1

Library of Congress Cataloging-in-Publication Data
Names: Jerry, Anthony Russell, author.
Title: Blackness in Mexico : Afro-Mexican recognition and the production of
    citizenship in the Costa Chica / Anthony Russell Jerry.
Description: First. | Gainesville : University Press of Florida, [2023] |
    Series: New world diasporas | Includes bibliographical references and
    index. | Summary: "This book delves into the ongoing movement toward
    recognizing Black Mexicans as a cultural group within the nation,
    focusing on this process in the Costa Chica region in order to explore
    the relational aspects of citizenship and the place of Black people in
    how modern citizenship is imagined"— Provided by publisher.
Identifiers: LCCN 2022051318 (print) | LCCN 2022051319 (ebook) | ISBN
    9780813069661 (hardback) | ISBN 9780813080123 (paperback) | ISBN
    9780813070438 (pdf) | ISBN 9780813072814 (ebook)
Subjects: LCSH: Black people—Race identity—Mexico—Costa Chica. |
    Citizenship—Mexico—Costa Chica—History. | Black people—Mexico—Costa
    Chica—History. | Black people—Mexico—Costa Chica—Social conditions.
    | Costa Chica (Mexico)—Race relations—History. | BISAC: SOCIAL SCIENCE
    / Anthropology / Cultural & Social | SOCIAL SCIENCE / Ethnic Studies /
    American / Hispanic American Studies
Classification: LCC F1392.B55 J47 2023 (print) | LCC F1392.B55 (ebook) |
    DDC 305.896072—dc23/eng/20221104
LC record available at https://lccn.loc.gov/2022051318
LC ebook record available at https://lccn.loc.gov/2022051319

The University Press of Florida is the scholarly publishing agency for the State University System
of Florida, comprising Florida A&M University, Florida Atlantic University, Florida Gulf Coast
University, Florida International University, Florida State University, New College of Florida,
University of Central Florida, University of Florida, University of North Florida, University of
South Florida, and University of West Florida.

University Press of Florida
2046 NE Waldo Road
Suite 2100
Gainesville, FL 32609
http://upress.ufl.edu

For Mari, Issak, and Miles

Contents

Illustrations

Map

Figures

Figures follow page 82.

Acknowledgments

Any list of acknowledgments for those responsible for the completion of this book would be incomplete. However, there are several people who have been instrumental to the completion of this project and therefore must be acknowledged directly. First I would like to acknowledge Mariana Palafox, Issak Jerry, and Miles Jerry, who have allowed me the space and time to pursue my work in Mexico. Without their support, this project would have been impossible. And I must acknowledge Loren Clay and her open heart, for which I am truly grateful. I would also like to acknowledge Bernardo Ramírez Ríos for being a willing thought partner and travel companion and for our countless discussions on Oaxaca. While not named directly in this book, his spirit animates many of the pages that follow. To the Blackness Unbound Collective, especially Ni'Ja Whitson, Vorris Nunly, Natasha McPherson, Joao Vargas, Dylan Rodríguez, Imani Kai Johnson, and Ayana Flewellen, for their willingness to create a community around Blackness at UC Riverside; a community from which I have benefited tremendously. I would also like to acknowledge Ramona Pérez and Jack Corbett for their introduction to Oaxaca and the Costa Chica region, as well as Alejandro Lugo for his continuous support and recognition of the need for a more robust theorizing around Blackness in Mexico. I must also recognize those in the Costa Chica who so willingly supported my work in the region, especially Lucila Mariche Magadán for her endless willingness to collaborate. Last, I would like to acknowledge the Fulbright García Robles Fellowship for their support of my research, as well as the Ford Foundation for a fellowship that helped me complete the very first draft of this book.

Introduction

Citizenship and Black Recognition in Mexico

In 2011, the Mexican government began to enact a methodology for officially recognizing Black Mexicans as an ethnic group. This methodology for recognizing Black Mexicans was conducted by the federal institution the Comisión Nacional para el Desarrollo de los Pueblos Indígenas (CDI) [the National Commission for the Development of Indigenous Communities], along with local branches of the Secretaría de Asuntos Indígenas (SAI) (now renamed the Secretaría de Asuntos Indígenas y Afromexicanos) [the Secretary of Indigenous and Afro-Mexican Affairs] to support the process of recognition at the state level. That same year, the United Nations, through resolution 64/169, proclaimed 2011 the "International Year for People of African Descent." In 2013, the UN would go even further, announcing resolution 68/237 and naming 2015–2024 as the "Decade for People of African Descent" (de la Fuente and Andrews 2018, 3). In 2011, during the Year for People of African Descent, the CDI and the SAI arranged several *consultas* (consultations/inquiries) in order to inform the African-descendant communities of the Costa Chica about the process of recognition and to gather information on the cultural repertoire of Black Mexicans within the region.

That year, the consultations were held in the administrative centers (what would be considered the Zócalo in Indigenous and Mestizo communities) in the Costa Chica towns of both Oaxaca and Guerrero. During the consultations, the townspeople were joined by local activists from the Costa Chica, a number of Mexican anthropologists and social scientists, as well as state and federal government officials for the ensuing discussions. For the most part, these discussions were presentations by both activists and government officials about the importance of official recognition and how it might impact the Black towns and their residents. On the part of the activists, the goal seemed to be the promotion of official constitutional recognition and the protections that such recognition might bring, both at the state and federal levels. For the government officials, the goal seemed more related to creating legitimacy in the eyes of the global community (Lara 2014). And for their part, the government officials used the opportunity to announce the project to the communities and then to arrange several follow-up visits (chapter 3) in order to begin the work of documenting the cultural elements that were imagined to be unique to the Black Mexican communities of the Costa Chica. On the part of the local townspeople, many seemed uninterested in the focus on legitimation through cultural and political recognition and were instead interested in how recognition might bring real material benefits to the communities, in the same way in which they understood Indigenous communities had benefited from a similar process decades earlier (Cunin and Hoffman 2014, xi; Lara 2014, 118).

The formal discussions about culture, political recognition, and the material needs of the communities usually lasted anywhere from one to two hours, with activists hanging around after the official event ended to talk with local townspeople about the related issues and to catch up with friends and family members from other parts of the region. The official conversations rarely involved deep discussion about slavery in Mexico, or the manner by which African descendants arrived in the Costa Chica, or racial discrimination, or the historic roles that Black people and Blackness had played in the production of the Mexican nation. However, at the less formal gatherings between locals and Black activists that would take place after the official meetings, activists and townspeople discussed these very issues as the activists attempted to inform local townspeople of the stakes involved in official recognition. It was at these meetings where I would get a sense of the disconnect between the activist agenda and the agenda of the state and federal governments. While the activists were interested in highlighting issues of racial discrimination and the continued impact of this discrimination on contemporary Black Mexicans (Hoffman 2014; Moreno Figueroa and Saldívar Tanaka 2016), the Mexican government was more interested in figuring out how to situate Black Mexicans, preferably as "Afro-Mexicans," into the contemporary multicultural landscape of the Mexican nation. For my part, it soon became clear that the broader recognition of Black Mexicans might not have anything to do with Black Mexicans. Rather, the government's intervention seemed more focused on managing the potential chaos associated with Black recognition and the potential threat that Black recognition posed to the general conception of Mexico as a nation of non-Black Mestizos. In this way, the project to recognize Black Mexicans as a multicultural ethnic group was/is partly an attempt to position the Costa Chica as a Black region, and the Black communities within the region in a way that functions as an extra-cultural space in relation to a normative White/Mestizo intra-cultural space (Wynter 1984, 41; Moreno Figueroa 2010). According to Mónica G. Moreno Figueroa (2010), the position of the Mestiza/o is not problematized enough, and therefore Mestizas/os naturally emerge "as a point of reference to speak of the 'other' and are considered, by others and themselves, as 'the' Mexicans" (391). Within this book, I argue that it is this now invisible and intuitive perception of the Mestiza/o as the point of reference for the recognition of the "other" that the demand for Black recognition necessarily calls attention to. Furthermore, I argue that restoring the balance created by this intuition of the Mestiza/o as "the Mexican" is a central focus animating the governmental project for the recognition of the "Afro-Mexican" as a cultural group. Through attempts to encapsulate Black Mexicans as a cultural group within the extra-cultural borders of the nation, the project for recognition is in itself a methodology of *mestizaje*, one that facilitates the continuation of the Mexican national project and reproduces the non-Black Mestizo as the archetypal Mexican citizen.

The 2015 Mexican inter-census counted 1,381,853 people of African descent in the country. This number represented 1.2 percent of the total national population (Perfil sociodemográfico de la población afrodescendiente en México, 2017). In 2020, perhaps due to a change in the phrasing of the questions on self-identification, which broadened the category to include a wider definition of Black identity, the count was seen to rise to 2.5 million residents (2 percent) (Censo de Población y Vivienda 2020 del Instituto Nacional de Estadística y Geografía [INEGI]). In general, African descendants are to be found in all states of the nation, with the lowest numbers found in the states of Durango, Zacatecas, Aguascalientes, Nayarit, Colima, and Tlaxcala, all of which reported less than 1,000 individuals in 2015 (INEGI 2015). According to the 2015 inter-census, the highest concentrations of African descendants were to be found in the states of Guerrero (229,514), Oaxaca (196, 213), Veracruz (266,163), and Mexico (304,274). This number accounted for 6.5, 4.95, 3.28, and 1.88 percent of the total state populations respectively. This means that, according to the census records, at least 40 percent of Mexico's African descendants resided in the Costa Chica in 2015. However, the accuracy of this number depends on several issues related to the difficulties with counting African descendants in the region (Telles and PERLA 2014; Villareal 2010; Saldívar and Walsh 2014), such as Black Mexicans' unwillingness to self-identify as African descendant due to the continued stigma associated with being Black in Mexico (Moreno Figueroa and Saldívar Tanaka 2016) and the confusion related to the numerous labels associated with Blackness in Mexico (Sue 2010, 2013; Hoffman 2014), as well as the geographic location of the respondents. For example, urban residents often resist racial identification, while rural residents show a stronger racial identification based on Blackness (Jones 2013). The 2020 census shows that the African-descendant population in Mexico is also highly concentrated within certain counties (*municipios*) within the states in which they reside. According to scholars, up to 6 percent of Mexico's Black population is concentrated in the Costa Chica (Vinson and Vaughn 2004; Jones 2013). Blackness in Mexico has widely been connected to the state of Veracruz, rather than the Pacific coast, where Blackness and Black people are popularly perceived within the context of the Caribbean (Jones 2013; Rinaudo 2014).

When I arrived in the Costa Chica to conduct long-term research in 2011, I found that the popular paradigms for understanding the historical and present African-descendant experience in other regions of Latin America were insufficient for understanding the current situation in which Black Mexicans found themselves (Hoffman 2014). For Black Mexicans in the Costa Chica, the context in which they imagine their own Blackness includes the local and the national, as rural locals' understandings of Blackness have yet to rely heavily on the notion of a Black diaspora. Wynter (2005) explains that the physical and discursive interaction between Black movements in the West (United States, West Africa, Caribbean) allowed for a common language to develop around the Black experience. The development of this common language required both physical movement as well as the movement of ideas and experiences. Due to the rural nature and limited mobility of Black Mexicans,[1] the perception of a common experience between global Black communities has yet to develop among rural Black Mexicans, and therefore the notion of diaspora has become less important in local everyday representations of a Black identity (Hoffman and Pascal 2006; Sue 2010). Sue argues that "the diaspora framing glosses over important differences within African-origin populations and imposes a broad analytic category that is at odds with certain social realities such as the case of individuals of African descent who feel little or no connection to Africa" or a strong global Black consciousness (2010, 290). However, from the perspective of the nation, and from the perspective of those non-Black Mestizos perceived as a metonym for Mexicanness (Williams 1989; Hernández Cuevas 2004; Moreno Figueroa 2010; Sue 2013; Telles and PERLA 2014), Blackness is definitely contextualized through the contexts of diaspora and racial difference and is rarely contextualized within the frames of the local and the national. This allows for the homogenization of the category "Black Mexican," by which the category of "White/Mestizo" (and Indigenous) is continually differentiated (see Wynter 1979, 152). This sets up a key tension between the state (and those who are allowed to represent/embody the state) and Black Mexican communities. This also sets up the potential for a failure of recognition (Taylor 1994, 35) of Black Mexican representations of self, as there has yet to develop a common representation of Blackness shared between Black and non-Black Mexicans.

Saldívar and Walsh argue that the 2010 census demonstrated that some 20 million Mexicans recognized some connection to Indigenous culture and that it is much more common for Mexicans to consider themselves carriers of Indigenous culture rather than members of an Indigenous group (2014, 470–71). This generic connection to Indigeneity through culture in Mexico is allowable to Mestizos because the nation is used as a common frame for both Indigeneity and Mestizoness (Saldívar and Walsh 2014). The same cannot be said for Black Mexicans whose difference continues to be perceived primarily through the lens of race (even when represented within the context of culture). Therefore, Black Mexicans' claims to Mexicanness are met with suspicion as their existence is perceived as always stemming from beyond the nation.

After realizing that the more popular paradigms of diaspora and culture were insufficient for understanding the Black Mexican situation in 2011 (Hoffman and Pascal 2006, 2014; Sue 2010), I considered an analysis that attempted to center Blackness and the Black Mexican experience as foundational to the production of the Mexican nation (and the ideal Mexican citizen/subject) rather than an analysis focused on Black communities as beyond the nation and as marginal by-products of the process of national consolidation that began in the late eighteenth and early nineteenth centuries and continues into the present. That is simply to say that I began asking the question of what role a Black subject position, if not Blackness explicitly, plays in the production of Mexicanness, as well as the reproduction of the ideal Mexican type: the Mestizo (Moreno Figueroa 2010). Several scholars have argued that an analysis of Latin America has long divided the region into two different paradigms: Afro-Latin American nations and Indo-Latin American nations (Villareal 2010; Sue 2010; Telles and PERLA

2014). Villareal, for example, argues that "experts on Latin American race relations often distinguish between countries in the region with a large population of African descent, where racial categories map onto a black-white continuum, and countries in which the primary distinction is between the indigenous population and the mestizo or mixed-race majority" (2010, 653). In these paradigms, Afro-Latin America is perceived to encompass primarily the Caribbean region and Brazil, while Indo-Latin America is seen to include Mexico, most of Central America, and the Andean countries (Villareal 2010, 653). One outcome of this division has meant that research on the "Indo-Latin American" countries has relied heavily on a Spanish/Indigenous divide to make sense of race and racial/ethnic relations within these countries (Sue 2013). This reliance on the Spanish/Indigenous divide has been responsible for what Hoffman (2014) refers to as the relatively impoverished theoretical basis for research studying Black populations in Mexico (86).

Heidi Carolyn Feldman (2012), reacting to the lack of visibility of Black communities through the Spanish/Indigenous divide of the Indo-Latin America paradigm, calls for a focus on what she labels the "black Pacific" (see also Whitten and Torres 1998). Feldman argues that Black communities in the Pacific may not fit into classic diaspora analyses such as the Black Atlantic model (Gilroy 1993), and that compared to Black Atlantic cultures such as Cuba and Brazil, Black Pacific communities can have few or no visible surviving African-descended cultural forms and therefore appear not to be "very African" in Herskovits's terms (2012, 45). Part of the issue here is that through an analysis of exclusion, Black communities in Latin America have regularly been compared to each other rather than through an analysis that considers Black communities and Black people in relation to the other non-Black communities and citizens within the countries in which they reside. The question of how we approach a regional entity such as the "Black Pacific" might also be problematic, as it assumes a paradigm borrowed from the regional approach of the Black Atlantic, and therefore may be overdetermined by the general conceptualization of that which it intends to complicate: the Black Atlantic diasporic paradigm. A more productive approach might be to simply ask, how do we discuss and make sense of the Black experience in the Pacific without privileging a Spanish/Indigenous divide? I believe this approach must include a focus on the relational nature of citizenship, not simply in its juridical aspect but in its more ideological and theoretical conceptualization as a broader set of social relations and form of subject making.

Both the diaspora and creolization paradigms common to an analysis of African descendants in Latin America embrace the issues of culture and cultural development in order to situate the notion of Blackness and Black people within the Americas. However, through the lens of culture, both paradigms view African descendants and the by-product of the Black experience in the Americas as an experience "apart," invoking the notion of exclusion and difference as a defining component of the historic Black experience, as well as a powerful (if not the privileged) component of the contemporary experience of, and identification with, Blackness throughout the region. The project of Black recognition, both as an official government-supported project and as a more grassroots community activist project within Mexico, has also found itself vacillating between these two poles. The government approach to the project of Black recognition within Mexico has attempted to makes sense of Blackness within the nation through the culturally accepted methodology of mestizaje, such as is evident in the cultural program and promotional campaign to rebrand the many African descendants within Mexico as Mexico's "third root" (*la tercera raíz*),[2] originally initiated by Guillermo Bonfil Batalla in the 1980s (Hoffman 2014, 93).

In 2011, the Mexican government relied on the CDI and the SAI to document what they considered to be a unique Black culture in the Costa Chica region. Part of this project relied on the conceptualization of Black communities as isolated from the broader nation. This perceived isolation and exclusion fit neatly within the historical conceptualization and production of the state of Oaxaca, and the broader southern region of the country (Mexico's "Indian South"), as being divided into several discrete cultural regions. This perception of geographic and social isolation also worked to support the belief that there could, in fact, exist a unique Black culture within the Costa Chica region. In the state of Oaxaca, the CDI partnered with the SAI to help implement the methodologies to create the official state and federally recognized ethnic group of Afro-Mexicanos. With the help of the SAI, the CDI organized a number of consultas geared at literally defining and documenting Black culture and setting a number of cultural parameters to geographically locate and ideologically situate the Black communities of the Costa Chica within Oaxaca's preexisting cultural cartography as well as the broader national landscape. The CDI's first general objective was "reconocer mediante un proceso de consulta a las comunidades de los pueblos afrodescendientes de Mexico y sus principales características" (recognition through a process of consultation with the communities of African-descendant peoples of Mexico and their principal characteristics).[3] The first step in this process was to present the methodology of the consultas to several politically active representatives of the African-descendant communities. At the first meeting in Jamiltepec, Oaxaca, CDI employees unveiled the plan to an audience of about forty individuals representing several Black towns, myself, and employees of the CDI and SAI. Taking its methodology directly from the earlier recognition process of Indigenous communities, the plan overlooked key racial dynamics that have historically shaped and defined Mexico's Black population. It excluded the activists and community members from these towns, as a matter of either institutional or social practice, from consultation on and collaboration in developing the methodology for the location as well as general recognition of the Pueblos Afrodescendientes (African-descendant towns/communities). The recognition of this exclusion on the part of the community representatives generated a lot of tension among the participants. Drafted by CDI representatives in Mexico's capital, the plan framed the process of recognition through the lens of the Mexican state's approach to multiculturalism and imposed a methodology, as well as a general racial and ethnic conception, on the Black communities. In Harris's terms, this constitutes a type of Whiteness as property that is "constituted through the reification of expectations in the continued right of white-dominated institutions to control the legal meaning of group identity" (1993, 1761). This is a concrete example of how mestizaje is transformed from ideology to methodology, as the Mexican ideology of mestizaje must be continually applied through real-world practice in order to maintain its hegemony over the other.

Local community members and activists were under the impression that this first meeting was to have been a "brainstorming activity," while the CDI expected that the "professionals" would present the plan, which would then naturally get ratified by the grateful representatives of the Black communities in attendance. However, the activist and community representatives appeared to be more aware than the government officials of the circumstances responsible for their own historical marginalization (see Trouillot 1984). After several hours, Black activists recognized that many of the elements within the proposed consultas, elements based on an intuitive belief in Africanisms related to traditional subsistence activities and the production of traditional cultural wares, were not relevant or simply excluded more important elements of the Black experience within Costeño (literally "coastal," but popularly referencing "racially Black") communities (Wade 2005). The approach taken by the CDI represents what Escobar (2008) and Restrepo (2002) refer to as the ethnicization of Black identity.

Escobar (2008) argues that cultural conflicts are often a reflection of ontological differences (14). This is a key issue in the project for Black Mexican recognition as employed by the CDI. In 2011, the CDI arrived to the consultation with an understanding of Black communities, and therefore Black people, that was not necessarily shared by the Black communities. And at the time, the representatives of the Black communities did not necessarily see their difference as a reflection of cultural differences. Rather, the activists and townspeople spoke of exclusion, racial discrimination, and a lack of resources. Despite the tensions between the two groups, I was left with the feeling, based on the reactions of the CDI representatives at the consultations, that the material was not going to change, as the "professionals" ultimately knew better.[4] The activists were quickly learning that government recognition in the form of multicultural recognition can be a double-edged sword and can often be conceived of in a way that suits federal agendas over the actual grassroots agendas of local communities (see Hale 1997, 2005; Postero 2007).

To be clear, I do not believe there to be, or have been, some type of heinous plot against the recognition of African-descendant communities on their own terms by the CDI. Rather, the CDI's presentation of its agenda to the Black communities was simply based on a number of preexisting logics and intuitions, or perhaps the collective unconscious (Fanon 2008; Hook 2004) that informs modern liberal governance, multiculturalism, race, and ethnicity, and the way that these logics are put to work to accomplish the larger state agenda. These logics, referred to as mestizaje logics by Moreno Figueroa (2010) in the context of Mexico, and more broadly theorized as "imperial debris" by Stoler (2008) and more pointedly the "afterlife of Slavery" by Hartman (2006), are an inheritance of the same intuitions that were part and parcel of the colonial administrative machine in Latin America. These logics were historically used to produce methodologies that were conceived, quite heinously, to have well-thought-out and intentional effects on Black communities as an overall mechanism for the production of White privilege and later the Mestizo state. It is the weight of this inheritance that Black communities in Mexico must carry through the process of official recognition. Contemporaneously, these intuitions work in very real ways to reproduce citizens in manners that maintain the status quo. In these subtle ways, the racial logics and legacies of colonialism continue to haunt current political mobilizations around difference.

While the focus on culture, wherever situated between the poles of creolization and diaspora, helps politically situate the many Black

communities within the nation in terms of mestizaje and multiculturalism, it ultimately reduces Blackness to a project of identity politics based on
difference, rather than legitimating Black Mexicans' claims to the nation.
Wade argues that "the maintenance of a racial hegemony happens through
the complex articulation of specific projects which are not necessarily coherently or intentionally racist or anti-immigrant or nationalist" (2001,
847). The recognition of Black people in Mexico based on the conception of
cultural difference does little to recognize the entanglements of Blackness
with Whiteness/Mestizoness, and the historic processes responsible for the
production of Black communities within the nation; rather, it reinforces
the racial hegemony of mestizaje. I argue that the lens of citizenship—that
is, the focus on citizenship as a theoretical notion and modern form of
subjectivization by and through the nation—holds the potential to offer a
powerful tool, beyond the above-mentioned poles and the ensuing problematic of identity politics, to help disentangle the many relationships that
rely on Blackness as a foundational oppositional condition by which the
modern citizen/subject, always intuitively read as non-Black within Mexico
and beyond, is allowed to exist.[5]

My intention with this book is to focus on the relational aspects of citizenship and the productive power of this relationship in order to think
about the present, as well as historic, experience of Blackness in the Americas. Sue (2010) explains that while many studies have focused on Blackness
in "Afro-Latin American countries, less research has been conducted on
how blackness functions (and the function of blackness) in mestizo American countries" (273). She goes on to argue that the Mestizo/Indigenous
divide leaves no conceptual room to explore the issue of Blackness within
these countries (2010, 273; Villareal 2010). The fact that the Mestizo/Indig-
enous paradigm has allowed for "Black" and "Mexican" to be perceived as
mutually exclusive (Sue 2010) should not allow us to imagine that a Black
subject position plays no role in the conceptualization of Mexicanness
(in both the Mestizo and Indigenous forms). My goal here is not only to
elaborate on the Black experience in Mexico but also to highlight the role
that Blackness, and a Black subject position, continues to play in the general conceptualization of citizenship and the reproduction of what Sylvia
Wynter (2003) refers to as the "norm-subject" or the ideal citizen type in
Mexico.

Broadly speaking, most of the work about Black Mexico has focused
on the history of colonial African descendants, discussions of diaspora, or
the impacts of the racial paradigm of mestizaje (that is, "race" and cultural

mixing) on the production of Black Mexican identities. Modern anthropological research on Afro-Mexicans began in the 1940s and 1950s with the pioneering Mexican anthropologist Gonzalo Aguirre Beltrán. While his work did much to make Black communities in the Costa Chica visible to social scientists, Aguirre Beltrán's work, much like the work of the CDI outlined in chapter 3, ultimately focused on outlining the cultural attributes, or lack thereof, of Black Mexicans and authenticating difference by attempting to pinpoint specific African survivals. This work acted to reify mestizaje as the prevailing racial paradigm of the postrevolutionary nation through Aguirre Beltrán's findings of a lack of African "authenticity." Ben Vinson III (2005) recognizes the development of a three-track system of research focusing on the Black experience in Mexico. Vinson explains that, on one track, many Mexican scholars have pursued the research path initially laid out by Aguirre Beltrán, focusing on how Blackness fits into the larger national discourse of mestizaje (García Orozco 2010; Diaz Pérez 1995). On another track, argues Vinson, international scholars (and some Mexicans) have focused on the Mexican case to better understand processes of slavery, freedom, and Blackness, within a broader global context. Last, Vinson sees the third track pursued by both Mexican and international scholars as attempting to understand the intricacies of Mexican colonial and nation-state hierarchies and determining how Blackness fits within such social organization schemes (2005, 5–6). I see my own work falling broadly into this last track, as I am looking to understand not only how Blackness fits into colonial and national-state hierarchies, but also how a Black subject position, and by extension Blackness and Black people, continues to be put to work for the facilitation and reproduction of such hierarchies. Scholars such as Herman L. Bennett, Ben Vinson III, and Nicole von Germeten have been important for uncovering historical accounts of the colonial Black experience and the roles available for Blackness in colonial Mexico. On the other hand, ethnographic work from scholars such as Laura A. Lewis and Bobby Vaughn detail how the racial paradigm of mestizaje, racial discrimination, as well as the potential for the development of diasporic identities among Afro-Mexicans, have shaped Black identities. These works have had a considerable impact on our knowledge of Black communities within Mexico and have done much to highlight the existence of anti-Black discrimination, racial stereotypes, and the differing social contexts in which Black Mexicans may or may not identify as "Black/Negro." However, by focusing on the construction of an exclusive Black identity (or lack thereof), these works often miss the ways that an "absent presence" (Wynter 2005) of a Black subject position in Mexico continues to act as a type of dark matter (chapter 2) by which non-Black subject positions and identities are continually reproduced within and through the mestizaje paradigm that frames the social and political relations of the modern Mexican nation.

Telles and Garcia argue that "by blurring racial divisions and denying racism, mestizaje ideologies undermine the formation of black and indigenous identities that are needed to sustain effective social movements for combating persistent social and cultural exclusion" (Telles and Garcia 2013, 132; Hanchard 1994; Telles 2004; Yashar 2005; Paschel 2016). This logic of mestizaje has also been perceived as limiting the production of Black subjects and Black subjectivities. I argue that the exclusionary and anti-Black nature of mestizaje continued to produce these subjects and subjectivities, even while limiting the social expression of Black identities. This is one of the reasons an exclusive focus on identity can be dangerous, as privileging identity as the unit of analysis overlooks the ways in which even resistance to Black identities can be predicated on an unseen but always present Black subject position in Mexico. By focusing too sharply on identity, it is possible to interpret the process of Black recognition in Mexico as an outcome of Black identity, rather than understanding Black identity (as well as other identities) as partly a political outcome of the process of Black recognition (Fields 1990, 2003; Paschel 2016).

An enduring Black subject position might be perceived as part of the social material by which all identities are formed (Appiah 1994, 154) in Mexico. Williams argues that "cultural anthropologists have become increasingly involved in an effort to define ethnicity, to explore the processes involved in the formation of categorical identities, and to disclose their meaning for the political and economic dimensions of social organization" (1989, 401). While identity studies have had a major impact in anthropology and the understanding of "new social movements" and "new political subjects" (Escobar 2008, 201; Paschel 2016; Huerta 2019, 2021), my goal here is not to define a Black ethnic identity or to explore the formation of a categorical Black Mexican cultural/political identity. Rather, I am interested in understanding how the production (and reproduction) of a Black subject position in Mexican society continued to endure (Andrews 2004), even as the public and popular recognition of Black people faded. Furthermore, I am interested in what role this subject position plays in the contemporary efforts to recognize Black Mexicans as well as contemporary reproductions of the Mexican nation and the Mestizo as non-Black. Williams explains that "the ethnic aspect of identity formation, like the other categorical aspects of any identity formation process, must be understood in relation to the societal production of enduring categorical distinctions and not simply in terms of individuals adopting and 'shedding' particular manifestations of those categorical identities" (1989, 428; Beaucage 1994; Escobar 2008). This relational approach outlined by Williams is key to my approach to the process of Black recognition in Mexico. A focus on the process of identity construction and Black agency (see de la Fuente and Andrews 2018, 12) is incomplete without an analysis of the role that a Black subject position plays in the broader frame of social relations within Mexico and how it is that that frame ultimately constitutes what are perceived as possible strategies for identity construction and individual and group agency.

According to Vinson, the discussion of Black Mexicans has followed the trajectory of the political development of the nation (2005, 1). This insight suggests that the conversation about Blackness in Mexico from the colonial moment to the multicultural present has been less about centering Blackness within the context of Mexico, and more about fitting Black people into a preexisting political framework that supports popular perceptions of the nation. Wade argues that "Indigenous and black minorities' growing consciousness of their own identity and position does not take place only from the bottom up, as it were" (2010, 115; see also Paschel 2016, 13). Rather, this process, argues Wade, is strongly mediated by a variety of non-Indigenous (and I would argue non-Black) people and institutions, which complicate any simple divide between grassroots, ethnic social movements and "the dominant society" (2010, 115). This argument suggests that the development of a Black identity must also contend with the ways in which non-Blacks are willing and able (or not) to engage with the historical and political development of a Black subject position by which their own identities have historically, although implicitly, been shaped. In Mexico, a huge majority of non-Black people are involved in and impacted by the official process of Black recognition. This necessarily means that the form of difference articulated by Black Mexicans and the constructions of Black Mexican identities has to be accepted (and is often conceived) by non-Black Mexicans who are also invested in the process of reproducing national (racial or otherwise) subjects. In Mexico, this process is deeply impacted by the national project of mestizaje, which has been so strong that it demands that the articulation of Black difference come in the form of cultural difference rather than an explicit racial difference.

According to Wade, Indigenous organizing in Latin America has been more successful than Black organizing (2010, 116). Wade believes that the reason for this has to do with "the historical institutionalisation of indigenous identity, which gave indigenous people a conceptual, political and often a territorial basis . . . on which to organise themselves" (116). The historical institutionalization of Indigenous identity has also allowed for the ideal citizen in Mexico to situate the place of Indigeneity into their own identities. This has allowed the ideal citizen to make claims to Indigeneity while simultaneously allowing Indigenous communities to make claims to both the nation and citizenship through the recognition of the historic location of an Indigenous subject position within the foundation of the nation. Black people in Mexico cannot rely on this historical institutionalization to make similar claims to the nation or to the ideal citizen (Wade 2010). I argue that the historic institutionalization of Indigeneity, and the rhetorical exclusion of Blackness from the Mexican narrative (Hernández Cuevas 2004), creates a situation in which the recognition of Black Mexicans must always be conducted in a way that does not disrupt the historic understanding of the ideal citizen as a unique mix of Spanish and Indigenous (Mestizo) and always non-Black. Where Black organizing has been most successful, it has required that Blackness be perceived as Indigenous-like (Wade 2005; Anderson 2007, 2009; Hooker 2005, 2009, 137–38; Ng'weno 2007, 2012; Restrepo 2002; Wade 1995). However, in general, the push for African-descendant rights in Latin America has been undermined by a refusal to recognize continuing racial inequality (Wade 2010; Hooker 2009; Moreno Figueroa and Saldívar Tanaka 2016) and the role that Black marginalization has played in the making and remaking of the nation.

Research on Blackness and Indigeneity in Latin America often failed to grasp the ways that Indigenous and Black groups were perpetually reconstituted and reimagined (Wade 2010, 60). My interests here are in the power dynamic involved in this process of reimagination and reconstitution, the investments that all citizens have in this process, and the productive power associated with this process as it relates to non-Blacks. That is, how non-Black Mexicans attempt to control this process as a method for maintaining an accepted social order. In this way, we can question the incentives that non-Black Mexicans continue to have for controlling the process of political and public self-making limitedly available to Black people. This process is not simply about reproducing Black people but maintaining the means of representation to reproduce the ideal Mexican, as well as the nation, as non-Black. As Harris argues, "definition is so often a central part of domination" (1993, 1763). The process of recognition underway in Mexico, then, as demonstrated by the CDI's approach discussed earlier and more in depth in chapter 3, is partly a strategy to restore the order of ontological Sameness and Difference (Wynter 1984, 41) and manage the social and political chaos created by the desire for Black Mexican recognition and self-representation.

Saldívar argues that even as our understanding of racialization in Mexico continues to expand, "studies continue to use the 'ethnic paradigm' in their analysis and explanations and fail to recognize the 'racial politics of culture' at work in Mexico" (2014, 104). The explicit recognition of racialization and racial discrimination in Mexico will, according to Saldívar, also require that we create theoretical and methodological tools for understanding these processes as "fundamental social forms of domination in Mexico" (103). I argue that these tools must also break away from the intuitions of mestizaje (Jerry 2021) and should not be considered as catchalls for understanding racial discrimination. Rather, these tools should be applicable to the different colonial tracings (Mallon 2011) unique to the positions of Indigeneity and Blackness (de la Fuente and Andrews 2018, 18) (as well as other racial and gendered positions) in Mexico and the differing roles that these positions have historically played in producing and reproducing the nation and the ideal subject. Wilderson argues that Black people have been historically burdened by "the ruse of analogy," which mystifies rather than clarifies Black suffering (2020, 41). Focusing on the specific role that the Black subject position continues to play in the social relations around race in Mexico will hopefully help avoid the analogizing of the Black experience with that of the Indigenous, or other marginalized groups, within Latin America.

African descendants in Mexico are currently being given form according to the multicultural values of the West, producing what is quickly becoming accepted as the "Afro-Mexican." According to Oliver, "within the colonial logic, the struggle for mutual recognition becomes part and parcel of the pathology of colonialism" (2004, 6). This can be seen to be true of the postcolonial moment, as well, as the project of Black recognition in Mexico continues to be motivated by the same colonial logic, now manifested as what Moreno Figueroa discusses as "mestizaje logics" (2010, 389), that gave birth to the social and political relations in which the project currently exists. The Mexican government's project of recognition is thus less about bringing African descendants into a "world of meaning" (Oliver 2004; Wilderson 2020) based upon their own values. Rather, the government's project is to hold in abeyance the conflict and the potential crisis of Whiteness (and ultimately citizenship) that the former slave's desire for a sense of their own self-worth could initiate (Oliver 2004). In this book, I argue that the government approach to Black Mexican recognition demonstrates that the management of this conflict requires that the Black subject remain subjected to Whiteness/Mestizoness as the means for reproducing Whiteness/Mestizoness and the current multicultural nation.

A focus on citizenship as a relational process, as well as one of producing national subjects, helps address the many racial entanglements that continue to produce the privileged Mexican "citizen," as well as the few socially acceptable strategies available for the recognition of Blackness as both a physical and cultural form. My work here is an attempt to go beyond previous approaches by asking how the current political project of Black recognition within Mexico can help understand the ways that race, and specifically Blackness, continue to be a foundational component of the production of modern citizenship. More specifically, this book asks how Blackness continues to be harnessed as a means of producing the nation and the national subject in its many, yet always intertwined, forms.

A Note on the People and Places of the Costa Chica

As of the writing of this book, there was yet to exist an official geography of Blackness in Mexico. While there have been several regions, states, and municipalities recognized as containing significant populations of Afrodescendientes (African descendants), much of this work being done through the official Mexican census and Mexican anthropologists as well as the less official work of the many Black mutual aid and political organizations within the country, the production and recognition of these spaces as a part of the broader cultural geography of Blackness in Mexico, continues to be underway. The lack of an official geography has meant that in some cases the local definition of spaces and places as Black towns, or *Pueblos Negros*, continues to be contested by many. My experience supports my opinion that this is also the case within the Costa Chica region. This is partly due to the fact that while many towns in the Costa Chica may be majority Black or African descendant, there are many Indigenous and Mestizos who have deep roots in the communities and continue to lay claim to the towns and the broader region as their own (see Lewis 2000, 2001). My use of the terms "Black towns," "Black region," or "Pueblos Negros" is not meant to overlook the legitimate historical and cultural attachments that non-Black Mexicans have to the region. Rather, I am using the terms to highlight the ways in which local Black activists have attempted to lay claim to the region as part of the process of official Black recognition, as well as the broader racial politics within the region that have required the development of a racial/cultural geography to legitimate the claims and being of Black Mexicans as part of this project of recognition.

Within this emerging racial/cultural geography in the Costa Chica, local activists have been working for more than thirty years (Huerta 2019, 2021) through a number of different mutual aid organizations to develop a dialogue around Blackness and to politically organize local communities in order to engage the local, state, and federal governments as a way of addressing the material needs of Black communities in the region. This has meant that local activists, mutual aid organizations, and everyday residents often share different understandings of the political stakes involved in the project for recognition, as well as the emerging strategies and definitions of Blackness that have animated the political movement for Black recognition in the region. Within this book, I have tried to highlight a variety of voices within this project, both activist and non-activist, the explicitly political and the mundane, as well as the experiences of the many Black men and women who are engaged in and impacted by the project of Black recognition.

While I have tried to attend to a variety of experiences of Black Mexicans within the book, the main focus here is on the existence of a general Black subject position, the impact of this unrecognized or invisible subject position on Mexican social relations, and the ways that this Black subject position frames the possibilities of the broader project for Black recognition. For this reason, this book does not attempt to offer a comprehensive theory or analysis of gender and gender relations at work within local relations between Black Mexicans in the Costa Chica. Kirin Asher's work (2009) on the politics involved around Black constitutional recognition in Colombia, for example, demonstrates the impacts that development projects within Colombia's Plan Pacífico have had on gender roles and relations within Black communities and the effects of these changing relations on the political organizing around Blackness in Colombia's Pacific Chocó region and beyond. Asher shows how development in the region focused mostly on providing economic opportunities in the broader labor market for Black men, impacted Black women and motivated these women to develop strategies to articulate their own needs and the unique experiences associated with being Black women in Colombia. Addressing the specific needs of Black Colombian women caused tensions within the broader male-dominated Black movement and was ultimately responsible for the development of

Black women as a political category and specific political subjects within the broader Black Colombian movement.

June Nash (2003) demonstrates the ways that similar economic development strategies in Mexico positioned Indigenous women within the domestic sphere and limited the economic opportunities available for women up until the neoliberal turn. However, during this turn, women who had been positioned within the domestic sphere as "keepers of Indigenous culture" were allowed new opportunities in the public sphere as the intuitive relationship between Indigenous women and culture positioned them to take advantage of the neoliberal commodification of culture through a developing framework of multiculturalism in Mexico. Similar to the example discussed by Asher (2009), the tensions involved with changing gender roles at this moment were also seen to be responsible for the articulation of Indigenous women as a political category, and the development of the "Indigenous Woman" as a unique political subject.

I am unaware of a comprehensive gender analysis such as that provided by Asher or Nash with regard to gender relations within the Black Mexican movement for recognition. However, Huerta (2019, 2020) does discuss the emergence of the Black Mexican woman as a specific political subject based on experiences of vulnerability that are specific to Black women in Mexico. Huerta (2021) argues that Black Mexican women have looked toward a US Black feminism in order to construct an Afro-Mexican Black feminism that has developed partly because Black Mexican women have realized the ways in which they are excluded from earlier versions of both Mexican and global feminisms (106). Huerta sees this recognition of the specificities associated with being a Black woman in Mexico as being responsible for the emergence of Black Mexican women as political subjects unto themselves (106). Huerta's work addresses social and cultural experiences of Black women within Black Mexican communities, economic and educational disparities between men and women, and the experience of domestic and structural violence and vulnerability.

Part of the issue here, according to Huerta, is that Black women have been historically viewed, both inside and outside of Black communities, as sexually available. The perception that Black women are sexually available (Huerta 2021, 113) is part of the broader historical positioning of Black women in Mexico, as demonstrated by B. Christine Arce's (2017) discussion of the conceptualization of the Mexican Mulata. Speaking of the popular imagination of the Mexican Mulata, Arce explains that "she is a beautiful mulata, possessor of an intense gaze that renders those men who look at her impotent to her charms. She lives on the edge of town and mysteriously prepares potions that have miraculous effects on her patients" (2017, 3). This popular notion of the hypersexuality of the Mexican Mulata, and Black Mexican women in general, contributes to common perceptions of Black Mexican women as always sexual and sexually available, and in turn contributes to the vulnerability of Black Mexican women. As Arce argues, when Black women are not seen through the lens of hypersexuality, then they are often pushed to the margins of existence.

Huerta's work also demonstrates the ways in which a recognition of the specificities of Black Mexican women's experiences has motivated Black women to reimagine their role in the Black movement in the Costa Chica. Huerta explains that until 2016, within the Encuentros de los Pueblos Negros, a biannual event bringing together local and international activists in the Costa Chica, Black Mexican women played a "traditional" role in the political meetings in the area, tending to the more "logistical" aspects of the meetings (2021, 194). However, she observed that in 2016 women began to articulate their own needs and experiences within the space of the political meetings and organizations. Ultimately, according to Huerta, Black women began calling for a common platform to address the gendered aspects of the movement (116). This has also meant that Black women in the Costa Chica are playing a bigger role in the contemporary production of Black material culture in the region. According to Huerta, Black women are now practicing versions of the cultural dances that have traditionally been practiced by men, such as La Danza de los Diablos (119). Huerta discusses this process as a type of hacking (120, note 23), in which women are inserting themselves into political and cultural structures. More than this hacking, women in the region are also engaging in the production of "African-inspired" dances as a way of stepping outside male-dominated cultural practices.

The long-term impacts of the push for Black recognition on gender relations within the communities of the Costa Chica and how these impacts will influence the development of new gendered Black Mexican subjects remains to be seen. While this book does not offer a comprehensive analysis or theoretical framework for focusing on the impacts of the project for official recognition on the gender relations within the Black communities of the Costa Chica, I have attempted to include both men and women as collaborators within this project. This has hopefully allowed me to present an ethnography of the process of Black recognition that resonates with the Black men and women with whom I work(ed) in the region.

Chapter Outline

While I use this ethnography to paint a picture of the places and people of the Costa Chica region, my main focus is on the process by which African descendants in Mexico are being interpellated as Afro-Mexican, and more broadly as Mexico's next officially recognized group of multicultural citizens, by the Mexican government and the ways in which this process relies on a type of subjectivization on the part of both African and non-African descendants. This process also relies on the tried-and-true strategies for cultural recognition previously developed by the Mexican government, in consultation and collaboration with anthropology and other social sciences, originally for use on Mexico's Indigenous populations. Therefore, this book is an ethnography of the process of becoming, as well as the process of racialization and subjectivization that accompanies this process, as a way to shed light on the role that a Black subject position continues to play in framing the potentials of being for African descendants in Mexico, as well as the reproduction of the nation-state and the ideal citizen type.

Chapter 1 gives a description of the places and people that make up the Costa Chica region. Within the chapter, I present a methodology that focuses on movement and crossing racial and ethnic boundaries. In this chapter, I highlight how a methodology of crossing borders while being Black uncovers the existence of an underlying but invisible Black subject position in Mexico.

Chapter 2 discusses the historical development of a Black subject position within Mexico and the role that this subject position played in the development of colonial social relations as experienced by African descendants. The chapter argues that a Black subject position continued to operate during the national period as a type of dark matter, and therefore continued to play a role in the postindependent and revolutionary imaginations of the nation. I argue that this subject position continues to impact the possibilities for the development of both Black Mexican and non-Black Mexican identities in the contemporary Mexican nation.

In chapter 3 I outline the process of officially recognizing Black communities and the process of "negotiation" that this project necessarily demands and sets into motion. The chapter discusses the government's motivations for recognizing Black Mexicans as a cultural group and argues that the strategy is also put to work as a way of reproducing the ideal type, the Mestizo, as non-Black. In this way, the process for recognizing Black Mexican difference reproduces the historic social relations around citizenship in Mexico.

Chapter 4 discusses my approach to citizenship as the social relations of production (Kazanjian 2003). I argue that rather than an individual relationship between the citizen and the nation, citizenship is better seen as a set of relations between citizens. The chapter focuses on the role that a Black subject position plays in this relationship and how the value of Blackness is reproduced and put to work, or employed (Comaroff and Comaroff 2009), within the social relations surrounding citizenship in Mexico.

Chapter 5 focuses on the way in which Black Mexicans narrate the experience of being Black in Mexico. These narratives help provide a sense of how Black Mexicans are experiencing the cultural and political project currently taking place and how a historical Black subject position informs Black Mexican identity within the Costa Chica. The narratives both contradict and reinforce negative stereotypes and shed light on activists' own feelings and beliefs as they engage with the value of Blackness within Mexico's contemporary racial economy.

1

Chasing Blackness

Racial Geography and a Methodology for Locating Blackness in Mexico

On a hot June day during the beginning of the rainy season in the Costa Chica town of Charco Redondo, I sat with local activist and self-identified "Negra" (Black woman) Lucila Mariche Magadán. Over the past couple of weeks, we had been discussing several topics related to her activist activities and thoughts on Blackness in Mexico: the process of Black recognition underway in the Costa Chica, the history of Black folks in the region, racial discrimination, and a host of other related issues. On this day, Lucila and I were speaking specifically about strategies for making Blackness visible within the broader cultural landscape of Mexico's southern region.

Charco Redondo (Charco), a small town of less than five hundred residents, sits roughly nine kilometers from the main Mexican costal highway route 200, and about eighty kilometers from the main costal center of Puerto Escondido. To arrive in this small town, one must travel the unpaved, and often flooded, dirt road that connects the main highway to the coast as well as some of the smaller towns in the region, including the towns of El Azufre and Chacahua. Charco itself, along with El Azufre, La Pastoría, Zapotalito, Cerro Hermoso, and Chacahua, sits within the Lagunas de Chacahua National Forest Preserve. Unlike the small town of Chacahua, famous for its undeveloped beach and backpacker tourism from Mexico and abroad, as well as day trips from Puerto Escondido, Charco receives very few, if any, tourists during the year. The town consists of several permanent cinderblock homes, as well as some smaller homes made of a mix of building materials, including cement and unprocessed wood products. The town does not have a *secundaria* or *preparatoria* (middle or high school). Neither does it have a full-time health clinic or grocery. In order to receive the basic services, residents must travel the nine kilometers to the main highway town of San Jose del Progreso, locally referred to as "Pueblo Nuevo" (new town). For more extensive services such as more advanced medical care, high school education, or government administrative services, residents must travel to the further urban centers of Pinotepa Nacional, Río Grande, or Santiago Jamiltepec. Most residents in Charco sustain themselves through a mix of growing several crops, such as lime and sesame, to sell at the local markets, or sell a mix of perishable products and packaged snack foods at their own *misceláneas* (small in-home markets). Several of the men in the town hunt in the surrounding area to supplement their diets with wild meats such as iguana, badger, armadillo, sea turtle, and the occasional small deer.

While in contemporary times Charco Redondo plays a limited role in the local economy, Charco and other towns in the region were once a part of a thriving colonial economy that depended on the production of cotton and cochineal dye for national and international markets (Chassen-López 1998, 100), as well as sugar cane and ranching (Castañeda 2012; Vinson 2001, 2005a, 2005b). Chassen-López (1998) explains that after 1550, enslaved Africans were imported to the region in order to work the large cotton plantations in the area. During this moment, the production of cotton and cochineal incorporated both the Indigenous communities of the Mixteca Costa, Amuzgo, Chatino, Mixteco, Nahua, and Tlapaneco (Lara 2014), as well as the African descendants of the Costa Chica into a larger regional economy. According to Chassen-López (1998), "despite ongoing mestizaje, hostility between the indigenous and Afro-Hispanic population arose from an early date" (100). The region continued to play an important role in the national and international economies after the War for Independence in the early 1800s. Even into the twentieth century, the region continued to be a major producer of cotton. During this time, the nearby port of Puerto Miniso played an important role in shipping agricultural products from the region, due to the failure of railroad projects in the area (Chassen-López 1998). Puerto Miniso is also a prominent feature in local narratives explaining the arrival of African descendants to the region. It is commonly cited that African descendants populated the area after seeking refuge on the coast when a ship carrying enslaved Africans ran aground near Puerto Miniso (Lewis 2012, 86). Older residents of Charco Redondo still remember participating in the modern cotton industry and the use of the nearby Río Verde to transport cotton and other agricultural products from the town to the main highway for delivery to Puerto Miniso. The narrative of enslavement is not a common theme in casual conversation in Charco Redondo. However, in our conversations Lucila explicitly mentioned the historical reliance on Black labor for agricultural production in the region, and the fact that the largest agricultural plantation in the town as well as the associated estate were owned by non-Blacks, or Blancos (Whites) as Lucila put it.

While many of the Mestizo residents of Charco Redondo would take issue with the idea of Charco Redondo as a Pueblo Negro (Black town), Lucila had no misgivings about her designation of the town as a "Black town," nor did any of the other Black residents. My own unofficial survey of the town revealed that most of the residents were indeed of African descent. However, at the time of this particular trip to the region in 2011, the Mexican government had yet to conduct an official census in order to count the number of "Afro-Mexicanos" or "Afrodescendientes" in the region. Moreover, a set of actual cultural, ethnic, or racial conventions that could clearly be used to categorize the town of Charco, or any other town in the region, as an ethnic and officially Black town had yet to be developed. Still, many of the Black residents within the towns of the Costa Chica refer specifically to the towns of the region as "Pueblos Negros." It was specifically the lack of conventions by which to officially categorize Blackness in the region that was the topic of my conversation with Lucila that afternoon, and it was a topic that also seemed to preoccupy Lucila more generally.

That afternoon as we talked, Lucila explained to me that she had been thinking of material ways to represent her town, as well as the towns of the Costa Chica in general, as Black towns. In Lucila's mind, this meant figuring out how to make a cultural connection, and perhaps later an identity connection, to a set of material artifacts that could then be used as a physical marker of Blackness, much in the way that material cultural artifacts have become synonymous with the many different Indigenous groups in the region. According to Lucila, she had yet to encounter any such artifact that could signal a distinct cultural difference that could represent Black residents apart from either the Mestizos of the region or the several Indigenous groups that historically have made their home in the Costa Chica. Lucila and I talked of these different bits of material culture that could be found throughout the region, such as different colors and types of pottery, specific colors and patterns of cloth used for clothing, or even the different food items, such as several insect species, that have become synonymous with Indigeneity within the several official state-recognized "cultural regions" throughout the state of Oaxaca. I would later return to Charco Redondo with a group of graduate and undergraduate students to collect several recipes that Lucila explained made up the common diet in the region, all of which are not specific to residents of the Black towns of the Costa Chica but are commonly seen as regional dishes more broadly. However, at that moment, Lucila and I continued to draw blanks regarding specific cultural artifacts that could indeed be seen to represent a cultural Blackness in some form in the region.

Lucila explained that she had been in touch with a Mestizo man in the town of San Jose Río Verde, a few kilometers up the main highway. This man, according to Lucila, was known for his beautiful jaguar head carvings. Lucila explained to me that she thought that perhaps this man might be able to teach the craft of the jaguar carving to youth in the area, which would ultimately be a strategy for creating a material artifact that could become representative of Blackness in the region. Lucila herself had been involved in several workshops, both individually and as part of a larger women's collective, aimed at teaching residents in the area ways of collectivizing and marketing products and skills as a strategy for exploiting the growing tourist economy of the region. Lucila thought that creating a recognized Black material culture would also allow the Black towns in the region to tap into the tourist economy that has been so important for Indigenous communities in the region as well as throughout the country. Lucila and I decided to take a microbus the next morning to visit the artisan of San Jose Río Verde and explore the possibilities.

After the artisan discussed his craft with us and showed us several examples of the jaguar heads that he produced, all very similar in appearance apart from the graphic designs painted on the wood figurines, Lucila realized that these figurines were like several others that she had seen in the many craft markets throughout the region. And while these figures may have represented a generic type of "Indigenous" craft production in the region, the figures themselves seemed to say little about traditions specific to Black, Indigenous, or even a regional Mestizo culture, beyond the generic recognition that the jaguar had been an important part of the broader regional ecosystem and Indigenous cosmology.

Lucila was deftly aware of the ways in which a multicultural economy required the ability for any material artifact to be both culturally significant and economically exploitable in order to be useful to the broader project of Black recognition underway in Mexico. I refer to the current process of Black recognition in Mexico as a "project of recognition" in order to highlight the intentional and calculated process associated with recognizing African descendants in Mexico as an official "multicultural" group. This also speaks to the ways that contemporary Black recognition articulates with previously employed hegemonic discourses of nation and citizenship in Mexico (Wade 2001, 2010). This project, a "racial project," as discussed by Omi and Winant (1994), truly began to develop momentum in 2011 as a response to the UN's declaration of 2011 as the year of people of African descent. Furthermore, referring to the process of recognition as a "project" highlights the fact that recognition of any form of Blackness in Mexico, whether racial or cultural, must contend with the existence of other previously constructed and accepted racial and cultural subjects. I argue that the ideal project of Black recognition in Mexico is one that allows for the production of a Black subject that leaves all other previously produced racial and cultural subjects (Mestizo and Indigenous), and by extension subject positions, intact. As Wade (2001) argues, "the maintenance of a racial hegemony happens through the complex articulation of specific projects which are not necessarily coherently or intentionally racist or anti-immigrant or nationalist" (847). For this reason, multiculturalism appears to be the ideal form for Black recognition in Mexico, as it aligns neatly with the accepted national ideology of mestizaje and allows for the maintenance of racial/cultural hegemony through the production of new cultural categories without necessarily unhinging others.

Multiculturalism as a manner of producing subjects, like the process outlined by Saldaña-Portillo (2003) and Asher (2009) in the context of development, seemed to have worked its way into Lucila's own understandings and expectations of/for difference and recognition. Lucila and I spent the next couple of days visiting several local markets in the region looking for any material forms of culture that might appear as potential candidates for the representation of a cultural Blackness within the region. Ultimately we were unable to find any such artifacts, nor were we able to find any Black artisans in the region producing any such artifacts that might be exploitable in this way. It later dawned on me that Lucila and I, spurred partly by the governmental project of recognition underway in the region, had spent the last couple of days chasing Blackness; in this context, a perceived multicultural form of Blackness that had yet to be invented, or perhaps uncovered, throughout the region. It is this process of chasing Blackness that is the main theme of this book.

Aimee Meredith Cox, discussing choreography and movement, asks how "movement might narrate texts that are not otherwise legible" (2015, 28). The choreography discussed by Cox can be utilized as an important method that employs movement to make the unseen visible. The process of chasing Blackness throughout Mexico allowed me to use movement as a methodology, where my own movement and attempted border crossings made the invisible visible. When speaking of choreography, Cox argues that "choreography suggests that there is a map of movement or plan for how the body interacts with its environment, but it also suggests that by the body's placement in a space, the nature of that space changes" (2015, 28). As I crossed the many ethnic boundaries of the region, I recognized firsthand the ways that Blackness, as an unrecognized racial and cultural form, interrupts the neatly organized ethnic geography of the region.

Chassen-López (1998) shows the official count of distinct ethnic groups in Oaxaca to be sixteen. This count does not include the developing recognition of Black Mexicans as an official ethnic group, which would increase the count to seventeen distinct ethnic groups within the region. Each one of the recognized Indigenous groups in Oaxaca is also seen to be associated with a recognized cultural geography, or what Wade (2010, 120) refers to as "customary territories." The customary territory associated with Blackness has only recently been officially incorporated into the multicultural landscape that continues to define Oaxaca as one of Mexico's most ethnic (read: Indigenous) regions. Even when ethnic geographies are present in the broader national landscape, "it is important to recognise that these spaces remain subject to the hierarchies of power and value inherent both in traditional ideologies of blanqueamiento, which favour whiteness and devalue blackness and indigenousness, and in more recent ideologies of multiculturalism, which tend to limit the nature of the space blackness and indigenousness can occupy" (Wade 2005, 255). The recognition of ethnic geographies in the state of Oaxaca supports broader notions of Mexico as a Mestizo and multicultural nation. Even though Blackness has recently been incorporated into the Mexican multicultural narrative, the fact that Blackness is not historically rooted within the country means that Black Mexicans continue to be conceived through a broader socio-racial order common in "Indo-Latin American" countries that associates Blackness with intruders and foreigners (Wade 2005, 150). And, where Blackness has been more significantly incorporated into regional discourses, such as Veracruz, the Black presence continues to be perceived through a transnational or diasporic context rather than being conceived as local/national (see Sue 2010, 2013; Hoffman 2006, 2014; Hoffman and Rinaudo 2014). My attempts to cross the many racial and ethnic borders in the state while being Black demonstrate the racialized dynamics of space (Cerón-Anaya 2019) in Mexico and the role that Blackness continues to play in the ways that people imagine and lay claim to space.

The inspections, both official and unofficial, that I was subjected to during my attempts at crossing the official ethnic borders within the region made visible the ways that Blackness continues to inform how non-Black Mexicans imagine what it means to be Mexican and how the placement of the Black body in these spaces challenges those conceptions. The movement of my own Blackness across these different boundaries and potential inspection points also demonstrated how non-Black Mexicans can embody the nation through their physical embodiment of mestizaje (Wade 2005) and create inspection points that act as powerful sites of reproduction. Through their own interrogations, non-Black Mexicans (both Mestizo and Indigenous) employed their ability to invoke the state and used these inspection points to exclude Blackness from the nation and to reproduce the nation as non-Black. Mallon defines the state as "a series of decentralized sites of struggle through which hegemony is both contested and reproduced" (1995, 9). These sites should not be limited to official (or even unofficial) state institutions, as state formation is also a cultural process (Guardino 1996, 2). It is important to recognize how small communities and the interactions between everyday people within these communities also become sites of the state. Therefore, ordinary non-Black citizens become capable of wielding the power of the state when confronted with Blackness (Wilderson 2020). In this way, Black Mexicans feel the weight of the state in everyday interactions with Indigenous and Mestizos but are rarely allowed to impose similar inspections on others. Embodying the nation, then, is about invoking kinship (Mallon 1995, 11) and a historic relation to others in the nation. The fact that Indigeneity has been woven into the fabric of the nation through a national origin myth allows for Indigenous claims to the national family. These national kinship claims are further supported by the official ethnic geographies of the nation and allow for inspections by Indigenous people to reproduce the boundaries of both the local and national community. The ethnographic material presented in the following pages of this chapter is not intended to develop a type of narrative authority problematized by Wade (2005) and others. Rather, my goal with the following ethnographic narrative is to utilize the practice of crossing borders (or attempted border crossings [Lugo 2000, 2008]) as an ethnographic tool that helps shed light on larger discourses and the ways that they are used to reproduce people and places.

Chasing Blackness in the Isthmus of Tehuantepec

In 2008, while conducting research and participating in a Mixtec language course in Oaxaca City, I traveled to the Isthmus of Tehuantepec, Oaxaca, to investigate a myth I had heard regarding Black communities located somewhere around the coastal urban centers of Juchitán Zaragosa and Salina Cruz. During this trip, it was explained to me by a Zapotec-language instructor and activist that there were communities of African descendants (simply labeled "Negros" by my would-be informant) living somewhere in the Isthmus region. By this time, I had been conducting a literature review and preliminary fieldwork on and off in Oaxaca throughout a period of about four years and had encountered similar tales. With my curiosity sparked by this "myth of Blackness," I decided to review maps of the region and then set out to find one of these "lost" communities. While this initial trip did not uncover any "undiscovered" Black communities, it opened my eyes to the shifting regional discourses on Blackness that exist in the overlapping social, cultural, and geographic landscapes within the region.

Shifting racial discourses in the region highlight the ways that Blackness currently has no geographical center within the states of Oaxaca and Guerrero and the larger Mexican nation. Rather, Blackness is made to fit within different regional discourses (Lomnitz 1999, 2001) depending upon historical relevance and contexts. While the concept of race may be firmly attached to the conceptions that people have of the nation and its various regions, trips across the many internal borders, exemplified by the officially and unofficially recognized ethnic/racial (Indigenous, Negro, or Mestizo) regions within Oaxaca, require that we pay close attention to the ways that local conceptions of race must be managed, and at times co-opted, in order to reproduce the broader racial perceptions of the nation, as well as those privileged racial subjects therein. The notion of chasing Blackness exemplifies my approach to this practice of reproducing racial subjects as a method for reproducing the nation and its application to Mexico, specifically to the state of Oaxaca and its Black population. Chasing Blackness! This is what I found myself doing that hot summer in 2008. I found it hard to believe that there might have still been communities of "Negros" hiding, or perhaps forgotten, within the coastal jungle of the Isthmus of Tehuantepec. However, while it may sound absurd or simply a product of the wild anthropological fantasy, due to the historic erasure of Black communities within Mexico (Hernández Cuevas 2004; Vinson 2001, 2005a, 2005b), the notion of a "lost" community of African descendants located somewhere within the "unexplored" wilds of Oaxaca should not be dismissed as beyond the realm of belief. If we situate this fantasy within the very real context of the racial narrative of the modern Mexican nation-state, we must confront the fact that many Mexicans are unaware of, and unconcerned with, the living and vibrant communities of African descendants that continue to flourish within their own country—even, in some cases, within their own back-yards. Such is still the case for many residents of Oaxaca and Guerrero as well as for non-Black Mexicans throughout the country.

In her book *Afro-Mexican Constructions of Diaspora, Gender, Identity, and Nation*, Paulette Ramsay (2016) quotes Padre Glynn Jemmott Nelson, a priest who had worked in the region for over thirty years, as he recalled his first assignment to Oaxaca. According to Ramsay, Padre Glynn, whom I also met and talked with in the town of San Andrés Huaxpaltepec, recalled that during his first month in Oaxaca (in the early 1980s), "on getting more precise information on where the black population was located, I trav-elled there for a brief look around. I spent a few days in the area and there and then decided that this was where I wanted to live and work. I wanted to remain and share the life and struggles of this little corner of Mexico where Afro-Mexicans seem to have been hidden from the world and even from other Mexicans" (Ramsay 2016, 18). This was the experience of Father Glynn in 1983, only twenty years or so before my own first "encounter" with the Black communities of Mexico. It should not be a surprise, then, that it seemed possible to me in the early 2000s that there may still have been Black communities somewhere in the Isthmus region of Oaxaca. In casual conversation, when discussing my research in Mexico, I am often met with the familiar response that "there are no Blacks in Mexico." And, even as the recognition of "Afro-Mexicanos" has created more visibility around Mexi-co's Pueblos Negros, Blackness is still operationalized as a myth in Mexico, more commonly related to distant Mexican history, folklore, and symbol-ism than to contemporary Mexico. Mexico's campaigns to expose the na-tion's Black population are still missing the general public and have yet to penetrate the imagination of Mexicanness, so it is understandable how the anthropological fantasy and a history of invisibility could come together to create the possibility of an "unseen" community of African descendants within the modern Mexican nation. Pushed by this "myth of Blackness," in 2008 I decided to see what I could find in the Isthmus region of Oaxaca.

My first modern cartographic glimpse of the region came from an out-dated map held in the Instituto Welte collection in the city of Oaxaca.[1] This map from the 1929 Rand McNally World Atlas, despite offering a slightly more detailed version than the previous colonial maps I had reviewed of the region, painted a very undetailed picture. This picture was only later elaborated upon by using the satellite option in Google Maps. The region had changed little from the era in which the 1929 map was drafted, or the colonial maps of previous centuries, for that matter, apart from the growth of the main centers of Salina Cruz and Juchitán. Armed with the tools of modern anthropology, my digital camera, backpacks, a photocopy of my US passport, and a few granola bars, I set out to locate these communities so rarely mentioned in the broader literature. However, no one could give me any specific details of where exactly I might find these communities of "Negros." Was I to look on the outskirts of the main Isthmus centers? Or, perhaps, I should explore the many tiny communities within the coastal jungle? I decided that it would be worth my while to do both. In the early morning hours on a hot April day, I arrived in Juchitán and decided to ask around to see what I could find. Most of the people that I spoke to were willing to humor my inquiries, even though they had no interest in my "expedition." Others gave me invaluable information—or so I thought—that would lead me to these communities just a little further south along the main highway. After referring to my copy of the outdated map, I decided that I would hop a bus and stop at the numerous communities located alongside the main highway and see for myself what I could find out about the unknown African descendants of El Isthmo (the Isthmus region).

Those familiar with the Isthmus region of Oaxaca might find it interesting that I would travel to the center of what has long been known as one of the most vibrant and political (Campbell 1994) as well as at times detested Indigenous regions in Mexico. Benito Juarez, for example, regularly touted as Oaxaca's "Indigenous president" and himself of Zapotec descent, talked of the "state of immorality and disorder in which the residents of Juchitán have lived since the very ancient times," as well as "the unruly character of these rascals" (Benito Juarez quoted in Campbell et al. 1993) when referring to the Isthmus Zapotec and the tradition of Indigenous resistance in the region. Campbell (1994) and others discuss the region in terms of a long-standing tradition of Indigenous struggle, resistance, and rebellion, lasting until the present moment. These representations of the Oaxacan Isthmus region reinforce the perception of Oaxaca as a conglomerate of distinct Indigenous, and therefore cultural, regions. However, the perception of these regions as autonomous Indigenous regions historicized by the political struggles, sometimes violent and sometimes hegemonic, between the Indigenous and Spanish—often still referred to by savvy politically minded locals as *Gachupines* (a derogatory term for "Spaniard" used in the early Independence era; see Guardino 1996)—overlooks the roles that African descendants and their possessed labor played in the settlement and building of the region. Dismissing the role of African descendants in the development of broader processes of production and economies of trade in the region, among others, erases the real impacts that African descendants had on the overall development of the later Mexican nation. These African descendants were instrumental in helping lay the foundation that allowed New Spain to violently emerge as Mexico in the early nineteenth century.

Tutino (1993) takes the African presence within the region seriously, if only as a historical moment. Discussing the impacts of several Spanish incursions into the region and the effect of Zapotec control over basic foodstuffs and the commercial production of elements essential to the local economy, Tutino (1993) argues that during the colonial moment "Zapotecs probably did not—and probably would not—serve as the core of permanent, dependent workers on the region's livestock estates. As a result, the major grazers had to invest in expensive slave laborers, now primarily Africans. During the late sixteenth and early seventeenth centuries, they [referring to enslaved Africans] were forced to come in sufficient numbers to introduce a third cultural tradition to Isthmus life" (48–49). The Mexican government, as well as academics embracing the preexisting paradigm of mestizaje and multiculturalism, have also turned to using a version of this third-space trope, as they prefer to rhetorically discuss Blacks in Mexico as the third root (*Nuestra Tercera Raíz*). This trope is quickly becoming the official language to discuss Blackness within the Mexican nation, at least from above (Sue 2010; Hoffman 2014; Rinaudo 2014; Hoffman and Rinaudo 2014). I soon found out that little remained of this third root and the historical presence of Blackness in the Isthmus. The descendants of those Africans who had been enslaved and brought to the region had either been absorbed through the process of racial mixing so prevalent in the national narrative or had simply sought refuge in other regions of the state.

I ended up that season in a small town by the name of San Francisco Viejo (San Francisco del Mar), inhabited by the few remaining Indigenous Huave speakers of the region. Needless to say, there were no signs of the long-lost Black community—or public accommodations—in this small town or in any other that I stopped through on this trip. I was lucky enough to meet an elder fisherman in the town who knew of a family that had made their way north to the United States. He told me that their unfinished house was available and that I could set up camp inside the cement shell and make use of the hammocks that had been set up in the empty rooms. I purchased a few fish from the fisherman and paid his asking price to prepare them for dinner. That night we talked about the loss of his language, the United States, and my motivation for arriving to his town.

The elder fisherman seemed to be unaware of any presence, historical or otherwise, of African descendants in the region. He also seemed unaware of the historical narratives discussed by Campbell (1994), the numerous contemporary Indigenous Zapotec activists in the main centers of Juchitán and Salina Cruz, the rich history of Zapotec resistance and struggle, or the broader cultural renaissance underway in the region (see Campbell 1994). This may have been because, as a member of a very small group of remaining Huave speakers in the region, my new fisherman friend seemed to be excluded from the broader politics of recognition underway in the area. Whatever the reason for this lack of knowledge, or perhaps lack of interest, on the part of my gracious host, as we talked I was reminded of how silly my story must have appeared to the average Mexican. Rather than traveling the coast, looking for sign of African descendants, and ultimately getting stranded in his small town, it seemed more likely to him, and others I met along the way, that I was an "illegal" immigrant from Central America, trying to stay under the radar as I made the dangerous journey up the Mexican coast toward a final destination of California in "El Norte." Ironically, until this point, I had been making my way southward along the coast, unlike my immigrant and migrant counterparts, many of African descent, who would be making their way northward. My new fisherman friend chose not to push the issue. But never did his belief that I originated from Central America stop him from offering me the utmost hospitality and the meager resources that he had at his disposal.

I had experienced a similar "logical skepticism" earlier that day, when trying to secure transportation to the small town of San Francisco Viejo where I was also accused of being an "illegal" from Central America. At this unofficial inspection point, I had to explain to my accuser, the owner of a small general store selling provisions and miscellaneous items in the area, that I was from California and looking to arrive in San Francisco Viejo in order to continue up the shoreline to the main town of Salina Cruz. He responded in a sly tone, untrusting my self-proclaimed origins, "You mean you want to get to California." Despite my best attempts to convince this man that I originated from California, putting on my best Californian accent and speaking in my West Coast Black English dialect (a strategy I used several times before and since), he would not allow himself to be fooled.

But, again, he did not try to impede my journey, and instead gave me instructions on how I might arrive to the small town where the land met the sea, and how I could encounter a *lancha* (a small boat with an outboard motor) in order to continue up the coast.

Being twice misinterpreted through the lens of illegality, I had to wonder: could it be that the rumors of Blackness that I had heard were a side effect of the silent callings of the United States that landed on the hopeful ears of the many Black Central Americans that attempt to make the journey northward every year to the United States?[2] Perhaps the discourse on Blackness in the Isthmus was simply one of illegality in the context of migration? Both the elder fisherman and my store-owning accuser were willing to become accomplices in my "illegal" journey northward. They even warned me of the dangers that would inevitably come along with such an expedition. They told me of the many Central Americans who were taken advantage of along the way: robbed, beaten, and even killed. Just a week before, a group of immigrants, perhaps Salvadorans, found themselves in danger in the rough seas right off the coast when the small launch that they were traveling in capsized and at least half of their party drowned. One member of the group, "a Black woman/una Negra," it was said, was seen coming out of the water modestly and unsuccessfully trying to cover her naked body as she asked for help from one of the locals. It seemed that this story was related to me from "a friend of a friend" after taking on the usual proportions of any tall tale. However, this tale should not be simply dismissed as local lore.

Interestingly, the narrative of the undocumented Black Central Americans utilizes a ship motif like the one discussed above. Laura Lewis discusses how the residents of San Nicolas, in Guerrero's Costa Chica region, utilize narratives of the "ship" sinking somewhere off the coast by the small town of El Faro (2001, 98). In this narrative, common in the Costa Chica region, the ship is used to establish local roots by tapping into the imagined routes by which Blackness arrives to the Costa Chica. In these narratives, the location of the shipwreck seems to change depending upon the local origins of the storyteller. The narrative of the capsized lancha in the Isthmus was utilized to accomplish a similar goal of establishing the routes by which Blackness enters Oaxaca from the south. However, in this narrative, the capsized lancha is used by non-Blacks to firmly establish the roots of Blackness beyond the nation. Although in different ways, the externality of Blackness is a key feature of both narratives. The narrative of the capsized boat also pointed to a broader transnational reality in which Blackness is criminalized. For example, in 2006, as I sat watching the night sky on a beach in the Lagunas de Chacahua national preserve in Oaxaca several kilometers northwest of the Isthmus region, a small prop plane, after a quick "fly by," dropped a mysterious cargo in the small bay. Minutes later, several Mexican military servicemen scrambled to investigate the shore as a small watercraft attempted to intercept the plane's jettisoned cargo. A friend would later explain that the origin of the plane was from Central America. Central American migrations through Mexico are also intertwined with the reality of the black-market economies that intersect the region. The view of me as an illegal Central American immigrant, shared by several people I met along the way, including the federal police that would repeatedly search my luggage and ask for my official documents, exposes a larger regional discourse (Lomnitz 1999, 2001) on Blackness and the ways that this discourse has been mapped out in actual social space (Lomnitz-Adler 1992, 19) in the region. Castañeda (2012), supporting Bobby Vaughn's ethnographic work in the Costa Chica (2005), explains that while Blackness in the Costa Chica is seen as entirely local, Blackness in Central Mexico is displaced to the United States. My experience in the Isthmus region points to another regional discourse on Blackness operating in southern Mexico, in which Blackness is displaced to Central America.

Mestizaje, as both a racial ideology and a methodology for implementing a form of White supremacy through racial mixing, has "mapped out" in both rural and urban spaces in Mexico. Part of this process relies on what Lomnitz, drawing on Mary Louise Pratt (1992), refers to as contact zones: "a kind of place within a system of functionally related places" (2001, 141). Within this functionally related system, a power hierarchy develops in which regional cultures, through the promotion of cultural and geographic zones, are used in the production and reproduction of the nation. Within traditional geography, zones are seen as internally homogenous spaces, while "region" refers to the functional integration of different kinds of zones (Lomnitz 2001, 130). Oaxaca, and the popular conceptualization of the state as comprising several distinct cultural groups and geographies, demonstrates how zones and regions are situated within broader discourses on the nation. In the context of Oaxaca's cultural geography, each distinct cultural zone is neatly buttressed against another, giving Oaxaca, along with Chiapas, the distinction of being one of Mexico's most important Indigenous, and therefore cultural, regions. What is important here is not simply the fact that these zones and regions are connected by and through real geography but that these zones and regions are also articulated by an underlying ideology. This ideology locally manifests itself as a form of anti-Blackness, which in turn is used to clearly define the borders of the region and the broader nation. The act of defining these borders and boundaries has a profound impact on the perception of Blackness within the accepted cultural zones of Mexico's "Indigenous" region. The discourse of Blackness in the Isthmus region of Oaxaca as one of illegality and foreignness is due in large part to the Central Americans, many of whom are Black, according to locals, who attempt to make their way clandestinely along the coast to the US-Mexico border (Blanchard et al. 2011; Briggs 2016; Menjívar and Abrego 2012).

In 2011, I returned to Oaxaca to do long-term field research in the Costa Chica and decided to follow up on my 2008 trip to the Isthmus of Tehuantepec to further explore my understanding of the regional approach to the discourse on Blackness. Again, I was confronted with the notion of foreignness and illegality. In the city of Oaxaca, I had been cautioned that I should be careful due to the recent drug trafficking activity and rumored kidnapping of immigrants taking place in the region.[3] While I did not experience any difficulty due to drug trafficking cartels during this trip to the Isthmus region, I was once again accused of attempting to make the treacherous journey from Central America to the United States. One man, a Mestizo Colombian who had lived in Los Angeles, California, for many years and now made his home in Oaxaca due to deportation, would not allow himself to be convinced (or perhaps fooled) that I was from California. I once again attempted to prove my origins by speaking with my best Black Californian English accent. The Colombian man explained to me that my Spanish accent did not sound like any Mexican dialect he knew and that he thought it was from Central America. He explained my fluency in English by reminding me that many Central American countries, such as Panama and Costa Rica, had a tradition of speaking English. Although I could not convince him that I was not an "illegal," he offered me firewood and a place to pitch my tent for the night, as well as a meal of seafood soup that his friend and landlord had made that evening. He even offered to hire a small boat for my passage across the lagoon and enthusiastically explained that we could leave later that evening. Remembering the anecdote about the shipwrecked Central American woman and thinking about my own personal safety, I accepted his hospitality with the caveat that we would leave in the daylight of the following morning. When I arrived at the other end of the lagoon, he told me how to find public transportation to the main town of Juchitán.

However, another group of locals cautioned me that I might not want to take this route, as the federal police would undoubtedly ask for my papers when we crossed paths—a situation I had experienced years prior when I had mistakenly left my passport in Oaxaca City, and a situation I have experienced many times since.

This last experience in the Isthmus region of Oaxaca solidified my understanding of conflicting regional discourses on race. While the idea of Blackness, or my own physical Blackness, did not seem to invoke any thoughts or attitudes about racial discrimination, the people around me perceived my Blackness as a foreignness and labeled it illegal. After their own personal inspections and comments, everyone I met was willing to assist me, even if some tried to economically exploit what they perceived to be my "situation." For example, one man in San Francisco Viejo offered to take me across the lagoon for the "affordable" price of $2000MX per person (roughly US$[2011]170), assuming that I was a scout for a larger party of illegally traveling Central American immigrants. He explained that there was room for fourteen in his small launch. The trip also solidified my understanding that the burgeoning Black movement to gain statewide and federal recognition in the Costa Chica still had plenty of work to do in order to make the efforts visible beyond the Costa Chica region. Although the discourse on Blackness in El Isthmo was similar to that in the Costa Chica—one of illegality and foreignness—the manner by which it was deployed was/is context-specific and influenced by geography and regional politics.

Chasing Blackness in the Costa Chica of Oaxaca

In the Costa Chica, I also found myself chasing Blackness. Hoffman argues that in the time of Aguirre Beltrán, "the Costa Chica seemed that last preserve of a black population that was gradually disappearing through racial intermixing" (2014, 91). The disappearance of Blackness, as foreshadowed by Aguirre Beltrán, has yet to come to pass. In fact, Castañeda cites the Minority Rights Group's estimate that the Black population in Mexico in the mid-1990s was a minimum of 474,000 (0.5 percent) and a maximum of 9 million African descendants (2012, 94). In contrast to the Isthmus, in the Costa Chica region it was easy to find people who appeared phenotypically of African descent. However, the issue was where to find those who explicitly self-identified as racially and politically Black. During my many trips to the Costa Chica, while many in the region would acknowledge being descended from "Africanos," they would regularly employ a strategy that Sue (2010) refers to as "racial distancing" and politely explain to me that if it were "Negros" (Blacks) I was looking for, I would have more success if I were to travel a little further up the road to another town, such as Santo Domingo Armenta, El Azufre, Corralero, or Collantes, where I would undoubtedly find "gente negra, negra" (very dark/black black). Sue (2013) argues that employing the rhetorical device of epizeuxis, the repetition of a word in immediate succession, is part of the strategy of racial distancing in which people who might be perceived by others to be racially Black shift the designation onto others who they argue are unmistakably racially Black, rather than simply dark due to skin color or environment. This strategy is often applied to the term *moreno* (dark-skinned) as in "moreno moreno," to politely recognize someone as racially Black rather than simply dark-skinned (Sue 2013, 39; Lewis 2001, 2003, 2006, 2012).

In the Costa Chica, many people I met would make the argument that they were dark-skinned simply due to exposure to the sun rather than their genetics. Part of the issue here was that Blackness in this case was defined simply as skin color, rather than an ethnic, cultural, or political racial category. Moreover, the stigma of being referred to as "Negro" often pushes people who are classified this way by others due to their skin color and features to deflect this racial signifier by explaining that there exists people "Blacker/mas Negro" than they are in some other town or region. Sue (2010) found the same to be true in Veracruz while attempting to locate Black Mexicans to interview for her research on racial identity. Discussing the racial distancing and the social phenomenon of what Godreau (2006) refers to as "the displacement of blackness," Sue argues that "in the process of rejecting the 'black' label for themselves, individuals or groups place the 'black' label on others" (2010, 275). Sue outlines an example like my own and explains that while in the city of Veracruz one of her informants arranged for her to speak with a man who others identified as "negrito." However, in the course of the conversation, the man explained to Sue that he in fact was not Negro but did in fact know someone who was. Sue then interviewed this second individual "only to be told that he too was not negro but, similarly, knew someone who was" (273). Sue argues that this was a common occurrence in her research. Harris (1993), in her work on Whiteness as property and passing in the Americas, discusses this strategy as a broader survival strategy due to the fact that historically, "race subordination was coercive and circumscribed the liberty to self-define" (1743). Harris goes on to explain that "self-determination of identity was not a right for all people, but a privilege accorded on the basis of race. The effect of protecting whiteness at law was to devalue those who were not white by coercing them to deny their identity in order to survive" (1743–1744). Those in the Costa Chica who utilized this survival strategy of racial distancing also incorporated another facet of this strategy, as they not only distanced themselves from Blackness but attempted to impose the racial signifier onto others as a way of including themselves in the category of "non-Black." None of the people I spoke with claimed to be White, or even Mestizo or Indigenous. Rather, they employed a strategy that moved the color line to include others supposedly darker and phenotypically more "Negro" than themselves.

My experience of chasing Blackness, elaborated upon by Sue (2010), demonstrates the difficulty of locating Blackness in Mexico. However, the process of chasing Blackness highlights the fact that a subject position for Blackness continues to exist in Mexico. While an identity position has yet to develop in order to articulate this subject position, examples such as the one above demonstrate how others position themselves against Blackness in order to make sense of who they are or how they want to be perceived by others. I argue that in this way, Blackness in Mexico operates as a type of dark matter (an absent presence as such; see Wynter 2003); an invisible yet felt subject position around which others position themselves. Lewis, in her work in San Nicolas Guerrero (2001, 2012), explains that her collaborators preferred the term *moreno* (dark-skinned), which she argues highlights an engagement with the mestizaje paradigm in a way that centers Indigeneity as opposed to Whiteness in the process of racial mixing and identity construction in the region (Lewis 2012). Focusing on racial distancing and the displacement of Blackness within the region, offers another way to approach this process of identity formation within the communities of the Costa Chica. Many Black Mexicans in the region refer to San Nicolas as one of the Pueblos Negros of the region. These same people also refer to the residents of San Nicolas as Black, utilizing both the terms *Negro* and *moreno*. The referencing of Indigenous mixing, found in San Nicholas and throughout the Costa Chica (if not Mexico more broadly), may not only be about biological or cultural affinities between African descendants and Indigenous in the region, but may also be an example of the tried-and-true strategy of deflection mentioned above; African descendants in the region recognize the value (negative value or disvalue) associated with Blackness, and therefore use Indigeneity as a strategy to distance themselves from this subject position.

Sergio Peñalosa, an activist and teacher in the town of Cuajinicuilapa, Guerrero, a short distance from San Nicolas, explained that he felt that this deflection was a type of self-discrimination (*autodiscriminación*), or self-hate brought about by the larger public stigma associated with Blackness. The idea of self-hate, or autodiscriminación, is becoming a discourse used by activists in the region to shed light on the invisible Black subject position and to promote a revaluation of Blackness within the communities of the Costa Chica. Sergio explained that when someone comes to the region because they have been told that there is a Black population, the people will often say "OK, good, but go to Santo Domingo [Santo Domingo Armenta] or Tapextla because, yes, they are really Black over there. But here, yes, we have slightly dark skin [sí estamos negritos], but over there, they have very dark skin [están negros-negros]" (personal conversation with Sergio Peñalosa). As part of his assessment of Blackness in the region, Sergio also incorporated the people of San Nicolas, located a short (*colectivo*) (unmetered taxi) ride away from the town of Cuaji, into the larger Black population, claiming that San Nicolas is also one of the Pueblos Negros of the region.

It may be impossible to prove or disprove the percentages around genetic admixture in the towns of the Costa Chica. Interestingly, I was told that there was a medical anthropologist in the region collecting genetic material in order to get a better understanding of the historic link between African descendants in the region and specific regions of the African continent. It is imaginable, especially within the prevailing racial economy of mestizaje, that this same material could be used to prove biological affinities with local Indigenous groups as well. In fact, in 2017 anthropologist Cristina Bejarano gave a talk at the University of California, Riverside, on how Mexican researchers were promoting the Mexican National Genome, and the ways in which this project promoted a type of somatic reductionism in support of the common interpretation of mestizaje and Mexicans as a by-product of Spanish and Indigenous mixing (Bejarano 2017). Ultimately it is the context, the system of value in which meaning is made of such genetic material, that allows us to make sense of racial mixing.

Sergio's and others' evaluation of the strategy of invoking racial mixing as a way of deflecting the social weight of Blackness demonstrates at least one other perspective on Blackness in the Costa Chica. The reliance on racial mixing, both figuratively and physically, to deflect the negative social weight of Blackness is a by-product of the anti-Blackness that is inherent to the Mexican brand of mestizaje. To demonstrate the perceived lack of value associated with Blackness in the region, Sergio shared with me a saying or sentiment that he says is common in the Costa Chica. Sergio continued, "Like people say, 'Blackness came by sea, so let's push it back to the sea, let's see if it goes back to Africa.'" Sergio himself did not share this desire to push Blackness "back to the sea" and is in fact deeply involved with the local and national struggles for Black recognition. Beyond the issue of self-discrimination, this strategy of deflection was an outcome of the fact that there did not exist an officially recognized geography of Blackness that actually rooted the "Black citizen" symbolically and/or physically within the Mexican nation.

Upon deeper analysis, the stigma associated with Blackness in the region, as demonstrated in following chapters, is only relevant within certain contexts. Ethnographic work on the process of constitutional recognition in Colombia (Arocha 1998; Paschel 2016; Wade 2001, 2010), for example, demonstrates the importance of recognizing the multitude of Black identities that exist within any particular region and the broader nation, as well as recognizing that racial identities are fluid and context-dependent (Derby 2003), rather than accepting the promotion of one identity over the other within a single context as a simple dismissal or disavowal of a larger subjectivity and subject position. Privileging subjectivity over identity enables us to ask how the construction of a moreno identity is not always about deflection, and how it could potentially represent the construction of multiple Black identities rather than the wholesale dismissal of the identity. For example, Sue argues that *moreno/a* is often used as a euphemism for the racial term "Black," and demonstrates how Black Mexicans in Veracruz vacillate, often times unconsciously, between the terms/categories of Negro and moreno (2013, 3). This demonstrates how the term *moreno* in Mexico is often used as both a racial term, one to invoke ancestry and groupness, as well as a color term to discuss individual descriptors (Sue 2013). In any case, there are several reasons for African descendants in the region to deflect the impositions of particular racializations (i.e., being interpellated as Black/Negro) and to impose those same racializations on an abstract group of people located somewhere further down the road. Interestingly, none of the people I spoke with, even those who utilized the strategy of deflection, refused to accept that "Negros/Blacks" existed and could be found in the region. This simple lack of refusal makes the invisible visible and demonstrates that a Black subject position exists within Mexico, even when there appears to be no proper racial subjects to occupy the position.

In the Costa Chica town of Charco Redondo, Lucila explained to me that after leaving the country she was almost denied reentry due to Mexican immigration officials' perception of her as a "foreigner." She explained to them that she was from Charco Redondo, a small town in the Costa Chica, but the immigration officials continued to accuse her of faking her passport and met her explanation of local origin with suspicion and accusations. The immigration officials then informed her that "there are no Negros in Mexico." This is another example of the notions of illegality and foreignness that are attached to both the public and official discourses of Blackness in the larger nation (Sue 2010). These discourses work to keep Blackness contained within some regions—the Costa Chica, for example—while simultaneously excluding Blackness from other regions—like the Isthmus of Tehuantepec. Through this geographic containment, Black Mexicans' claims to belonging are tenuous and contested in several ways, as they are only "allowed" to exist in limited sanctioned geographical regions. Unlike Mestizos, who can claim the nation as property through the physical and symbolic embodiment of the Mestizo Mexican nation, and can therefore act on behalf of the state, Black Mexicans can only lay claim to very specific geographic zones, affording them limited access through a type of conditional belonging. Therefore, Black claims to citizenship in Mexico are only supported when they appear within the sanctioned geographies of rurality and cultural difference. Outside of these geographies, they are interrogated at the boundary/border of the multiple contact zones that continue to frame their existence as the quintessential "other" within the Mexican nation. This demonstrates the role that Blackness plays in determining the possibility for supposed membership. Sue argues that "the supposition found in the literature—that Latin Americans conceptualize race in a fluid manner—is only partially correct. This assumption is accurate only if we confine our discussion to a local population; when the conversation is broadened to include those outside of the local population, there are fixed, clear and concrete definitions of blackness" (2010, 292). For non-Black Mexicans, Black as a racial category is a fixed category that corresponds to a broader subject position that is utilized to recognize those who do not belong. Through these interrogations, the Mexican ideal is continually reproduced as anything but Black. This is further demonstrated by the popular use of terms such as "Afro-Mestizo" and "Afro-Mexican" by non-Black Mexicans to make a distinction between themselves and Mexicans of obvious African descent.

Process and Movement as Methodology

More than an ethnographic representation of the racial and cultural geographies developing around Blackness in the Costa Chica and Isthmus regions, my ethnographic vignettes highlight the difficulty developing a methodology for researching any aspect of Blackness beyond the imposition of preexisting, and perhaps ill-fitting, paradigms. The fact of Blackness (Fanon 2008) may indeed be a social fact in any region affected by the colonial importation of enslaved Black Africans or within any former colonial power dealing with immigration of African descendants. However, the meaning and manner by which we utilize this fact in developing methodologies for the study of the experience and contemporary possibilities for Blackness must incorporate regional discourses, definitions, and experiences of the production of Black subjects. The Isthmus and Costa Chica regions of Oaxaca are both affected by the conceptualization that Blackness is not rooted (Gilroy 1993; Greene 2007) within the respective regions. The notion of the ship (see Lewis 2001 for examples in the Costa Chica) plays an important role, similarly to other regions in the Americas, in the popular narrative explaining and helping to legitimate the African-descendant presence in the Costa Chica region. While the ship may be less relevant in terms of a historical presence in the region (Vinson and Restall 2009), the ship is used to make sense of the routes of Blackness to the nation, while simultaneously ensuring the continued perception of Blackness as *the* mode of foreignness. During my trips to the two distinct regions, while Blackness was recognized as belonging within the Costa Chica by those from the region, it was expressed as something that could be better exemplified, or perhaps personified, in some other town always a bit further down the road. Similarly, in the Isthmus, Blackness could be found traveling through the region, but always originating from some other point outside the country.

The differing manifestations of this discourse of foreignness within the Isthmus and Costa Chica regions during my many research trips made the task of developing a methodology for ethnographically interpreting Blackness a difficult endeavor. Hoffman (2014) argues that North Americans often arrive to the Costa Chica with well-constructed discourses validated in our home environments. During my initial fieldwork, I realized how these discourses informed my own methodology. Originally, my intention was to visit the Costa Chica and situate myself in a Black town, where I would do ethnographic fieldwork on the development of the "Black Movement." However, I soon realized that this strategy was complicated by the fluidity of Black identity in the region and the fact that Blackness continued to be a moving target, creating what Sue refers to as a "wild goose chase" (Sue 2010, 273; Jones 2013). While many people I spoke with agreed that there were similar cultural elements shared within the region, the negative historical and racial stigma associated with Blackness precluded many of these same folks from taking ownership of a Black identity.[4] Though many have discussed the cultural elements binding the community within the region (Vaughn 2001; Lewis 2000, 2001, 2006; Ramsay 2016), an ethnography of the production of a political Blackness has proved to be more difficult. This difficulty lies in the challenges presented by an actual ethnographic approach to "process" as opposed to an ethnography of some particular people or place. Here I mean to make a distinction, like Palmié and Stewart's distinction between an "historical anthropology" and an "anthropology of history" (2016), from a processual anthropology (the focus remaining on anthropology itself) and an actual anthropology of process (the focus turning toward a social/political process). I argue that this switch in focus from thing to process allows for the application of anthropological theorizing to the relational nature of concepts such as Blackness and citizenship, rather than relying on the static forms necessary for ethnographic treatments of the political byproducts of these relations (i.e., citizens and non-citizens). In many cases, the a priori assumption of Blackness (or lack thereof) is applied to a group of people, and then ethnographic work is conducted accordingly. What to do, however, if the process of laying a foundation for a politically racialized "becoming" (Hall 1994) and the production of Black political subjects (Paschel 2016) is still taking place?[5] This was the question I had to ask in 2011, the global year of people of African descent (UNESCO 2011), as the Mexican government and local activists went about the messy business of officially recognizing Blackness in the Costa Chica.

By referencing a foundation for being, I do not mean to argue that racial and ethnic identities are static once established. Rather, I mean to demonstrate that there is a process of racial identity construction underway in the Costa Chica that relies on a preexisting ontological position of Blackness. For this reason, an ethnography of process may be more useful than a snapshot of the ethnographic present in helping imagine the potentially infinite possibilities for the construction of Blackness in Mexico, as well as the historic relations that then enact the historical and political frames that limit the ways Blackness in Mexico can actually take shape. This approach brings to light the struggle over the possibility of changing the value associated with Blackness and the Black subject position in Mexico as well as the instrumentality and utility that people apply to the concept. It highlights the fact that Black people (as well as non-Black people) must constantly be reproduced by and through political, social, and economic relations and negotiations. The process of negotiation points to the creation of a community as the conglomeration of multiple events (see Lugo 2008, 257, n2 on "event"). Looking at particular events (Sahlins 1985, 1993; Hartman 1997; Sewell Jr. 2005; Jerry 2021) and the ways that groups and individuals strategically approach these events calls attention to the actual process of community construction and subject formation. Therefore, a research methodology regarding the Costa Chica, at least at this stage in the racial/ ethnic political life of the region, must be different from a methodology designed for an ethnography of a preexisting culturally or racially "Black" community where a foundation for the historical construction of the political Black subject had previously been developed. My methodology is directly informed by the tradition developed by previous anthropologists such as Michelle Zimbalist Rosaldo (1980), Renato Rosaldo (1989), Trouillot (1984, 1992, 1995), and Sahlins (1985). It is my opinion that due to the discipline of anthropology's more recent privileging of studies on identity and agency, as well as a general trend for disciplines such as anthropology, sociology, and ethnic and cultural studies to see Black and Mexican as mutually exclusive (Sue 2010; Jones 2013), a processual approach to the role that Blackness plays in the overall production of citizenship has yet to be applied to Mexico.

During my fieldwork in the Costa Chica, one of the first questions that I had to ask myself was: Where and how was the current idea of Blackness coming about in the Costa Chica? This question is directly related to a historical approach to the construction of a racialized group of people, but it more importantly focuses on the place and space of a current conception of Blackness. I found myself looking for the current sites of production and transmission of Blackness. I found that these sites were located in multiple places and were also politically charged, as they included a large majority of non-Black Mexicans. For example, the consultas organized by the Comisión Nacional para el Desarrollo de los Pueblos Indígenas (Commission for the Development of Indigenous Communities) (CDI) to discuss a methodology for "investigations into Black towns [comunidades negras]" were headed by White Mestizos, apart from the official inclusion of one Morena worker from the Oaxacan Secretaría de Pueblos Indígenas (Secretary of Indigenous Affairs[6]) (SAI).[7] With the broader goal of rhetorically incorporating the communities into the multicultural web of the Oaxacan state and the larger nation, these consultas were designed to ultimately categorize the African-descendant communities of Mexico (las comunidades Afrodescendientes de México) in order to "officialize" Black racial and cultural difference, as opposed to Indigenous and Mestizo, for the overall project of state and federal recognition. These consultas, then, were official sites of contemporary racial/ethnic subject making, as they attempted to solidify difference in a way that would be meaningful within the preexisting framework of mestizaje and multiculturalism that reflected the preexisting state and federal discourses on Blackness.

Take, in sharp contrast to these official state consultations, a more grassroots example. In the town of Pinotepa Nacional, I witnessed a concert that highlighted African music and storytelling, in the Spanish language, by a West African activist by the name of Sebastian Esomba, then living in Guadalajara, Mexico. Sebastian was usually referred to by my collaborators in the region simply as "Esomba," which seemed to authenticate his general Africanness. Esomba was slowly amassing pieces of imported African material culture for an African museum that he was constructing in the city of Guadalajara. He entertained the crowd in Pino, which is the regional shorthand for "Pinotepa Nacional," an important regional commercial center for both Black and Indigenous communities in the Costa Chica, by playing "West African" music on African instruments and telling the popular West African tales of his childhood in Spanish. He also mixed genres and sang well-known Mexican songs in West African styles. The Black activist organizations in the region sponsored this event, after a non-Black representative from the Secretaría de Asuntos Indígenas de Oaxaca (Secretary of Indigenous Affairs Oaxaca) unofficially introduced Esomba at a meeting between activist organizations in Cuajinicuilapa, Guerrero. This concert represents an unofficial site of racial and cultural production. However, this unofficial site is no less important, as it potentially corroborates some of the state and local discourses on Blackness, even as this strategy attempted to maintain the means of racial/cultural representation in the hands of Black activists (as opposed to the state). These sites of racial production were politically charged, and both the official consultas and Esomba's concert in Pino are potentially at risk for popular scrutiny as they incorporate outward notions of race that may not speak to the lived experiences of local inhabitants. These types of sites, which I will explore in depth in later chapters, became important in my research—more so than the location and identification of cultural elements—in thinking about the process of racial subject making. Pinning down these sites of racial production and exploring the ways in which they are capitalized on and exploited in the process of reproducing not only Black Mexicans but Indigenous and Mestizos as well is hopefully one of this book's contributions to the ethnography and conversation around Blackness within the Costa Chica.

Many of the institutions responsible for creating and maintaining the perception of racial/ethnic difference within Mexico represent federal and state apparatuses such as national museums and institutes like the National Institute of Anthropology and History (INAH), the Commission for the Development of Indigenous Communities (CDI), and the Secretary of Indigenous and Afro-Mexican Affairs (SAI). These institutions are some of the formal bodies that promote state conceptions of race and ethnicity and continue to be responsible for defining Blackness from the top. Other important institutions are the regional Afro-Mestizo Museum (El Museo de las Culturas Afromestizas) in the Costa Chica, as well as the numerous mutual aid societies, such as Black Mexico (Mexico Negro), AFRICA, Cimarron, and many others, that developed at the grassroots level and have brought together a limited number of activists in order to support local communities and to capitalize on the contemporary trend of identity politics within Mexico. At the time of my research in the Costa Chica, there were several organizations, both active and defunct, formed around the notion of Blackness in some form or another. These organizations are responsible for defining Blackness from the bottom and engaging with the dominant conceptions of race that have become prevalent within the nation.

As the Costa Chica is part of a larger system of migrant networks, transnational organizations are also important to the process of racial construction. One such organization within Los Angeles, California, is La Organización Afro-Mexicano (The Afro-Mexican Organization). This mutual aid society was founded in order to deal with the specific social problems and cultural issues that Costa Chican migrants face within the Los Angeles area, as well as to raise funds for community projects within the Costa Chica. Important to my focus in Los Angeles was to explore in what ways La Organización Afro-Mexicano interacts with Oaxacan Indigenous organizations in Los Angeles and how this interaction does or does not reinforce the specific types of social relations and discourses that have become prevalent within Mexico and the Costa Chica region.

To see how the discourses of mestizaje and multiculturalism are manifested, I employed a combination of participant observation and both short and extended open-ended interviews focusing on the multiple conceptions and experiences of Blackness, as well as the official process of Black recognition. Interviewees included several of the activists and employees of the above-mentioned institutions. My initial investigations, seriously beginning in 2007, allowed me to create a spatial/ethnic map of the region (Cotton and Jerry 2013), and I divided my time between several communities, including Cuajinicuilapa, Corralero, Chacahua, Charco Redondo, and Puerto Escondido, to mention a few. I focused my attention on the active sites of political construction and transmission among Black Mexicans within the Costa Chica. These sites included the regional Museo de las Culturas Afro-Mestizos (Cuajinicuilapa, Guerrero), museum exhibits and academic talks/conferences in Oaxaca City, local schools, small "town hall" meetings, activist organizational meetings, a local Black community radio station, and the local organization Mexico Negro (based in El Ciruelo, Oaxaca). Participant observation at these sites provided a unique opportunity to understand how Black Mexicans within the Costa Chica are internalizing or confronting contemporary processes of racialization and how historical ideologies and practices are incorporated or excluded from the construction of current Black identities. These sites also make visible the tensions prevalent between generations and political actors; one tension being the signifier that should be adopted for racial identification: "Negro," Afro-Mexicano, Afro-Mestizo, Moreno, and so on.

My focus was on the group settings created by the consultas organized by the CDI and the meetings between the Black activist groups within the Costa Chica. I have treated these meetings as group interviews, for which the groups kindly afforded me permission to participate and record. The group setting allowed me to get a sense of activists' and townspeople's thoughts and feelings on the broader conversation around Blackness and Black representation, and I used the individual interviews with activists to elaborate on questions that came from these "group interviews." While I have been visiting and conducting research in the region since 2003, my 2011 visit to Oaxaca lasted for a period of ten months, and geographically spanned the city of Oaxaca to the small Costa Chica towns on the Pacific coast of the states of Oaxaca and Guerrero, as well as a few exploratory trips

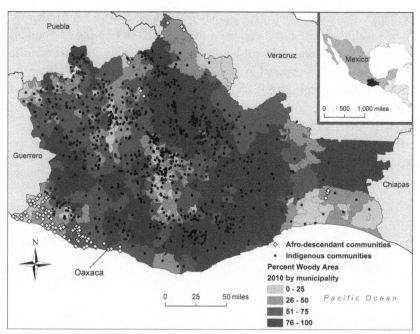

Map 1. Geographic location of Black communities in the state of Oaxaca. Sources: INE-GI Archivo Histórico de Localidades, CIESIN, ESRI, Google Earth, thematicmapping. org. Mexican Datum 1994 UTM Zone 14N. Date: January 28, 2013. Authors: Nicole Marie-Cotton, Sarah Wandersee, SDSU, "Drawing the Lines: Racial/Ethnic Landscapes and Sustainable Development in the Costa Chica," *Journal of Pan African Studies* 6(1): 210–226 (2013).

to the Isthmus de Tehuantepec region and the cities of Veracruz and Jalapa in the state of Veracruz.

Arriving again in the Costa Chica at the beginning of 2011, I soon realized that my original methodological approach of locating and documenting Blackness in the Costa Chica during previous research trips put me in a position to continue to "chase Blackness." African descendants in the Costa Chica are also chasing Blackness as they attempt to reimagine the value that this concept has traditionally held and to make new sense of the preexisting racial economy in which this value has historically been put to work. I have found that a logic of cultural difference, based on colonial logics of race, especially Blackness, limits the potential value and use of race and ethnicity (i.e., difference) as effective political tools toward a project of full inclusion. My intention in this text is not only to elaborate on a political economy of race but to also demonstrate the existence of a separate ideological (or perhaps symbolic) economy (i.e., a racial economy) in which race takes on its own value system and therefore continues to be a framing component of peoples' social and political being. It is this economy that frames the Black experience of citizenship in the Americas. This project asks how the current political project of Blackness within Mexico can help understand the ways that race continues to be one of the formative components of modern citizenship. I also aim to understand in what ways a persistent racial economy continues to position Blackness as the overall means for the reproduction of the Mexican nation.

2

Dark Matter, Ideology, and Blackness in the Conceptualization of Mestizaje

Many have discussed the role of Whiteness in the process of mestizaje, as both an ideology for nation building and racial/cultural mixing, in Mexico (Vasquez 2010; Harris 1993; Hernández Cuevas 2004; Joseph and Buchenau 2013; Jones 2018; Sue 2013). However, in research focusing on so-called Indo-Latin American countries, these discussions have focused primarily on the production of the Mestizo as a by-product of the cultural and racial mixing between the Indigenous and Spanish (Moreno Figueroa 2020). Often overlooked in the conversation are the ways in which Blackness, assumed to be either erased altogether or (more generously) assimilated into the material and social fabric of the nation-state, continues to operate as a subject position within the Mestizo nation even as explicit representations of Blackness in the country cease to exist. The perception that Blackness does not exist when the Black body is out of sight allows for the assumption that Blackness plays no role in the conceptualization of the nation or the ideal type, the Mexican Mestizo. While mestizaje became a tool to erase Blackness from the modern nation by privileging the biological mixing of Spanish and Indigenous, Blackness remained a subject position in Mexico and continued to act as a specter in Mexican society. This specter can better be perceived as a type of "dark matter," in that the invisible dark matter of Blackness, as a consequence of what Winant (1994) discusses as the "Big Bang" processes that would lead to modernity (cited in Wynter 2003, 265), continues to dictate the material outcomes of social relations within the nation. As a consequence of a growing Black movement and government responses to this movement, the dark matter, and the social relations of citizenship dependent on this matter, is currently becoming visible in Mexico and must now be reckoned with as African descendants' attempts for recognition and legibility make the subject position of Blackness explicitly visible to the Mexican nation as well as the states in which Black Mexicans continue to reside.

Lomnitz argues that postindependence nationalism in Mexico appropriated the pre-Hispanic world in a similar manner to the European appropriation of classical antiquity. According to Lomnitz,

the Aztecs served as the forerunner of independent Mexico; the colonial period was a parenthesis that served to bring Christianity and certain traits of civilization, but it also barbarously degraded the condition of the indigenous peoples. Therefore, in principle, the glorification of the pre-Hispanic past did not imply claims on behalf of the contemporaneous Indians because their habits and condition were seen to be the result of colonial degradation. Thus, in the early postindependent era, modernization could readily be made to trample over indigenous traditions without challenging national identity. (2001, 132)

In his 1829 book *Mexico*, H. G. Ward demonstrates the ways that this strategy of appropriation of the Indigenous past, and Indigeneity itself, was put to work by the Mexican Creole elite during the Mexican War for Independence. Ward argues that "from the first breaking out of the revolutions, the Creoles were obliged to court the alliance of the mixed classes, and in all their proclamations, we find them representing their own cause, and that of the Aborigines, as the same" (1829, 26). This strategy also required the rhetorical appropriation of Indigenous history and the employment of this history for the actual production of the nation. For example, Ward recognizes the "apparent absurdity of hearing the descendants of the first conquerors (for such the Creoles, strictly speaking, were) gravely accusing Spain of the atrocities, which their own ancestors had committed; invoking the names of Moctezuma and Atàhualpa; expatiating upon the miseries which the Indians had undergone and endeavoring to discover some affinity between the sufferings of that devoted race and their own" (26). Gillingham also recognizes how pre-Hispanic pride lay at the center of early nationalist discourse, explaining that "when Morelos declared Mexico independent in 1813, he invoked the 'spirits of Moctezuma, Cacamatzin, Cuauhtémoc, Xicoténcatl, and Catzonzin' to witness that the rebels were 'about to reestablish the Mexican Empire, improving its government'" (2011, 150). This rhetorical strategy allowed for independence-era leaders to be referred to as the "children of Moctezuma" and to invoke the Indigenous "hero" Cuauhtémoc in Independence Day speeches from the 1840s to 1870s. This shows how Indigeneity was seized upon as one of the building blocks of the nation, even if a national identity around this foundational feature was slower to develop (Gillingham 2011, 151).

Bulmaro, a Black activist, educator, and engineer from the Costa Chica town of Cuajinicuilapa, also recognized how narratives about the Indigenous "ruins" of Mexico separate a noble Indigenous past from contemporary Indigenous people. Bulmaro explained to me, "Then they [Spaniards] arrived here, they found very well-planned streets . . . those from Mexico City. And they ask themselves, 'What is this?' Like a very cool drainage system that is still working these days. And how did they do this? With knowledge. Those pyramids which are so well planned. I mean, the Sun pyramid was something they could not explain. So, they [Indigenous peoples] were amazing, but they [Spaniards] never said they were peoples who'd mastered sciences." Bulmaro's recognition is in line with the separation between the Indigenous as a historically relevant people and contemporary Indigenous people as a degraded by-product of colonialism. Echoing modern Western society's claims to ancient Greece and the Roman Empire, the ideological distance between those Indigenous who built the Pyramid of the Sun and the many impoverished and marginalized Indigenous peoples of today allows the Mexican state and its associated progeny, the modern Mestizo, to claim the past in order to historicize the origins of the greatness of the nation without sacrificing the state as a modern entity.

Sergio, a high school teacher and member of the mutual aid society and activist organization "Mexico Negro," recognized the opposite strategy for the rhetorical use of Blackness in the present as a strategy for creating a baseline for underdevelopment. Discussing the ways in which Blackness is presented in modern textbooks, Sergio explained, "In a textbook we do not see more than half a page about Afro-descendants. They talk about slavery and all that, [and] at the end they talk about a comparison between the developed and the underdeveloped countries, and they place Africa as an underdeveloped country [sic] in the comparison." Sergio went on to explain that as part of this strategy, textbooks in Mexico made material comparisons between Mexico and Africa by comparing, for example, pictures of hospitals in the two places. Sergio told me that in order to present Mexico as a modern nation, textbooks show a picture of a "twenty-first-century hospital" in Mexico. In juxtaposition to the modern Mexican hospital, in order to demonstrate the contrast between Mexico as a modern nation and Africa as undeveloped, these same textbooks present a picture of a hospital in Africa "that has been made of wood, and such things." Much to Sergio's frustration, the textbooks never mention that while there may be some rural hospitals in Africa such as those made of logs and other unmanufactured materials, there are also many similar medical facilities in rural areas of Mexico. Sergio went on to explain, "I mean, not all that is presented about Africa is like that, and not all that is presented about Mexico is like that. So, there is a distortion of reality. Children are seeing a reality that is not objective, right?" This lack of objectivity mentioned by Sergio is one of the by-products of the Mexican ideology of mestizaje as it is put to work as a methodology for educating Mexican youth. Furthermore, the use of rural hospitals in Africa as a comparison to reinforce a perception of Mexico as a modern nation is representative of a strategy that employs the perception of Blackness as the epitome of the undeveloped and uncivilized and utilizes this perception as the baseline for determining what is modern. This strategy is employed through everyday encounters between students and educators to reinforce the perception of Mexico as a modern nation and of the African continent, and by extension Black African descendants, as modern Mexico's polar opposite.

Historically, this modernization required the invention of the new nation as aesthetically and temporally in line with other modern states of the West (Kazanjian 2003). The need to present Mexico as a modern yet distinct nation allowed for the utilization of Indigeneity as one of the two symbolic pillars, alongside Whiteness in the form of Spanishness, of the postindependence Mexican state. Wade argues that the ideology of indigenismo (a form of mestizaje discourse) "used indigenous people to confer uniqueness on Latin American national identities in a global world and this is still common today" (2010, 101; Telles and PERLA 2014, 20). However, the explicit use of Indigeneity alongside Spanishness as the symbolic means for the production of the Mexican nation, and the associated ideal Mestizo Mexican citizen (Telles and Garcia 2013), should not allow us to assume that Blackness, as an ideal and a material reality in the nation, plays no role in the imagination of the nation postindependence. I argue that in the postindependence nation the ideal of Blackness becomes dark matter, allowing a new relation between Whiteness and Indigeneity to exist. At this moment, as the reliance on African descendants as the physical and symbolic means of production of the colonial period (the enslaved Black body) gave way to the use of the noble Indigenous past to create a symbolic origin myth for the modern nation, Blackness began to be erased from the legitimated, recognized history of the nation.

While Blackness has been positioned through the invention of modern racial thought and racism as the opposite of modernity, it has long been recognized that Blackness is the actual basis and by-product for modernity (Du Bois 1968; Trouillot 1992, 1984, 1995; Gilroy 1993). Blackness, then, has never been worked out of the ideology of the modern Mexican nation, or our conceptualization of modernity in general. Nor was it imagined out of the system of value that continued to inform the postindependence present in Mexico. In a conversation with Sergio in his classroom in the town of Cuajinicuilapa, Sergio recognized the disconnect between the historical use of Blackness as the physical means of production and the negative stereotypes presently associated with Blackness. Sergio explained, "No, Negros also work, because they were brought here [Mexico] to work. I always say they were not taken here on vacations, right? They were forced to build the economy of a country that was being created, right?" Sergio's comment is a direct response to the present negative perceptions about Blackness that Sergio and other Black Mexicans must confront on a daily basis regarding Blackness as representative of backwardness and laziness in Mexico. This perception is often articulated through the trope of the *hamaquero*—someone who can always be found (in a Black costal community) resting in a hammock. Further evidence of the ways in which outward conceptualizations of Blackness continue to be drawn upon to juxtapose the modern nation are visible in a discourse of anti-Blackness that continued to inform Mexican culture up into the twentieth century, most notably in Vasconcelos's eugenic work, *La raza cósmica: Misión de la raza iberoamericana* (1997). More mundane yet equally malignant are the use of iconic characters such a Memín Penguin (Moreno Figueroa and Saldívar Tanaka 2016) and the "African Bushman" caricature used to advertise the popular Pan Bimbo treat, Negrito.[1] In postindependence Mexico, the appropriation of Indigeneity by the Creole elite plants the seeds for what would become the official rhetoric of mestizaje as the dominant ideology of the nation. The development of this ideology, combined with a preexisting colonial valuation of Blackness, later turned into an actual strategy—or, better said, a methodology—that allowed for the almost complete erasure of Blackness from the popular national memory.

This erasure emerges through the promotion of particular postindependence national traditions that rely on "traditional" Indigenous elements as a means for representing the new nation (Hernández Cuevas 2004). The National Museum of Anthropology exemplifies this strategy (Lomnitz 2001, 133). Lomnitz recognizes tradition to act "like the country's spiritual dimension, which is incorporated as an aesthetic into a unique modernity that is the country's present and, above all, future" (2001, 133). This aesthetic, as well as the Mexican present and future, is realized not only through the exclusion and erasure of Blackness from state and national projects, but also through a more mundane discourse on Blackness as the polar opposite of modern, which underscores the intuitive logic of Black and Mexican as mutually exclusive (Sue 2013). This discourse of mutual exclusivity, as well as the cultural exclusion and erasure of Blackness from Mexican history, frames the current project for Black recognition, as well as the ways in which this project can take form in Mexico.

Rather than recognizing the role that African descendants have played in the development of the contemporary Mexican nation and the national culture (Hernández Cuevas 2004), and therefore Mexicanness, Black Mexicans are currently being recognized as a distinct cultural group apart from the average Mexican. This strategy has been operationalized in Mexico through the notion of the Third Root (Ramsay 2016; Hernández Cuevas 2004; Sue 2010; Hoffman and Rinaudo 2014; Hoffman 2014; Rinaudo 2014). Relying on the logic of mestizaje, the rhetoric of the Third Root positions Blackness as one of the historical elements of the Mexican nation. However, an underlying Black subject position that supports the perception of Black and Mexican as mutually exclusive limits the Third Root discourse, and therefore Blackness, from being incorporated into the Mestizo as an ontological position and the representation of the ideal Mexican. Rather, the Third Root strategy has produced the Afro-Mestizo/Afro-Mexican as a distinct cultural group within Mexico.

According to Hernández Cuevas, in some instances it might be more appropriate to refer to the African element in Mexico as the "first root" (2004, xiv). However, because of the intimate social relations between Africans and the Spanish in the colonial moment, it has become almost impossible to distinguish the African contributions within Mexican society. Hernández Cuevas's work explains how African ethnic contributions were plagiarized by the Criollo elite. Here, plagiarism acts as a mechanism for appropriation. But in the context of the production of the nation and the subsequent exclusion from the ideal national citizen, Hernández Cuevas suggests that plagiarism can be seen as a process in which Blackness is utilized as the means of production, in that the "African Mexican cultural expressions that became icons of modern national identity were separated from their African origins and ascribed to Spanish and Amerindian origins alone" (2004, viv). This has made it difficult to recognize distinct African/Black Mexican cultural forms, if they indeed do exist. The current strategy of cultural recognition requires that Black communities in Mexico speak the language of culture as a way of proving a type of difference—cultural rather than racial—that is acceptable to the larger nation-state. Through culture and tradition, Black Mexicans in the region are seen as taking their rightful place as one of the cultural elements of the nation while not threatening the preexisting narratives of the modern contemporary Mestizo Mexican state and people as being non-Black. Ironically, as cultural recognition allows for the material visibility of Black communities in Mexico, an unrecognized Black subject position allows Blackness to remain the dark matter by which the Mestizo nation is perpetually reproduced. In the current strategy for cultural recognition, the lack of acknowledgment of an enduring Black subject position allows for the perception that contemporary Black Mexican communities have survived in spite of mestizaje rather than as a direct consequence of the racial and ethnic dimensions of the historic national mestizaje project.

The Colonial Black Subject Position and Discordant Identities

The Black presence in Mexico, then the colony of New Spain, dates to the early sixteenth century with the arrival of the Spanish conquistadors. Ben Vinson (2001) and Matthew Restall (2000) document Black participation in the settlement process as well as the incorporation of Africans and their descendants into the colonial economy and militia groups aimed at domestic defense. While the presence of these Africans and their descendants is well-documented demographically, the question of community building and the colonial impact on the development of Black identities within these groups remains underexplored. Vinson's and Restall's historical research points to how the caste system impacted the creation of a diverse set of racialized Black social and political groups and situated these groups within an institutional racial and ethnic hierarchy. This archival research also sheds a dim light on the ways in which African descendants within Mexico historically interacted with these hierarchies in order to form their own communities. Among the many forms of nomenclature used to distinguish Blacks from their non-Black colonial counterparts—"Spaniards," "Mestizos," and "Indigenous"—the most utilized terms were "Pardo," "Negro," and "Mulatto" (terms used to reference percentages of African genetic admixture). While these were clearly utilized as racial terms (Sue 2013), they were applied differently between Spaniards and Blacks in both personal and institutional capacities (Vinson 2001). Closer examination draws attention to the varied historical experiences of race among Indigenous peoples, Blacks, and Spaniards within specific historical eras (Omi and Winant 1994).

This section briefly focuses on the presence of these groups within Mexico and the development of Black communities or a racial consciousness within colonial Mexico as a consequence of a colonial racial and caste hierarchy. While they were diverse, evidence demonstrates that these communities would have had some sense of individual and communal identity based on their own perceptions of racial affiliation, as well as the imposition of a broader Black subject position in the colony. For African descendants, racial identities and the experience of an explicit Black subject position within the space of colonial social relations would have been part of the political, social, and cultural lenses through which the later Mexican War for Independence would have been contextualized.

Herman Bennett's research shows that in 1640, the year the Portuguese slave trade to the Spanish Americas "officially" ended, colonial Mexico contained the second largest population of enslaved Africans and the highest population of free Blacks within the Americas (2003, 1). Within a century of Cortés's expedition into New Spain, Portuguese slave traders had brought 110,000 enslaved Africans to the region. By 1646 the census counted 116,529 persons of African descent in colonial Mexico, and by 1810 the free African-descendant population numbered over 600,000, or 10 percent of the total population (Bennett 2003, 1). By this time, the free African-descendant population considerably outnumbered that of the enslaved population within Mexico. While the numbers of free African descendants alone do not speak to the existence of a consciously unified community, the numbers are important to understanding the potential for the mobilization of unifying racial and ethnic ties among Black people at the time, as well as the potential for the production of shared subjectivities based on common experiences within the colonial racial hierarchy.

While the imposition of racial hierarchies was also utilized by African descendants, the large population concentrated in certain geographic areas created opportunities for communities to develop among individuals around caste markers (Vinson 2001; Von Germeten 2006). Rather than seeing the mobilization of Blackness as a strategy simply to counter the institution of slavery, it is important to recognize the everyday meanings of race and ethnicity as well as the ways in which communities mobilize around familiarity in order to maintain and re-create community in the face of larger institutional forms. While acknowledging that the meanings of race are constantly negotiated on both institutional and social levels, my intention here is to focus on the social outcomes of everyday experiences of race. As Bennett argues, "Africans and persons of African descent created communities that expanded the boundaries of the households in which they served as slaves and bridged cultural divisions. Yet even as 'Angolans' formed communities with individuals from 'Lamba Land,' for example, they retained their newly imposed ethnic identities" (2003, 82). Bennett's argument here highlights the use of community in two distinct ways. While African descendants began to create networks among themselves based on a sense of generic racial Blackness (Gomez 1998) (and all the value that this term referenced within the colonial racial economy), the use of imposed ethnicities helped maintain ethnic boundaries that were meaningful on personal levels and perhaps also helped maintain a sense of a shared past.[2]

Bennett goes on to show that these ethnic boundaries also influenced the choice of marriage partners within these multilevel communities (2003, 82). Maintained ethnicities, combined with broader institutionalized social hierarchies, also allowed for the utilization of experiences and recognition of other Black bodies as sites of familiarity, which in turn fostered the fortification of ethnic and racial communities. Within these communities, the caste system played a role in internal communal hierarchies. However, the caste system itself may have been utilized in different capacities from within. That is, Black communities may have operated around an ideological centering of Blackness, rather than the simple acceptance of a pathological centering of Whiteness within their daily lives. Napolitano uses the concept of "prisms of belonging" in order to demonstrate how people express differently situated selves under different circumstances, and the ways in which "heterogeneous perceptions, feelings, desires, contradictions, and images . . . shape the experiences of space and time" (2002, 9). While pointing to the variance of experiences within communities, Napolitano's concept can also be applied to the varied experiences of society and social phenomenon between groups that lead to vernacular experiences of the same phenomenon (Gilroy 1993; Hanchard 1999; Napolitano 2002; Neyazi 2010). Therefore, colonial hierarchies may have been experienced in different ways between social and racial categories. That is simply to say that the value of these racial and social categories would have been experienced in different ways, and even contested, according to specific social contexts.

Bennett (2003) demonstrates that identity for African descendants was not a preordained essence in the New World but rather was carefully constructed. This careful construction of identity drew upon experiences within the context of slavery and other institutional exclusions and inclusions, but it was undoubtedly also formed by experiences of family, community, and internal understandings of selfhood. My intention here is not to explore historical identity formation among African descendants.[3] Rather, I highlight the ways in which a Black subject position and the process of racialization were felt differently and employed differently within institutional and communal capacities according to one's own location in the colonial racial hierarchy. Much of the historical literature on race and mestizaje in Mexico overlooks this contextualization of Black value and assumes a lack of value and that Blackness acted as anti-value in all social contexts. This approach to Blackness allows for a general acceptance that African descendants resisted affiliation with each other and were preoccupied with "Whitening" as well as the potential for assimilation at the dawn of Mexican independence. However, historical work such as Vinson's and Bennett's recognizes how Blackness was employed, and perhaps embraced, within Black communities, allowing for community cohesion and the maintenance of Black communities even as the developing system of mestizaje allowed for the popular and institutional erasure of Blackness from the national narrative. As witnessed by the existence of contemporary Black communities in areas such as the Costa Chica, a local sense of community on the part of African descendants has persisted into the present. With this recognition, the continued existence and reproduction of Black communities within Mexico appears to be less the consequence of Black communities miraculously escaping the modern project of nationhood in Mexico, and more realistically the result of a deliberate internal, as well as external, social process.

Vinson discusses the importance of confraternities and *cabildos* (local municipal governing councils) in preserving and developing facets of Black culture within Mexico while simultaneously providing material assistance to freed Blacks in times of need (2001, 2; Von Germeten 2006). African descendants in Mexico also used confraternities and community organizations to highlight their incorporation into larger Spanish society. Von Germeten's historical work (2006) demonstrates how different Black confraternities within Mexico provided for community needs and fostered social mobility. She explains that participation within confraternities may not have been an individual's only source of personal or communal identity, but that race did influence an individual's experience within a confraternity. Confraternities were created based on identities formed both before and after enslavement. According to Von Germeten, "some confraternities characterized their members as from a specific African place of origin and others extended membership only to mulattos or Blacks, making a distinction between individuals identified by these racial labels" (2006, 192). She goes on to argue that confraternity founders worked hard at preventing anyone with a different racial designation than that of the confraternity from becoming organizational leaders (192).

Later, confraternities of the eighteenth century were subject to the same effects of the caste system as the broader society. The eighteenth century brought with it a shift in the labels of confraternities, as they integrated members of different castes. No longer were the confraternities of this period labeled Negro or "Black," but they reflected the Spanish authorities' preference for the term *mulatto*. If we take seriously the ways in which many African descendants in the Costa Chica continue to reference themselves and their own communities as "Negro," then we can see that the term does not disappear but instead becomes applied internally by African descendants within unofficial contexts. This coincides with the use of "Negro" within communities of non-Blacks in Mexico, as well, as "Negro" continues to be used as a pejorative when referring to actual African descendants by non-Black Mexicans.

The militia also played an important role in reinforcing Black identities. Ben Vinson asks two important questions: first, "given that colonial Mexico was a society where 'racial drift' and even 'passing' were possible, did the mulatto or pardo [someone of African, Spanish, and Indigenous descent] ever feel a racial identity as such," and second, "did free-coloreds bond or feel a race-based affinity, especially considering that racial discourse during the colonial period was largely defined by and worked for the benefit of others" (2001, 4)? Vinson's questions explore the ways in which Blackness was experienced from the bottom, or inside, rather than from the top, or within an institutional context. The militia may have provided more opportunities for African descendants than civilian life. And within this context, Blackness became even more salient in the lives of militiamen. Vinson argues that "by enrolling in the free-colored corps, soldiers participated in an institution that was often segregated and defined by race. As a result, upon joining, race assumed added meaning in their lives, perhaps more so than for the average Mexican colonist" (2001, 4). Joining the militia allowed for the creation of new networks with other persons of color (2001, 4). While the logic of Whitening and mestizaje held that the eroding of connections based on affinities with Blackness enabled social mobility, for militia members mobility came with an even more pronounced Black identity. The opportunities brought about by militia service were sometimes the basis for internal rifts among African descendants. This reinforces the notion that racial identities were strongly predicated upon the intense desire for privilege, but when threats to the soldiers' rights emanated from outside their own organization, militiamen utilized a unified front (Vinson 2001). While the caste system infiltrated even the militia units, militiamen themselves negotiated the meanings of these different nomenclatures and employed them within different contexts. Vinson argues that the use of the same terms, *Pardo* and *Moreno*, varied between the crown and soldiers, and that this variance in use reflects separate racial outlooks (2001).

This difference in racial outlook between Black and non-Black is important for the continued existence of African-descendant communities within Mexico, especially given the caste system and the implicit encouragement of social mobility through "Whitening" later promoted within the developing system of mestizaje. The use of "Whitening" as a strategy for social mobility may have been only part of the reality of race for Mexico's African descendants. Bennett argues that "for Africans and their descendants, the imposed patterns of social stratification and their own community boundaries were very different phenomena" (2003, 125). This highlights the ways in which African descendants in Mexico were not only subjected to the caste system but were also aware of the processes involved in the project of racialization and therefore utilized the same process to create communities based on shared racial subjectivities and positioning around a Black subject position in the colonial era. Colonial communities, while affected by the racial hierarchies at play within the caste system, may have also incorporated individuals from the various castes while simultaneously maintaining racial or ethnic identities. As Carroll (1991) notes, the family played a large part in the socialization process, and undoubtedly the changing racial dynamics within this same institution in Mexico would be responsible for allowing for the recognition of racial and communal ties. In other words, while racial mixing may have allowed for the adoption of strategies for social mobility within an institutional context, within a communal context race may have bound Black communities together rather than facilitating their disintegration. The focus on the impacts of mestizaje in Mexico has overlooked how this process is still at play within contemporary Black communities of the Costa Chica and has yet to be addressed by much of the research on Black Mexico or the project for Black recognition underway in Mexico today. The creation and maintenance of Black communities and Black social networks speaks to the historic vitality of Black communities, as well as the existence of multiple Black identities. Part of this Black community work relied on the reproduction of a clearly marked Black subject position within the economic and social relations of colonial New Spain.

According to Aguirre Beltrán, by 1793 "Afro-Mexicans approached . . . roughly 10% of the entire population" (1989, 222–30, cited in Vinson 2005b, 60). Vinson (2001, 2005b) demonstrates that there was a well-developed negative discourse about Blackness into the independence moment. He argues that of the 370,000 documents in the national archive focused on the period of 1521–1821, 9,000 contain discussions of the African-descendant population. According to Vinson, "blacks appeared most frequently in documentation that focused on the themes of deviance, social control, and the colonial economy" (2005b, 61). Vinson goes on to highlight the obsession with Blackness as a central feature of the colonial caste structure. Vinson explains,

amidst the literally hundreds of possible racial combinations within the caste system, fifty-three have been surveyed as being applicable to Mexico. Black racial categories accounted for at least thirty-six of these, including lobos [wolves], zambos [bowlegged], saltatrás [a step backward], tente en el aire [suspended in the air], and the no te entiendo [I don't understand you]. The vast majority of these classifications were never used in common language. But they served to exhibit the fears that colonials had about black admixture in disrupting the natural order. Blacks (Negros) were perceived as being "sexually vicious," "lazy," "drunkards," "vile," "untrustworthy," "naturally turbulent and defiant," as well as "cruel and malevolent." (Israel 1975, 73; Aguirre Beltrán 1989, 185–89; cited in Vinson 2005b, 64)

According to Vinson, these stereotypes in conjunction with the nomenclature of the caste system demonstrate that race mixing did not necessarily negate the negative traits associated with Blackness. Rather, race mixture was thought to intensify the worst qualities of racial stock.

Vinson's work clearly shows that over the course of three centuries, the Black population, while perhaps not motivating the production of individual texts, remains a relevant theme informing colonial Mexican society on the eve of Mexican independence. The War for Independence does not change the discourse associated with Blackness or the ways in which Blackness operated as an underlying theme in Mexican society. The war, however, would create the need for the rhetorical development of a new national citizenry (Jerry 2021) and the ideal national subject, the Mestizo.

And while the production of this new national Mestizo subject relies on the explicit embracing of both Spanishness and Indigeneity, a Black subject position continued to endure, albeit implicitly, within the postindependence national period.

The Move to Independence and the Effect of Mestizaje as Ideology

Mexican independence brought with it the question of nationality. While perhaps not threatening the existence of Black communities and identities per se, Mexican nationalism threatened the explicit institutional recognition of Blackness within Mexico and began a process of popular erasure facilitated by the appropriation of Indigeneity as the foundation for the Mexican nation; it also brought about the explicit conceptualization of the new Mexican citizen as a unique new world hybrid between Spanish and Indigenous. There are at least two dimensions of mestizaje as ideology: one being the conceptualization of mestizaje as a principle for national development, and the other being mestizaje as a principle for intermarriage (Telles and Garcia 2013, 131). According to Telles and Garcia, the first dimension is closely related to the national narratives developed by elites during the periods of nation-making in Latin America and maintains that race mixing is good for the nation (2013, 131). In Mexico, this principle was utilized as a way of inventing the prototypical Mexican citizen as a mixture of Indigenous and Spanishness. During this moment, Indigeneity was utilized symbolically as one of the foundational pillars of the nation. This symbolic incorporation created the need to assimilate the Indigenous as a way to sanitize Indigeneity and the perceived negative characteristics associated with colonial stereotypes of Indigeneity. This sanitization allowed for elite claims to Indigeneity without sacrificing the claims to modernity that were needed to legitimize the new Mexican nation.

The postrevolutionary period in Mexico would seize upon the form of indigenismo/mestizaje developed during the national period as a way of creating an ideal racial subject that was in line with the ideological subject imagined during the national period. This strategy required a reimagination or reconceptualization of the value associated with Indigeneity (Saldívar and Walsh 2014), and therefore mestizaje, in the postrevolutionary period, attempted to value the Indigenous contribution to the racial character of the nation rather than do away with Indigenous communities through the previous postindependence strategy of assimilation. Vasquez suggests that in the aftermath of the Mexican Revolution, artists, philosophers, and government agencies utilized indigenismo as a counterargument to Eurocentrism by privileging the heritage of Indigenous populations (2010, 191; Joseph and Buchenau 2013, 107). During this moment, government agencies sought to expand the presence of Indigenous peoples into a "new Mestizo national vision" and began attempts to address Indigenous communities' social and economic needs (Vasquez 2010, 191). Vasquez argues that "through government funding and encouragement Mexican historians continued to inscribe Spanish and Indigenous peoples as creators of a modern Mexico, while simultaneously downplaying the roles of African-descended peoples as subjects and citizens" (2010, 191). While the transition from the postindependence to the postrevolutionary approach to mestizaje challenged previous conceptions of Indigeneity, the negative value and subject position associated with Blackness endured. This is to argue that the War for Independence and the Mexican Revolution may have very well been perceived and experienced by Spanish, Mestizo, and Indigenous alike as an actual event in the terms laid out by Marshall Sahlins (1985, 1993; Wynter 1984; Sewell 2005; Hartman 1997). However, for African descendants, these historical happenings may have been more of a non-event (Hartman 1997) as the underlying Black subject position and the set of social relations in which Black value was constructed and put to work continued to influence how Black Mexicans could experience the new national environment.

Ted Vincent (1994) argues that the Mexican War for Independence was not only a struggle for national independence but also a social revolution. According to Vincent, "those of African heritage in Mexico had special incentives to fight, were encouraged to join the struggle, and provided many participants and leaders" (1994, 257). His insights highlight the existence of vibrant Black communities at the beginning of the war and even their mobilization around issues of race as well as the discrimination imposed by the caste system. In this sense, African descendants' involvement in the independence effort should be understood as a conscious and calculated project. While Vincent overlooks the importance of communal ties after the war, as he argues that African descendants' involvement in the War for Independence was aimed mostly at the possibility to assimilate, he points out the lived consequences of race during the first decades of the nineteenth century. The imposition of the caste system not only created racial boundaries but also, as demonstrated by Vinson, allowed for resistance predicated on issues of race and racial affiliation. According to Vincent, Hidalgo, during the first months of the conflict, declared the abolition of slavery and caste laws. After Hidalgo's death in 1811, Morelos took up the cause, calling for the banning of slavery and caste distinctions as well as elaborating on Indigenous rights (Vincent 1994, 259). Vincent suggests that for the "darker" people of Mexico, the revolution spoke of equal opportunity and social integration (1994, 259).

The question of integration becomes important throughout Latin America and the Caribbean as a succession of colonial states gained independence throughout the nineteenth century. The beginning of the century witnessed Haiti's independence (1803), with struggles in Mexico (1810) and Colombia (1819) following shortly after. Brazil and Ecuador initiated their own national periods in 1822. With the beginning of these national periods in Latin America came the question of defining not only the nation but also the ideal national subject, the citizen. For many of the newly conceived Latin American countries, this issue is represented by "the Indian question." For these new nations, the question became how to deal with the inclusion of the Indigenous while simultaneously promoting the nation as modern.

One of the strategies imposed to answer this question was the adoption of policies of "Whitening" through immigration (Telles and Garcia 2013; Wade 2010; Larson 2004; Paschel 2016) to genetically weed out the biological influences of the "inferior races." In Colombia, for example, it was hoped that assimilation could be achieved through intermarriage and mortality (Larson 2004).[4] According to Larson, this strategy was predicated on the sense of Whiteness as a pathway to modernity, while non-Whites symbolized the opposite end of this spectrum, anti-modernity. Paschel (2016) shows that in Brazil, Black Brazilians were the most impacted by immigration policies that incentivized foreign immigration as a mechanism for Europeanization, as Blacks were displaced by immigrants. This demonstrates how the transition from the colonial reliance on Black people as the physical means of production through slavery to a model of liberalism in the national period does not naturally allow for Black incorporation. Rather, it simply ensured that Blacks would remain, by and large, unemployed and marginalized.

In Mexico, the Creole elite adopted Indigeneity as a progenitor of the nation itself. During this period, the embracing of Indigeneity as a symbolic pillar of the nation created the potential for Indigenous communities to capture some of the value created by nationalization. But what role does Blackness play in this equation, either explicitly or implicitly? The adoption of Indigeneity as a rhetorical strategy for producing the nation allows for the potential imagination of the Indigenous as educable and ultimately incorporable within the nation. Blackness, however, continued to represent the eternal other: the non-Mexican. The Mexican approach to the incorporation of the Indigenous by way of assimilation through labor and education in both the national and revolutionary periods, as well as the lack of any similar program focused on African descendants, is a stark example.

According to Vincent, a series of laws were drafted shortly after Mexican independence, which reflected the rhetorical importance of racial equality during this period. These laws were not specifically drafted to protect certain groups such as earlier colonial decrees focused particularly on Indigeneity (Lewis 2012, 4). Law #303, for example, prohibited public officials from speaking disparagingly of any citizen's ethnic background. Another example comes through law #313, which prohibited the use of race in any government document and in church recordings such as marriage, baptism, and death records (Vincent 1994, 272). While these laws may have been interpreted as successes for Indigenous peoples and Blacks within Mexico—as Vincent argues that incorporation within the larger social system was one of the main goals of African-descendant participation in the conflict—these concessions may have played out only officially. Furthermore, the institutional dismantling of the caste system did not necessarily correlate with the end of race-based discrimination for Mexico's Black communities.

Saldívar and Walsh argue that "when Mexico became an independent nation in 1822, the old social order and classification of its inhabitants was replaced by liberal notions of universal citizenship, private property and nationhood. Legally all casta identities were replaced by the figure of the universal citizen, but three dominant categories would persist in everyday practice as well as in statistics: White/European, Indigenous and Mestizo" (2014, 456). This is the political environment in which Blackness became invisible within Mexico. However, this does not mean that Black Mexicans and a Black subject position are not reproduced within the national period. Saldívar and Walsh highlight how the caste system gets folded into the concept of race to define the new nation. They argue that

after the casta system and slavery were officially abolished in 1829, casta categories were largely abandoned in registers of births, marriages and deaths. Concepts of bodily, geographical and cultural difference continued to thrive, however, under the rubric of race. The idea of nation was political and geographical, but also corporeal and cultural. In this context, casta was folded into, and eclipsed by, race as the register upon which difference was evaluated. And while casta was a technology of governing socioeconomic boundaries that was derived from ideas about the history of conquest and the genealogy of families, race was a concept that oriented ideas about the evolution of national populations. (2014, 461)

Again, we see the impact of colonial debris here as the social relations of the colonial period become the foundation for those in the national period.

This debris would continue to inform conceptualizations of the nation and the norm-subject into the postrevolutionary moment. Vasconcelos's work clearly reveals that even by 1925, a point at which the nation was again explicitly engaging in the work of nation building (Telles and Garcia 2013) by questioning the meaning of Mexicanness, the Black subject position and the question of race in Mexico was still very much a hot topic, at least among the new revolutionary elite. Wade sees nationality as a relational term and argues that nations are forever "haunted" by their various definitional others (2001, 851). I think that in the context of Blackness, the concept of dark matter is more appropriate than the notion of a haunting, as it highlights the relational character of nationality and allows for the recognition of interaction between the living and those who are perceived to be socially dead. Independence-era legal proclamations may have worked more to segregate Black communities and to limit Black Mexicans' claims to discrimination rather than to limit actual discriminatory practices against them, therefore leaving the actual Black subject position within the racial hierarchy intact.

The legal mechanisms that limit the explicit institutional recognition of a Black subject position, and the value associated with that subject position, do not limit the negative valuation of Blackness by non-Blacks from being used as a mechanism for determining a Black subject position as the baseline for social mobility through Whitening within the social relations of mestizaje (Cerón-Anaya 2019). My own experience in both Mexico and the United States offers a lucid example of how Blackness facilitates social mobility for non-Blacks. Discussing my interest in African descendants in Mexico, Mexican nationals, as well as Chicanx and Mexican Americans in both Mexico and the United States, repeatedly shared similar anecdotes. People self-identifying as non-Black Mexicans would often explain to me, "One of my relatives is 'Negro' or 'moreno,'" often followed by the qualification "más Negro que tú" (even Blacker than you). This strategy serves to create boundaries between a general racial "us" and "them," even within the same family, as a direct relative's racial signifier from the previous generation may have no effect on the speaker's current affiliation (Sue 2013; Hoffman 2014).[5] The ideal of mestizaje, and the two racial poles associated with the process, emerges as both ideology and methodology, as many of these same respondents would be quick to appropriate the Indigenous blood of their ancestors into their own contemporary personal and political identities, as Indigeneity does not threaten the possibility of Whiteness in the same ways that Blackness does. Ultimately, the racial system of value that is mestizaje allows for Indigeneity and Whiteness to be compatible (Wade 2001; Greene 2012). However, Whiteness and Blackness continue to act as two opposite poles on the spectrum of value in Mexico. This example highlights the processes of Whitening involved within the discourse of mestizaje (Lugo 2008; Safa 1998, 2005; Whitten and Torres 1992, 1998), as some view Blackness as an escapable quality or condition, while those unsuccessful or devoid of access to this strategy may view Blackness in more than simply phenotypic terms. This process depends on geography, as well as local communal and regional discourses of race. For example, many in the Costa Chica who would be phenotypically considered non-Black claim to be Black by association. My extended time in the Costa Chica shows this social phenomenon becoming more and more common now that the movement for recognition is gaining momentum.[6] The 2015 inter-census lent credibility to this hypothesis, as it added questions on African-descendant identification (which should be seen as different from identity), however nebulous. The official 2020 Mexican census continued this trend of attempting to count those who self-identify as Black in some form or another.

While racial mixing during the nineteenth century in Mexico is not promoted strictly under the rhetoric of mestizaje, postindependence indigenismo plants the seeds for the later institutional version of postrevolutionary indigenismo in the form of mestizaje (Telles and PERLA 2014, 41). Martínez-Echazábal argues that mestizaje "is a foundational theme in the Americas, particularly in those areas colonized by the Spanish and the Portuguese" (1998, 21; Knight 1990, 83). During the nineteenth century, according to Martínez-Echazábal, mestizaje was a recurrent trope, linked to the search for "lo Americano." Martínez-Echazábal goes on to explain that, during what she refers to as the period of national consolidation and modernization (1920s–1960s), "mestizaje underscored the affirmation of cultural identity as constituted by 'national character'" (1998, 21), specifically for my interests here, Lo Mexicano. Joseph and Buchenau suggest that we should question the exceptionalism created by concepts such as Lo Mexicano or even Mexicanidad (2013, 10). However, my use of the term here is not intended to highlight the exceptionalism of the ideal Mexican type based on insular local developments. Rather, I use the term to reference an ideology that is employed to produce Mexican nationalism, and which is encapsulated by the invention of the ideal Mexican citizen. Vinson argues that "after the revolution, Mexico placed a heightened emphasis on the hybrid nature of its population to demonstrate the strength of its national character" (2005a, 3). Rather than a new invention, the heightened emphasis on mestizaje and racial mixing after the revolution was an elaboration on the theme (Arrizón 2017; Knight 1990, 83) of racial mixing, both physically and rhetorically, that had already been in place pre-revolution. The heightened emphasis on mestizaje during the revolutionary period is also an elaboration on the value placed on Blackness that had carried over into the independence and later revolutionary period. Sue explains that there were three pillars of postrevolutionary ideology: 1) mestizaje, the embracement of race mixture and lauding of the Mestizo; 2) non-racism, the contention that racism does not exist in the country; and 3) non-Blackness, the marginalization, neglect, or negation of Mexico's African heritage (2010, 14). However, just as Indigeneity was seized upon as an ideological or symbolic pillar for the postindependence construction of the nation and then reevaluated in the context of the postrevolutionary national project, I argue that non-Blackness was also a pillar of postindependence ideology in the national period. This theme was later elaborated on, but not invented, in the postrevolutionary period by such scholars as Vasconcelos, Gamio, and other revolutionary thinkers. Knight (1990), for example, argues that Porfirian-era indigenismo was the mestizaje discourse of the nineteenth century, which expanded on a discourse created in the early part of the same century. This discourse is mostly an ideological mestizaje utilized for the purpose of nation building, a strategy that relied on the appropriation of Indigeneity to produce the archetypal national subject. This is an important point for thinking about the role that Blackness has played within conceptualizations of the nation throughout Mexican history, as it allows us to recognize that at the very foundation of the nation is the conceptualization of Mexico as non-Black (Sue 2010, 14). Furthermore, the process of "excluding Blacks from the national image was a process that was long in the making" (Vinson 2005a, 3). This must be considered when thinking about the contemporary possibilities for Black recognition in Mexico.

Mestizaje and Whiteness

With the help of Vasconcelos (1997) and others, the postrevolutionary twentieth century gave birth to the images of the Mestizo and the Mulatto (Martínez-Echazábal 1998), within the context of nation-state consolidation. Vasconcelos and others, while promoting a project of equality through mixing, ultimately endorsed a broader project of eugenics and Whitening. Sue (2010) argues that the contradiction of mestizaje is that it appears to challenge the notions of White superiority yet promotes Whitening. Another contradiction pointed out by Sue is that "while mixed race brown skinned individuals became the esteemed national representative, the white phenotype was (and still is) very much prized" (18). However, the privileging of the White phenotype in mestizaje is less of a contradiction if we allow for the possibility that the Mestizo is a variant of or position within Whiteness, and that mestizaje was actually conceived as a methodology for achieving Whiteness.

Castañeda, drawing on Hernández Cuevas's insight on the pathology of mestizaje (2004, 101), explains that mestizaje "turned the members of a mainly dark population against one another, made a whole country and its people ashamed of their African heritage, and propagated the whitening mentality that infects a considerable portion of Mexican Mestizos up to the present" (2012, 96). Mestizaje in Mexico was used to create a brand of Whiteness that could exist outside of the United States and other European brands of Anglo Whiteness. Knight (1990) explains that indigenismo (referring to postrevolutionary mestizaje) tended to reproduce many of the racist assumptions of the preceding "Westernism" which it formally opposed. "It did so because, even when it reacted against Porfirian racism, it continued to operate within the racist paradigm—it could not, in other words, break out of that paradigm, but chose rather to criticize and invert several of its basic tenets. Like Marx, shackled to Ricardian political economy, the indigenistas could shake the bars of their conceptual prison but not escape from it" (87). In this way, mestizaje becomes a discourse of Whiteness and White supremacy (Telles 2004, 4), not just a process of racial Whitening, and therefore produces the Mestizo itself as a White form.

This form of Whiteness is easily disguised, as Mexican politics, both in Mexico and the United States, have been waged in part by positioning Mexico, and *the Mexican*, in opposition to a type of Protestant Anglo Whiteness (Knight 1990, 95) that supposedly categorizes Whiteness in general, not only in the United States but more broadly. Therefore, Mexican, and by association the Mexican, is perceived to be non-White in relation to US Anglos. However, this is complicated when Blackness is added to the formula. Knight suggests that the official ideology of mestizaje has perpetuated a kind of instrumental Indianness, but this Indianness stands at odds with a social reality in which "White/mestizo depreciation of supposed Indian attributes keeps alive the old pattern of negative Indian identification" (1990, 100). Greene (2012) explains, however, that Whiteness and Indigeneity can be mutually constitutive. Greene, writing on the use of Indigeneity as a national symbol in Peru, argues that "the abstract representation of 'the Inca' in Peru serves as a central discourse of nation, civilization, and citizenship. It is thus necessarily conflated with discourses of whiteness, modernity, democracy, and liberalism in contemporary Peru" (2012, 283). This is a prime example of how Indigeneity becomes employed as a hegemonic tool to support Whiteness. Greene refers to the outcome of this process as a type of "Inca Whiteness." In his analysis, Greene uses the term "Whiteness" as it is used by critical theorists such as Lipsitz (2006) and argues that Whiteness is "essentially a representation of power, prestige, and privilege that is ideologically associated with a particular narrative of world history that is deeply Eurocentric" (2012, 286). He goes on to indicate that the key to this approach is that it allows us to recognize that "the power of Europe's whiteness is its ability to constitute itself as different and in so doing constitutes other non-Europeans or nonwhites as different and whiteness itself as the implicit norm" (286).

Whiteness, drawing on Greene's analysis, can be seen partly as the ability to claim the nation as your own, and to determine the image that is reflected in the national mirror. It is obvious that Indigenous people and communities in Mexico have not been able to exploit the value of Indigeneity in the same way as the White/Mestizo. For example, while the Indigenous may occupy a privileged othered position in Latin America (Wade 2010; Hooker 2005), this has not necessarily translated into better material or economic positions, as Indigenous groups represent the lowest socioeconomic status of all ethno-racial groups in Latin America (Telles and PERLA 2014, 33). However, the ideological incorporation of Indigeneity has created a powerful political tool by which Indigenous groups' political claims on the nation are legitimated. This is a key difference between Indigeneity as an "instrument" for the production of the nation and Blackness as "the means of production," as Indigenous politics can potentially capture the value of the nation that they help create as instruments, whereas Black Mexicans as the means of production cannot.

Helen Safa argues that "although mestizaje affirmed race mixture, it maintained White supremacy through a hegemonic discourse of blaquea-miento [Whitening]" (1998, 5). However, mestizaje also fosters the creation of communities and consciousnesses based on race and ethnicity, even while institutionally employing hegemonic processes of "national" homo-geneity. As noted by Bennett and his discussion of the disparity between ra-cial boundaries utilized by the state and local communities, while mestizaje may have been utilized on an institutional level to appropriate privileges and resources, it may have been less important for the development of local racial identities. Furthermore, as Blackness is still allowed a value within the social and racial system of mestizaje—albeit a negative value—mes-tizaje does not preclude the development of racial subjectivities. In fact, for those unable to "escape" their own Blackness, whether through mixing or due simply to outward impositions, mestizaje is responsible for the repro-duction of Black subjectivities and a Black subject position. The difficulty in recognizing these subjectivities, and the identities they help create, within the mestizaje paradigm is due simply to the lack of official ways of publicly recognizing Blackness. The issue is ultimately a lack of legitimate forms of representation (Taylor 1994; Lucero 2008) and visibility. The active with-holding of these legitimate forms of representation and visibility from Afri-can descendants should be perceived as one of the many methodologies of mestizaje and seems to have created a Du Boisian "double-consciousness" within Mexico's African-descendant communities.

The Neoliberal Moment and Political/Cultural Mobilization

Most recently, mestizaje has been drawn upon to promote heterogeneity rather than homogeneity. Martínez-Echazábal argues that "since the 1980s, the concept of mestizaje has come to play an important role in the rec-ognition of the plurality of cultural identities" (1998, 21). The neoliberal moment in Mexico was ushered in by the economic collapse of 1982 and brought with it a broad program of structural change, subsequently labeled with the convenient shorthand "neoliberalism" (Lomnitz 2008). The neo-liberal turn rearranges the relationship of social groups who were previ-ously grouped by class to resources and opened up the space for future identity politics as a strategy for the acquisition of resources and opposi-tion to neoliberal reforms furthering privatization (Baca 2008; Berger 2001; Hale 2005; Speed 2005). Gwynne and Kay (2000) suggest that the adoption of neoliberal policies within Latin America is based on the logic of a "lack of alternatives" argument, in which neoliberal policies are seen as the only option for Latin American countries to compete within the global market. The adoption of this alternative produced a deep fracture in every Latin American country between groups that were thrown at risk and those that benefited under conditions of free trade and the shrinking state (Lomnitz 2001, 24). Within Mexico the key neoliberal reforms were implemented between 1983 and 1992 and relied on the force of the old revolutionary party, "yet the state's shortage of resources and its limited and well targeted aims for reform meant that its principal negotiating chip during this painful reorganization of the economy was a calibrated democratic transition" (Lomnitz 2008, 54).

While individual rights and citizenship are important to this democratic transition, the focus on the individual is counter to Indigenous organization and community development and negates the development of communal identities based on claims to Indigeneity, ethnicity, and culture. While the previous liberal era promoted the erasure of communal identities within the context of the nation, neoliberal reforms adopted a strategy of incorporation that Hale has labeled "neoliberal multiculturalism" (Hale 2002; Postero 2007). Within the neoliberal multicultural model, proponents of neoliberal doctrine proactively endorse a substantive yet limited version of Indigenous cultural rights to deal with their own problems and to advance their own political agendas (Hale 2002, 487). Within this project, the state advances multicultural rights in order to reconstitute civil society and Indigenous culture in its own image, shearing them of radical excesses and inciting them to do the work of subject-formation that would otherwise fall to the state itself (Hale 2002, 496). While neoliberal projects recognize Indigenous community rights and cultures, this recognition comes with defined limits.

According to Hale, multiculturalism can be used to reinforce neoliberal doctrine rather than to promote collective empowerment. Multiculturalism, within the context of neoliberalism, thus becomes a hegemonic tool for incorporation (homogeneity) rather than the embracing of heterogeneity. Multiculturalism, writes Hale, "is the mestizaje discourse for a new millennium, offering a parallel mix of opportunity and peril" (2002, 491). This suggests that both mestizaje and multiculturalism rely on the same system of racial and ethnic value. Telles and Garcia further recognize that "by raising awareness of racial and ethnic inequalities, multicultural policies may increase the salience of mestizaje as an ideal for improved race relations" (2013, 136). While the reorganization of the economy may have reimagined people's relationships to resources and the state, the value associated with the "other" and the Mestizo, as the individual embodiment of the nation/state, remained static. Ultimately, Hale argues that cultural rights movements have little choice but to occupy the spaces provided by neoliberal multiculturalism and that they often have much to gain by doing so. However, when groups do occupy these spaces, they must assume that they will be articulated, in the Gramscian sense, with the dominant bloc, unless the decision forms part of a strategy of resistance from within and is part of a well-conceived political alternative (Hale, 2002).

The Zapatista movement serves as an example of the multicultural politics ushered in by the neoliberal moment. The Ejército Zapatista de la Liberación Nacional (EZLN) (Zapatista Army of National Liberation) chose the latter option offered by Hale as a strategy of mobilization, working for political and structural change rather than absolute incorporation and relying on an older national discourse (Duran de Huerta 2000). Lomnitz argues that the Zapatista movement "cast itself as a prolongation of the radical struggle of Emiliano Zapata in the armed phase of the Mexican Revolution" (2003, 23) in order to contest the meaning of the nation, who represents it, and who is a member. This strategy is only possible within the context of mestizaje and the fact that Indigeneity as a subject position had already been worked into the common sense associated with the Mexican nation. The Zapatista strategy tapped into the fact that in Latin America, "indigenous ethnic identities and nation-states are highly interdependent and, in some sense, mutually constitutive" (Wade 2010, 99; see also Telles and PERLA 2014, 53). This allows for political groups like the EZLN to take back the symbol of Indigeneity from the Mestizo state (Gillingham 2011, 217). The same cannot be said for Blackness and a Black subject position within the context of the historical national origin myth. Telles argues "that the Zapatista rebellion challenged the relationship between the state and indigenous peoples" (Telles and PERLA 2014, 47). However, it must be recognized that Indigeneity as a preexisting national symbol was the key to the Zapatista strategy of attempting to force the government to make good on its own rhetoric. In some ways, the Zapatista calls may have also signaled a desire for the return of a previous colonial form of Indigenous separation/ autonomy in which an Indigenous republic was allowed to operate alongside a separate Spanish republic (Guardino 1996, 27). The Zapatista rebellion, whether successful or not, attempted to seize the symbolic means of production from the state by tapping into the value of an Indigenous subject position. An important question is whether or not this same strategy is possible for Black communities in Mexico. Through the Zapatista strategy, nation building and mestizaje become bottom-up processes (Berger 2001; Wade 2001, 2005, 2006; Hale 2005; de la Cadena 2000). The Zapatistas, suggests Berger, use a revised form of Mexican nationalism to make claims for themselves to rights of citizenship and, in the process, seek to reshape the nation and the state in a time-honored practice in Mexico (2001, 154). Important here is the ability for the Zapatista movement to invoke the nation based on claims of citizenship while simultaneously projecting an Indigenous identity. This strategy has been successful partly due to the way in which the Mexican nation has been defined since the independence era as a Mestizo nation, relying on an "honored" Indigenous past. In this way, the Zapatista movement, although potentially risking co-optation, successfully called on citizenship through the subversive practice of embodying the nation through Indigeneity, while maintaining an Indigenous identity that does not conflict with revolutionary definitions of nationality. In this strategy, Indigeneity is used to tap into a position usually secured by Whiteness/Mestizoness—that is, the norm-subject (Wynter 2003). That is to say, through practices of embodiment, the nation is claimed by Indigeneity as an actual property for legitimating claims to Mexicanness and citizenship. Ironically, the Zapatistas are using the ideology of mestizaje against Whiteness and the privileged Mestizo. The multiculturalism utilized here speaks to the "true" origins of the Mexican nation-state as well as the revolution, a strategy withheld from Black Mexicans as the preestablished racial logic limits the ability for African descendants to embody the nation and therefore excludes any legitimate claims to the nation as property, as well as claims to legitimate citizenship.

The Zapatista strategy was also supported by the fact that in the 1970s the Mexican state had abandoned its approach to Indigenous integration, and once again pushed the glorification of Indigenous traditions and culture as a strategy to reignite nationalist feelings and to regain legitimacy (Saldívar and Walsh 2014, 468). In the 1970s, the federal state increased its presence in Indigenous regions with the rapid growth of local offices of the National Indigenous Institute (Instituto Nacional Indigenista [INI]), the promotion of bilingual education in rural schools, and the creation of the General Office of Indigenous Education in the Ministry of Education (Saldívar and Walsh 2014, 468). According to Saldívar and Walsh, "the increased presence of the state in indigenous communities generated strong criticism of the role that the state and anthropology had played in the integration and disempowerment of indigenous people after the revolution" (2014, 468). This criticism led to the denouncement by critical anthropologists and Indigenous organizations of the negative impacts that state policies and the project of modernization since the Mexican Revolution had had on Indigenous communities (Saldívar and Walsh 2014, 468). This changing political climate beginning in the late 1970s, however, does not challenge the ideology of mestizaje. Rather, mestizaje and the accepted value associated with Indigeneity are put to work in order to highlight what are perceived as state abuses of Indigeneity. Subcomandante Marcos's invocation of difference and inclusion in the context of Indigeneity (Duran de Huerta 2000) is supported by this broader political environment, and Zapatista claims resonated with the foundational logic of mestizaje. This in turn allowed for the Zapatistas to politically employ a logical argument that positions anti-Indian sentiment as ultimately anti-Mexican.

African descendants within Mexico, following Indigenous/Zapatista and other African-descendant struggles in Latin America, have begun to exploit the political spaces created by neoliberal restructuring. However, this exploitation has had to deal with broader government agendas in the region and the underlying logic of mutual exclusivity between Blackness and Mexicanness. The Museo de las Culturas Afromestizas de Cuajinicuilapa (Museum of Afro-Mestizo Cultures of Cuajinicuilapa), which highlights the historic African presence within the region and more broadly the nation, is just one example of the several competing racial projects currently underway. Discussing his opinion of the museum, Nestor, an activist and self-identified "Negro" in the town of Pinotepa Nacional, Oaxaca, explained to me that "it is necessary to rescue the past and put it into relation with the present. Why? Because the issue of discrimination that is lived in the pueblos due to poverty and due to our color is a very burdened load." Nestor seemed to recognize the disconnect created by the present governmental strategy for recognition of Black Mexicans in the region and the tendency to recognize the present existence of African-descendant communities without recognizing the history of the production (and current reproduction) of these communities within the region and broader nation. Nestor continued, "That is why a lot of people sometimes deny their past time and again. And that happens with our people . . . So, it is certainly necessary [to know] from where our population has arrived. We should foster a project that rescues this issue, a museum, right? Unfortunately, I want to tell you that if you go to Cuajinicuilapa, the project for the museum was a project very . . . very ideal. But it has gradually been abandoned."

For Nestor, the abandonment of the museum acts as a metaphor for the abandonment of what he refers to as the "comunidades Negras" (Black communities) of the Costa Chica. "It has been abandoned gradually. They made it like redondos [round houses supposedly typical of early African settlement in the region], but now they are abandoned. The only thing that the museum has is that it is just a museum . . . the space, some masks, some paintings, and that's all . . . But what it was in essence has been abandoned as time passed."[7] The museum seems to have been a product of the larger La Ruta del Esclavo (The Slave Route) project carried out by the UNESCO beginning in 1994.[8] The museum in Cuaji focuses on the routes, rather than the local roots, through which the enslaved were brought to Mexico during the colonial period. The focus on routes is utilized to make sense of the present existence of African descendants in the region, and many of the cultural elements within the museum speak to an African past that currently has little relevance to Black Mexicans in the region. The routes project, by focusing on the arrival of African descendants rather than the historic lived experience of Black Mexicans in the country, reinforces the sense of externality associated with Blackness. The continued acceptance of Blackness as external to the nation also creates the logical expectation of a contemporary difference that the state-sponsored project for recognition is attempting to capture with their methodology of cultural recognition. The broader project for recognition refuses to address the social gap between the past and the present, which is painfully obvious when walking through the small museum. It is this social space between the past and the present, and the history of race-based discrimination, that ultimately makes visible the dark matter within the ideology of mestizaje that is physically represented by the "comunidades Negras" of the Costa Chica region.

Referring to the museum and the contextualization of Blackness within colonial history, Sergio, a teacher from the town of Cuajinicuilapa, explained,

The most common thing is to present the historic part because, well, history is already written, and it would be impossible to change it. However, we are in this museum, and maybe if there was a budget for the Black population in Mexico, if there was a budget for . . . updating it, right . . . we could avoid . . . begging for resources for this space. It is true that the government participated here, at three levels. The federal, the state, and local government have participated here. But I do not feel that the economic impact is visible. Because all this museography that we see was part of a project, the project La Ruta del Esclavo. They did not make this specifically for here, they already had it and wanted to take it out to some other place. This building [referring to part of the museum complex] was not specifically constructed for the museum, it would have a different design, right? This was constructed for the establishment of the ISSSTE [Institution for Social Security and State Workers], but for certain reasons the project was not carried out, and they gave . . . well, they lent us the building. On the other hand, the staff of the museum does not get paid by them, I mean, the museum needs to do activities so they can pay them. Therefore, the government is not really interested in opening those spaces for the visibility of the Black population. Mexico is part of that project, La Ruta del Esclavo, and obviously, it has to justify, in some way, being part of that project, doing something, and this is one of the activities, a justification. But they came and they left it here, and here it is, abandoned. (personal conversation)

Sergio recognizes how the Mexican government is attempting to utilize the incorporation of Black communities to present Mexico as a modern nation interested in the global struggle for human rights. However, Sergio also identifies the ways that this strategy necessarily omits the gap between the racial past and present in order to continue to reproduce Mexico within a preexisting logic that reinforces the accepted national origin myth of Mexico as a non-Black Mestizo nation.

Bulmaro, another educator and activist in Cuajinicuilapa, recognizes this process as well. At his Universidad del Sur (UNISUR) building, a small local grassroots university in Cuajinicuilapa, Bulmaro explained, "we were part of the idea for the museum and the Mestizos took it up. That is the problem. The Mestizos took it up, turned it upside-down, and they named it Museo de las Culturas Afromestizas, right? So, we don't feel related to it anymore." Bulmaro also recognizes the effects of mestizaje and how the underlying value system limits the potential legibility of Black movements in the region. As we spoke in one of the UNISUR buildings that also houses a local community radio station, Bulmaro pointed out that local activists themselves decided to shape the UNISUR building as a round house. Because its meaning is always contested depending on context, the roundhouse reflects the stakes of recognition and representivity, "the belief that an organization truly speaks and acts for a particular constituency" (Lucero 2006, 33). The roundhouse is a cultural symbol of the present within Bulmaro's and local activists' own politics, a space that contains the present struggle for recognition and the recognition of the historical discrimination of the African-descendant communities within the region. However, within the context of the larger national ideology and state methodology for recognition, the roundhouse is a historical relic, which ultimately becomes useful for recognizing Blackness as a historical but separate component of the Mestizo nation. This is reinforced by the government's use of "Afro-Mestizo" within the official title of the museum, an ethnic title that seems to be meaningless to all but government officials and "well meaning" but out of touch Mestizos.

Conclusion

Bennett, Vinson, Restall, Von Germeten, Vincent, and others demonstrate the development of vibrant Black communities based on an explicit Black subject position during the colonial period. Postindependence and revolutionary nationalisms create the need to clearly define the national subject in Mexico. Mallon (1995) sees nationalism as "a broad vision for organizing society, a project for collective identity based on the premise of citizenship—available to all, with individual membership beginning from the assumption of legal equality" (4; see also Beiner 1995). Mestizaje, first in the broadest sense as an ideology for nation building, and then in the more specific context of racialization, was used in Mexico to enact this collective identity by creating an ideology for the realization of the nation and an ideal type: the Mestizo. We know the role that Indigeneity has played in the broad vision of Mexican mestizaje. However, we have not asked what role Blackness has played in this broad vision. Rather, it has been simply assumed that Blackness plays no role in this vision of the nation. If we ask what role the conceptualization of Blackness has played in the broader envisioning of the nation (that is, the nation as non-Black), then it may be seen that a project for Black recognition cannot be enacted without a real interrogation of the ideology that is responsible for Black exclusion in the first place. Mallon (1995) argues that "nationalism would become a series of competing discourses in constant formation and negotiation, bounded by particular regional histories of power relations" (4). While the historical development of mestizaje as an ideology for defining the nation may rely on competing discourses, in order to be legible these discourses still rely on a set of shared values and facts. The value of Blackness within all versions of Mexican mestizaje, and the associated Black subject position, seems to be the constant within these discourses. As Robinson (2007) makes clear, the "negro" (in Robinson's terms) is necessary for facilitating other transactions. Focusing on the Spanish/Indigenous divide inherent in the process of Mexican mestizaje has allowed for the question of whether Black people can be Indigenous or Mestizo to appear to be a logical question. However, theoretically and analytically, it has already been concluded that both the Indigenous and the Mestizo are non-Black positions. This has been accomplished through the work of citizenship and nation building that has relied on the historical continuity of the value of Blackness in Mexico. The project of producing and reproducing the Mexican national subject, or norm-subject (Wynter 1984), relies on the ideological erasure of a Black presence and an explicit Black subject position within Mexico as a way of reproducing the non-Black Mestizo as the prototypical Mexican citizen. While this erasure may have been successful within an institutional context, on a communal level, racial discrimination and the continued experience of an implicit Black subject position continued to be important to the historic maintenance of African-descendant communities from the national era up to the present.

As Indigenous struggles show, the neoliberal period has provided the impetus for struggles of citizenship and inclusion based on Indigenous rights. African descendants in Latin America have followed the lead of Indigenous groups in attempting to take political action to secure collective rights. However, due to the underlying value of Blackness within the Mexican mestizaje discourse, Black Mexicans are confronted with specific obstacles that do not exist for the Indigenous communities of Mexico. Alberto Melucci (1985) argues that a strict focus on political mobilization overlooks the cultural characteristics and everyday meanings of cultural and political identities. While neoliberal multiculturalism demands that groups politicize identity, the successes to these struggles depend on the broader roles that different subject positions have historically played in the making of the nation. Within Mexico, strategies to secure citizenship and collective rights based on politicized Black identities will not succeed without recognition of the real, continued existence and maintenance of a Black subject position throughout Mexican history, despite mestizaje-driven racism and the continued attempts of an ideological erasure of Mexican Blackness. To borrow from Napolitano's concept of "prisms of belonging," "prisms have a refractive and, to some extent, elusive nature: what we can see through them depends on the angle we are looking through" (2002, 10). Looking through the prism also entails a sense of looking back, which in a political sense allows us to reimagine how we have arrived at our present locations.[9] Highlighting culture, as a process of mediation or negotiation and not a set of material artifacts or behaviors, is important to this process. For Black Mexicans, Bonfil-Batalla's concept of Mexico Profundo may take on another meaning. That is, Mexico, viewed through one of Napolitano's prisms, is partly defined by an experience of Blackness. This is key to locating Black culture and the consequences of processes of racialization within Mexico, as well as understanding the current Black movement within the Costa Chica and the nation's overall attempt to incorporate this movement into its current conception of the multicultural milieu that is the Mexican nation.

The following chapter is an ethnographic example of the way in which the Oaxacan and Mexican governments are attempting to incorporate (and perhaps co-opt) the Black movement into the broader nation. This incorporation has brought about several tensions between activists and government employees. In some ways, activists and local residents rely on a more quotidian cultural, as well as historical, sense of Blackness in order to imagine their official participation and recognition within Mexico. However, government officials themselves rely on the rhetoric and strategies developed by mestizaje and multicultural logics as a foundation for the project that incorporates Black Mexican difference into the present national imaginary. The actual products generated at these points of tension between quotidian experiences of being and official projects of recognition expose problems with the officialization of difference, to which the following chapter is dedicated.

Figure 1. Andrés Rodríguez Robles preparing iguana. Photo by the author.

Figure 2. Teresa Mariche Hernández. Photo by Mariana Palafox.

Figure 3. Virginia Magadán Gallardo. Photo by the author.

Figure 4. Lucila Mariche Magadán. Photo by the author.

Figure 5. Marcelo García Zaguilan. Photo by Mariana Palafox.

Figure 6. Rosendo Vargas Morga. Photo by the author.

Figure 7. Agustín Bernal Salinas.
Photo by the author.

Figure 8. Ricarda Acevedo Mariche. Photo by Mariana Palafox.

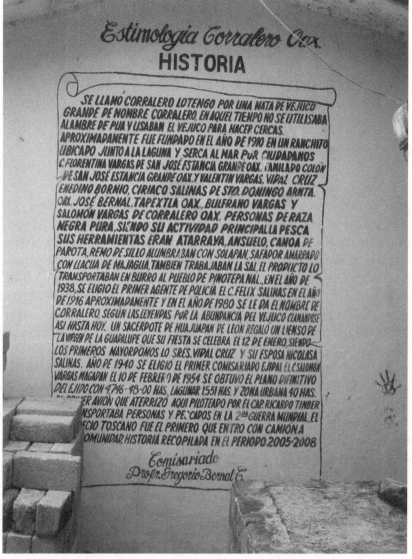

Figure 9. Historical origins of the town of Corralero. Photo by the author.

3

Recognizing Culture and Making Difference Official

The perception of difference as a naturally occurring phenomenon obscures the larger historical processes and social relations that have actually produced racial and ethnic difference, and which continue to bind people together through these social relations (Fields 1990, 2003). Colonial institutions originally drew these lines of difference as a technology for dealing with the day-to-day practical management and discipline of colonial subjects (Bhabha 1994, 2002; West 2002). These lines were no less important in the imagination of the modern nation-state (Goldberg 2002; Omi and Winant 1994), and the new form of subject-making (citizenship) associated with this new political invention (Kazanjian 2003). Thinking about the ways in which the symbolic and geographic lines of difference continue to be redrawn (Cotton and Jerry 2013) and how state and nongovernmental organizations (NGOs) actively work to make difference "official" exposes the fetishization of difference, as well as the real productive power associated with this fetishization, and helps uncover the web of political, social, and economic relations responsible for the continued reproduction of the exclusion of Black Mexicans. This chapter serves as an ethnographic example of the ways that the Mexican state and NGOs are working to make "Blackness" an official form of cultural difference in Mexico. This chapter also focuses on some of the potential pitfalls of this project and the ways that the official recognition of Blackness in Mexico can potentially empower African descendants while simultaneously reproducing the same logics of difference responsible for their social and political exclusion. This chapter focuses specifically on Oaxaca, as most of the CDI-sponsored consultations during my fieldwork took place in that state. These consultations also attracted many activists and members of mutual aid groups from the neighboring state of Guerrero. I have also conducted field research in

Guerrero, and therefore the voices of several activists and educators from the state of Guerrero are included within this discussion.

The Scene

> This process of consulta [consultation] . . . is mainly directed by the government, and maybe it is paying attention to the requests that we [Black activists and mutual aid groups] have been making for fifteen years. But maybe it is also paying attention to what is happening at the international level, with the UN Declaration of the International Year for People of African Descent. Therefore, they are doing something to justify in some way . . . their [Mexico's] belonging to the international body. (Sergio Peñalosa, activist and educator in Cuajinicuilapa, Guerrero)

The United Nations' declaration of 2011 as the "International Year for People of African Descent" is, in many ways, the ideological backdrop for political activities regarding the social, cultural, and political recognition of Mexico's African-descendant population that has intensified over the last decade. Political action around this struggle has been active since at least the early 1990s, since Padre Glynn Jemmott Nelson helped begin the local mutual aid organization Mexico Negro in 1993. The year 2011, the International Year for People of African Descent, is also when the states of Oaxaca and Guerrero significantly stepped up their attentions and began putting serious resources into the subject of recognition for Black Mexicans. As noted by Sergio Peñalosa, a Black activist from Cuajinicuilapa, Guerrero, in the opening quotation, the instrumentality and utility (Vinson 2005a, 2005b) of African descendants and the Black communities of the Costa Chica in the Mexican government's increased efforts to create a responsible global image by recognizing Black communities in 2011 is not lost on local activists. Sergio's comments reveal that activists are aware of the historical trend of putting Blackness to work for the production of the Mexican state. In its deceleration, the UN states, "around 200 million people who identify themselves as being of African descent live in the Americas. Many millions more live in other parts of the world, outside of the African continent. In proclaiming this International Year, the international community is recognizing that people of African descent represent a distinct group whose human rights must be promoted and protected."[1]

In this same year, the state governments of both Oaxaca and Guerrero began to strategize ways to seriously include African descendants within the states' racial, ethnic, and cultural milieu by recognizing African descendants' existence and rights within their respective state constitutions[2] (Jones 2013). A comment by a non-Black Mestizo director of the Comisión Nacional para el Desarrollo de los Pueblos Indígenas (CDI) (National Commission for the Development of Indigenous Towns), to whom I refer as Mariano to ensure his anonymity, clarified this as we talked about the broader project of consultation undertaken by the CDI. Mariano explained to me the process and methodology employed by the CDI, adding, "And maybe it is so because it is the international year, the international year of the Afro-descendants, and maybe that gave the opportunity to start doing this kind of work." The process of official recognition necessarily included setting several parameters, both social and geographical, as well as inventing definitions of Blackness that were seen as suitable as a means for official recognition. This process of defining Blackness and setting parameters brought several groups to the table and involved negotiation between federal and state governments, local NGOs, a number of Mexican anthropologists, and several politically active and not so active community members. Within this forum, official forms of difference were being created in 2011 in the rural coastal towns of Oaxaca and Guerrero.

The methodology for the state-organized portion of the project of Black recognition, as explained to me by a CDI employee, was borrowed from preexisting methodologies developed for the inclusion of Indigenous communities within the state constitution. Mariano explained,

> There was a reform where the Indigenous population was mentioned. Where they said that it is pluricultural, I mean, all that because the indígenas [Indigenous] themselves have been fighting to get that recognition. I think it was only around 2001, because there was a reform for the Indigenous population too. But not for the Black population. It never showed up. It was only for the Indigenous populations that things were done. We have even identified the number of existing etnias [Indigenous ethnic groups]. But the población negra is not mentioned for any reason whatsoever.

Mariano went on to explain, "The CDI, within their duties, has made this poll, but with the Indigenous population. So, in previous years, it has made like five, five consultas. In our case, we did here [Oaxaca] a consultation about Indigenous rights, a poll on traditional knowledge, that was here . . . So, the CDI was charged with a survey specifically on the Black population. In this case, Veracruz, Oaxaca, Guerrero, Michoacán, and I don't remember the other one . . ."

This borrowing of methodologies highlights the Mexican government's approach to cultural diversity/multiculturalism over the last several years. This methodology also reflects a common approach taken by some Mexican academics and anthropologists (Aguirre Beltrán 1958; Dávila 2007; Dávila and Lézé 2007; Diaz Pérez 1995), which focuses on culture and demographics, as well as issues of poverty and discrimination, and attempts to create comparisons between Black populations in Oaxaca, Guerrero, and Veracruz. Built into such methodologies are several issues that created tensions between local Black activists and state organizations and forced local community members to think seriously about their own identities as well as the ways in which they understand their own cultural and social development. Nestor, an activist from the town of Pinotepa Nacional, Oaxaca, found the consultations necessary. However, he believed the methodology and the government explanation for the consultas to be a bit ridiculous and even disingenuous. Nestor explained,

> So, we say that if we have a culture then we need the government to recognize it. The CDI is asking us questions, and within those questions they ask us which is the geographical location? When they ask this question, part of me is laughing and part of me starts getting a headache. You say that the government does not know where the Negros are. Like, the government does not know where Cuajinicuilapa is. I mean, can you imagine in the twenty-first century they are coming to us to ask where the Negros are, right? Where are we? In which geographic part of Mexico are we? They ask us if we have authorities [local leaders].

As his frustration with the rhetoric surrounding the consultas makes clear, Nestor understood the stakes involved with recognition. The ways in which the first stages of the recognition process were being undertaken helped maintain a particular narrative of Blackness within Mexico—a narrative of African-descendant communities as simply the forgotten consequence of history rather than the product of a process of exclusion and invisibilization brought about by the invention of the modern Mexican nation and the subsequent iterations of that national project. Through this rhetoric, the federal government is attempting to appear as a benign authority rather than the maleficent progenitor of historical racism and discrimination, as the lack of knowledge on the geographic location of Black communities seems to suggest no involvement in the actual historical circumstances surrounding the current geographic locations and material realities of these communities.

Sergio also saw the need for the consultas. But, while Sergio had high hopes, he was a bit skeptical of the process and of the overall focus on ethnicity and distinct cultural elements. Sergio talked to me about the real need for such a process toward recognition, but he was aware of the potential for recognition to be used in a way that could maintain exclusion rather than work for true inclusion. Sergio explained,

> Yes, I believe that in practice, it is [necessary], because they [Mexican government] do recognize cultural traditions of people of African descent, but that's all. I mean, to make something fancy during an event, or to say, "We are doing something for the popular cultures." But let's look for the essential: where are those people of African descent? Let's look for the public policies that benefit those Afrodescendientes [African descendants], let's look for the constitutional spaces where their rights are taken into consideration and are respected. This does not exist. We have not been socially recognized.

Both Nestor and Sergio demonstrate an awareness of the potential pitfalls associated with official recognition. However, they and their respective mutual aid activist organizations, Enlace de Pueblos y Organizaciones Costeños Autónomas (EPOCA) (Network of Autonomous Coastal Towns and Organizations) and Mexico Negro (Black Mexico), seemed to be at a loss for a way to get the government representatives and the African-descendant communities of the region on the same political page.

The Comisión Nacional para el Desarrollo de los Pueblos Indígenas is the federal arm that took on the development and implementation of the methodologies that would be used to locate, in a physical and metaphorical sense, the Black communities of the Costa Chica. Again, Mariano, seemingly speaking to Nestor's frustrations, told me that

> The survey aims at knowing where they are, in which places. By now, we are identifying at a glance only eleven municipios [municipalities] and seventy . . . like eighty, eighty-five localidades [small towns]. But that is only because we think they are there. There is not much information, well, in general, I can assure you that they work in agricultural production . . . and fishery. But if you ask me what they

need, well, I don't know exactly, because the little we know, it is about the Indigenous population. About infrastructure, roads, production, education, health. And we are already proposing some actions to deal with these problems [for Indigenous communities]. But with the Black population, we don't have a diagnosis, and I believe that with this consulta we would be identifying where the communities are, and with that information they need to submit the corresponding petition.

While Mariano's comment seems to be about locating Black communities as a first step in the process of recognition—in other words, producing the multicultural citizen through the production of an official racialized geography—the document used as a template for the consulta process (discussed later in the chapter) focuses mainly on a repertoire of cultural difference to recognize the Black populations of Mexico as culturally and ethnically distinct from the general Mestizo population as well as the local Indigenous communities in the region. Ironically, there is no need to confirm the racial uniqueness of this population, as racial difference speaks, although quietly, for itself. However, the production of the culturally distinct other—the cultural and therefore conditional citizen—requires an invention of a whole other kind. Wade (2005) recognizes mestizaje as involving the maintenance of enduring spaces for racial and cultural difference alongside spaces of sameness and homogeneity. For the CDI, the first step for cultural recognition required the production of an official space for Black racial and cultural difference. This demonstrates how mestizaje can be transformed into a methodology to map ideology onto geographic space.

The brochure circulated to the activist organizations of the Costa Chica by the CDI to promote the "Consultation for the Identification of Mexico's Afro-Descendant Communities" (Consulta para la identificación de las comunidades afrodescendientes de México) asks three important questions: Who are we? Where are we located? How do we identify? The intention of the consulta is very clear: "For the recognition of our communities and our rights." The brochure uses the inclusive pronoun "we," which includes all community members and ultimately a racial and ethnic symbolic community of African descendants (Nuestro Pueblo)[3] within the CDI project. Simultaneously, this use of the pronoun "we" also put the community on board, at least rhetorically, with the CDI-sponsored project and its official approach. Moreover, the project simultaneously recognized a group of people without considering the processes that were responsible for the "social forgetting," or now political recognition, of this group. At the moment of invention, history is allowed to take a back seat while a people can be brought into the present and be legally (officially) recognized without the social recognition of the processes that have made this group invisible for so many years, in effect creating this group out of cultural thin air. Once the three aforementioned questions are answered, the business of applying rights to this "new" multicultural group would be able to begin in earnest.

The brochure continues with a list of rhetorical sub-questions that were developed to help elaborate on the three main questions and which ultimately found their way in some form into the list of subjects addressed by the consultations themselves. Added to the list were "What are our main productive/economic activities? What is the origin and history of our community? How do we organize (socially and politically) our community? Where are the geographic boundaries of our community? In what way do we prefer to be referred to or identified? What are the roles of our own authorities?"

The single question on the brochure that deals with any type of historical perspective asks about the "origin and history of our community" (¿Cuál es el origen e historia de nuestra comunidad?). Further analysis of the sub-questions associated with this section of the consulta document suggest that this is not speaking of the origin and history of the people within the community but the actual geographic community itself. This may take on a different connotation when applied to some of the Indigenous communities who were "allowed" (somewhat tenuously throughout different political periods) to occupy and maintain traditional spaces, apart from the lands that were taken and developed as colonial centers (Lomnitz-Adler 1992; Menchaca 2001; Vinson and Restall 2009; Guardino 1996; Wade 2010; Saldívar and Walsh 2014). For Black communities, the question of origin and history is inseparable from the origin and history of the Spanish and later Mestizo communities in the region.[4] The question of a unique and separate community history and origin is imaginable, at least symbolically and ideologically, for Indigenous communities because Indigenous groups are historically (even if within another historic or political context) autochthonous to the region. However, for African descendants the question of history and origin necessarily calls for the historicizing of African descendants within a broader colonial, and later Mexican national, history and politics. As Wilderson argues, "the prior reference of the worker, a time before the Enclosures, for example, or of the postcolonial subject, a time before the settler, are simply not available to Black people" (2020, 217). The

Mexican government's attempts to recognize a unique Afro-Mexican culture overlook the reality that there is no "before Mexico" (conceptualized as the before of conquest) for Black Mexicans by which an authentic and uniquely Black/African culture could be based upon.

The conception of the history of Black towns must be intertwined with the racial and ethnic realities of the colonial and later national moments in Mexican history in order to get a realistic picture of the history and origin of these contemporary communities. Asking the question of history and origin of African-descendant communities brings up several important questions that the CDI did not intend to address and was not equipped to answer, especially within the parameters set forth by the consultations. While Indigenous and Black communities have different colonial histories, both groups are, without a doubt, products of the colonial moment and are therefore both colonized peoples. However, colonial understandings of biological and cultural difference historically placed Black and Indigenous communities in different functions in relation to the Spanish crown (Blacks being simultaneously party to and product of the machine of colonial dominance). Therefore, approaches to space and place have to make linkages to the specific racial and ethnic experiences of geography and the ideological interconnections. The Mexican process of recognizing and "officializing difference" overlooks these issues.

Escaped enslaved African descendants historically claimed and developed communities in what had been Indigenous lands. For example, the small pueblo of Charco Redondo, on the outskirts of the Lagunas de Chacahua National Forest, is one of several towns incorporated into the larger state of Oaxaca through the county seat (Municipio) of San Pedro Tututepec, commonly referred to as Tutu. Tutu is an important symbol within the region, as it is home to a local Indigenous community museum, Museo Yuku Saa (Cerro de Pájaro/Bird Rock/Mountain), and continues to be a strategic source for grounding Indigenous identities within the coastal region. A friend and Black activist, Lucila Mariche Magadán, explained to me that after any heavy rain, anyone could wander through the small town of Charco and find a number of Indigenous artifacts as random as shards of pottery and as specific as fully preserved figurines. Several residents in Charco corroborated her claim. While I have not been able to validate the cultural origin of these "artifacts" (most probably Mixteco, Nuu Savi in the Mixtec language), their existence below the surface serves as a metaphor for the multiple connections between African descendants, Indigenous, and Spanish (and now Mestizos) in the region. While the Spanish approach to colonization of Indigenous lands utilized a strategy of partial domination and incorporation by transfixing colonial capitals on preexisting Indigenous political and ceremonial sites, escaped enslaved African descendants sometimes necessarily relied on a similar strategy that involved "homesteading" on and in preexisting Indigenous communities. The heavy downpours of the rainy season in Charco unearth the foundations and colonial connections that the federal government, through the CDI's process, continues to overlook and perhaps build upon.

The Major Players (in the "Official Process" for Recognition)

Apart from the everyday residents of the Costa Chica, at least five governmental organizations/institutions and at least thirteen local (in both Oaxaca and Guerrero) mutual aid organizations and NGOs share this political, social, and cultural scene. After discussing the organizations and their individual goals and intentions with Heladio Reyes, a non-Black Mestizo and current head of the nongovernmental organization Ecosta Yutu Cuii and then *presidente municipal* (municipal president) of San Pedro Tututepec, I was able to get a sense of the tensions and labor involved in the project of making difference official.[5] This process has been a negotiation, perhaps not one of equality, between the government and the many local organizations created by local Black activists and advocates. Ecosta is mainly an ecological organization founded by Heladio Reyes, who also holds a degree in agricultural engineering. According to Heladio, Ecosta began to officially direct some of its energies and resources at African-descendant issues and "los Pueblos Negros" in 1997. During my fieldwork in 2011, Heladio and the rest of Ecosta planned a gathering to bring communities throughout the Costa Chica together to discuss some of the issues important to Black communities, as well as some of the issues focused upon by the CDI consultas. Ecosta envisioned a "Red de Pueblos Negros" (Network of Black Towns) in order to limit the political and social tensions that plagued the organizations and hampered the effectiveness of the grassroots projects. This network was also imagined as a way to re-localize the conversation on Blackness in the region, as the "Encuentro de los Pueblos Negros" (Meeting of Black Towns) events that had become common in the region began to take on a more international character.

Heladio played an instrumental role as liaison and intermediary between the CDI and the Costa Chican communities in the network of Black towns' first meeting, and he provided a platform upon which local communities could deliver their perspectives and concerns to the ears and voice recorders of the CDI. One activist told me that Heladio's experience and position as a twice-elected municipal president made him a very respected member of the community and allowed him the unique ability to mediate conflicts and tensions between local NGOs and community factions. While Heladio was born in the Costa Chica, in Santa Rosa de Lima, his racial and cultural Mestizo background also allowed him the ability to act as mediator between both groups. Heladio was perceived as being knowledgeable about coastal issues and having an allegiance to coastal towns rather than a desire to cultivate state or federal governmental connections. Heladio, when asked to get involved in low-level disputes, presented himself in a politically neutral manner. He made it clear to all present, at least publicly, that his only interest was to facilitate the important discussion between los Pueblos Negros and the CDI and that his place was not to make decisions. While Heladio Reyes and Ecosta Yutu Cuii began focusing on the ecological issues of los Pueblos Negros in 1997, it was not until later that they began to help with the organization and promotion of Blackness as a political and cultural identity within the Costa Chica.

I asked Heladio why, since there were already several local Black organizations in existence, he found it necessary to add to this mix and direct some of Ecosta's already limited resources to Black communities. He explained to me that several organizations were less effective than they could be due to political tensions between the organizations and the effect that political affiliations had on productive collaboration. In some cases, this affected the priorities of some organizations, allowing the goals of rights, representation, and recognition to be overshadowed by personal or professional aspirations and politics. A meeting to discuss the consultas in Cuajinicuilapa, Guerrero, where Heladio was forced to mediate between two organization heads due to a difference in official political party affiliation highlighted his point. Heladio Reyes, sitting between the two leaders who engaged in indirect cross talk, relayed each leader's questions and concerns to the other although we were all sitting less than two feet apart from each other. Official political affiliations were so strong (the Institutional Revolutionary Party [PRI], and the other the National Action Party [PAN]) that the two representatives at the table were unwilling or unable to speak to each other. In this case, interpersonal tensions led to a lack of collaboration and productivity between groups and individuals who at the very basic level shared the same overall goals and intentions. Activists explained to me that at the time of this research at least twelve local organizations shared the political environment around Blackness in the Costa Chica. These organizations included Mexico Negro, Museo Comuniatrio Negro, AFRICA, Cimarron, EPOCA, Colectivo Pinotepa, Socpinda, Ecosta, ODECA, Afro Desc, and Colectivo Makandal. Several of these organizations came about as spin-offs from the original organizations after the centrifugal force of political differences or differing agendas among participants became too much to bear.

The Formula for Officially Mapping and Recognizing Cultural Space

The practice of mestizaje and racial mixing has mapped out in both rural and urban spaces within Mexico, allowing for modern urban spaces to become the natural geography of the Mestizo, while rural spaces remain the territory of culture, tradition, and authenticity. In the multicultural era, mestizaje has been put to work through a geographical hierarchy of power in which regional cultures are used in the everyday reproduction of the multicultural Mestizo nation. In this way, spaces of difference are utilized as constitutive features of the nation (Wade 2005, 249). This geographical hierarchy supports the ideology of mestizaje by allowing Mestizos to point to their living roots, while simultaneously embracing a more culturally and racially sanitized modernness. A key issue here is how and under what circumstances rural "cultural" communities, as well as the individuals who represent these cultural communities in urban (read modern) spaces, are allowed access to the means of representation that surround, and therefore determine, the interpretation of these regional cultures within sociopolitical and economic contexts. Embedded in this issue is the fact that the representation of cultural communities in Mexico is also used as a method to indirectly reproduce and represent the modern Mexican Mestizo.

This dialectical relationship demonstrates how the process of Black recognition is a process of citizenship in which citizenship is not simply an issue of access or belonging but a relation between different social actors and categories—a relation that requires exclusion as a method for producing includability (Kazanjian 2003; Wynter 1984). As Wynter demonstrates, it is the mode of difference alone of the "other" that enables the mode of sameness (1984, 34). This process is heavily dependent upon accessing the means of representation within society and the power to represent oneself as an ideal type within the nation while simultaneously constraining the ability of others to represent themselves as a reflection of the nation (Williams 1989). Access to the means of representation and the ways in which

Blackness and the African-descendant body can be represented as signs or core elements of national culture (Wade 2005) within the multicultural discourse of the Mexican nation serve as the main points of contestation within the current project for African-descendant recognition, both locally and at the federal level in Mexico. This tension was exacerbated by the fact that the majority of those involved in the conversations around Blackness in the Costa Chica were themselves non-Black.

The document used by the CDI in 2011 to orchestrate the community gatherings and facilitate the collection of data for the official recognition of African descendants was labeled the Carta Descriptiva (descriptive charter). The actual title for the document is "Talleres para la Identificación de Comunidades Afrodescendientes de Mexico" (Workshops for the identification of the Afro-descendant communities of Mexico). The Carta Descriptiva should be viewed as a "constructed text," as referenced by Mallon, who argues that "if we privilege documents as repositories of information, forgetting or ignoring them as constructed texts, we return to the deduction of consciousness, culture, and socio-political practice from abstract, sometimes implicit categories that often masquerade as 'objective history'" (1994, 1506). Through the officialness of the text, the cultural difference associated with Blackness is made to appear natural. The document utilized what Eisenstadt regards as a primordial approach to ethnicity, in which an ethnic group is perceived as a "stable group of people who have in common relatively enduring characteristics of culture (including language) and psychology, as well as a unity of conscience" (2006, 109). As a foundational logic, the Carta Descriptiva utilized the understanding of "cultural difference" as the way to recognize a distinct people, or *pueblo*. While the pluralization of the word "communities" speaks to the recognition of multiple localities in which African descendants reside, the singular use of *pueblo* (as in *Pueblo Negro*), often used to refer to a broader "Afro-Mexican" people, limits the possibility for the existence of multiple distinct Black groups. Unlike Indigenous communities, who can be viewed as separate ethnic groups, and therefore pueblos/peoples, African descendants in Mexico are recognized as one people, which speaks to the implicit recognition of Blackness as a racial, rather than ethnic, category. Hoffman (2014) argues that the classic cultural indicators (language, clothing, "traditional" social organization) do not work for Blackness in Mexico (94). Even still, the CDI document implicitly takes Indigeneity as the foundational form of acceptable cultural difference within Mexico, as it focuses mainly on the anthropologically accepted characteristics of Indigenous communities in relation to the contemporary modern national citizen. To make the document feel more personal to the workshop participants, the personal pronoun "I" and the inclusive pronoun "we," both used in the form of verb conjugates, were used in conjunction with the third person. This gives the Carta Descriptiva a fractured character, in which African descendants were both included as part of the national body and simultaneously set apart from that same imagined community.

The document for the workshops lists several specific thematic areas, each with their own set of specific questions, enabling a systemic way to categorize Blackness, as well as demarcating the cultural and regional boundaries associated with the African-descendant communities of the coast. These thematic categories include Demografía (demography); Economía (economy); Identidad, Lengua, Indumentaria, Cultura, Culinaria, Arte, e Historia Colectiva (identity, language, native/traditional dress, culture, culinary practices, art, and collective history); Ciclo Festivo y Vida Ritual (festival cycles and ritual life); Territorialidad (territorial dispersion); Autoridad o Formas de Gobierno y Sistemas Jurídicos Propios (authority or forms of governance and our own legal systems); Adscripción (social attributes or characteristics); Articulación (geographic and social connections to region); and Invisibilidad, Racismo, y Discriminación (invisibility, racism, and discrimination). This last thematic category appears to be the only category that deals with the historic exclusion of the comunidades Negras. Furthermore, all but the last thematic category appear to be conceived of as ways to link the communities to cultural traditions and authenticity rather than modern Mexicanness. This intuitively leaves the Mestizo as the inheritor of the modern nation, and therefore the rightful manager of cultural difference within the country. By utilizing conceptualizations of the rural peasantry, this strategy also locates Blackness outside a context and an analysis of modernity and supports the logic of Blackness as outside of the modern capitalist mode of production through which the nation was conceived (Ranger 1983; Trouillot 1984).[6]

The first thematic objective of the Carta Descriptiva is Demografía (demography). This section is intended to identify "the elements related to a framework of persons, homes, and groups of persons that establish and maintain relations of diverse types, constituting a network of established and recognizable relations, whether contiguous or occasional, that can be differentiated from others." The objective goes on to explain that these elements should be regularly expressed or practiced and recognized within institutional forms such as kinship, sexual and age divisions, and geographic neighborhoods, among others. Ultimately, the document seeks to establish specific forms of organization, whether real or symbolic, that differentiate African-descendant communities from other locally and nationally recognized groups.

Questions within the demography thematic objective include "¿Cuáles son los localidades, rancherias, o parajes que se relacionan con nosotros dentro de nuestra municipio?" (Which locations, ranches, and places can be linked to us within our municipality?), "¿Con que otras localidades, rancherias, y municipios tenemos relación que no son de nuestro municipio?" (With which other localities, ranches, and municipalities beyond our own municipality do we have relations?), "¿Hay indígenas y blancos en nuestra localidad?" (Are there Indigenous and Whites in our locality?), and "¿Hay morenos viviendo en la cabecera?" (Are there Blacks living in the municipal seat?)[7] These are only a few of the questions in this thematic section, but they follow the broader intention of the section in attempting to officially situate the African-descendant communities of the Costa Chica within some systematic organizational framework. The questions attempt to recognize symbolically important places within the communities or larger municipality, as well as the larger geographic and social relations that link communities in the region. It is revealing that the official document makes a clear distinction between Whites and Indigenous people, and that it recognizes a potential power dynamic where African descendants may not have a say or influence in the day-to-day interactions of those in the county seat, simply due to their lack of presence or even exclusion from the real estate associated with political power in the region.

The questioning of whether Indigenous people and Whites live in the Black communities demonstrates the Mexican government's recent recognition of a racial framework that continues to exist within Mexico but often goes unnoticed within popular discourses due to the overarching racial economy established by mestizaje. In the context of Indigenous and Mestizo relations, the term *Blanco* (racially White), as a racial signifier, is unnecessary, as one can simply rely on the dichotomy of "Indigenous" or "non-Indigenous" to interpret class relations, where the Mestizo occupies the privileged, unmarked position. However, incorporating Blacks into the racial/ethnic mix necessitates the use of other racial signifiers, namely White, that have been allowed to exist only intuitively in everyday political and social relations. Once the social location of "Negro" is incorporated into the conversation, Mestizo is uncovered as the White position within the Mexican racial economy. This should not be interpreted as a US import or foreign infiltration into the Mexican racial system of classification. Rather, the use of *Blanco* in the Carta Descriptiva is representative of the ruptures (Ferguson 2003) that often occur in any political economic system, a rupture that forces the broader public to make sense of the contradictions and paradoxes that exist in any system that is taken for granted. The residents of the Costa Chica recognize the dichotomy of a Black and White racial framework as an organizing frame both internally and externally (see also Sue 2010, 2013). The consultas and talleres of the CDI and the official project of recognition, in the form of a production of an official racial geography, impose this frame on the residents of the Black communities in the Costa Chica. Through this project, the dark matter of Blackness is becoming visible through the new borders and boundaries of race in addition to the official geography of Blackness that is being produced in the Costa Chica.

Racialized geographies act as the necessary property for racialized groups to make claims to citizenship in the multicultural nation. The production of an official "Black geography" is the first step in the process of establishing citizenship. As the nation has long been accepted as the rightful domain of the Mestizo, and in general a Latin American mode of Whiteness, the production of racial geographies is an important strategy for anchoring "others'" claims to citizenship in real geographic space without threatening claims to the broader nation as a Mestizo property. Nestor explained to me,

> And some people are not interested. Some say, "Why are you interested in the *Negro* issues? I mean, why are you interested? Why say if people are *Negros* or not, if we are all Mexicans." Yes, we are Mexicans. We are Mexicans! We recognize we are Mexicans but . . . there are Indigenous Mexicans that have a culture, a tradition that is recognized or taken into account. We, as población Negra [Black population], we have a culture, we have a tradition, we have history, but it is not recognized as such. Thus, as we are not recognized, we are not even given the support to create history and to rescue the little that remains.

The Indigenous culture and history that Nestor describes also coincide with an official geography of Indigeneity. It is within this geography that Indigenous history and culture are allowed to be (re)produced. A key difference here is that Indigeneity has also been worked into the national origin myth. Indigenous culture and history are allowed to cross the sanctioned borders of Indigeneity through cultural forms that have been appropriated or employed for the sake of reproducing the nation and the Mestizo. This is clearly demonstrated by the ways in which Indigenous culture has historically been used to attract tourism to many of the urban tourist centers of Mexico. Without an official geography, this same process cannot be set into motion for African descendants in the Costa Chica.

Another example from Nestor, discussing a meeting between government officials, academics, and Black communities, elaborates on the importance of geography as a requirement to be perceived as a legitimate citizen. Nestor recounted this meeting to me:

> Some days ago, we went to an interview, there were . . . two engineers from SAGARPA, one engineer from SEDART . . . A representative of FAU and representative of Chapingo, of the Universidad Autónoma de Chapingo. We were a team of technical staff, engineers, each of them had to introduce themselves. Your name, where do you come from, what do you do . . . all those things. So, we introduced ourselves. But unfortunately, one compañero Negro was the last to introduce himself. His name is Rudolfo Prudente, he is from Santiago Llano Grande [town in the Costa Chica]. But he has not lost his accent [su tono] . . . he went to study to become a seminarian, he went to study philosophy, and he never changed his accent—bandeño, as people say here. Bandeño is what people from Llano Grande are called. He never changed his accent. When we finished introducing ourselves, the representative from Chapingo told him, "Can you tell us your nationality?" A professor from Chapingo! Professor from Chapingo, one of the most prestigious universities in Mexico! We were all surprised. We said, "Well, he is Negro, he is from the Costa." It makes me laugh. She said, "I am sorry, I heard a Peruvian accent."

Without an official racial geography for Blackness, the idea of the nation as the real property of the Mestizo is never disrupted or disputed. Rather, all sorts of illogical rationalizations become more plausible than the simple acceptance of Blackness as authentic to the Mexican nation. For that reason, a university professor from "one of the most prestigious universities in Mexico" can easily misidentify African descendants in her own country as Peruvian. This is the invisibility faced by Black folks in the Costa Chica, an invisibility that underwrites the question of demography in the Carta Descriptiva.

The communities in the Costa Chica, comunidades Negras, have not relied on the government to make their presence known. Almost all the

Black NGOs in the region have their own meetings in different communities throughout the Costa Chica. More often, these meetings are sponsored by one organization but well attended by members of other political organizations. The goal of these organizations is to use their meetings as a way of both attracting visibility about Blackness within the Costa Chica and educating Black communities in the Costa Chica about Blackness beyond the borders of the nation. For many within the Costa Chica region, Blackness is uniquely Mexican, and little, if anything, is known about Black communities beyond the racial borders of the Costa Chica. For example, a young woman I met in Charco Redondo whose mother had left to the US years earlier refused to believe that I was from the US, as she associated the US with Whiteness. She explained to me that if I was not from Mexico, then I must naturally be from Africa. Sergio Peñalosa, an activist from the town of Cuajinicuilapa, described the importance of the Black community organization meetings in the region. Sergio explained,

Fifteen years ago, people were less aware of the existence of other Black communities in other parts of the world. Today, some people are still unaware because not everybody comes to the encuentros [meetings] or reads books or watches TV. But there is a percentage, even if it is very small, that through the encuentro de los Pueblos Negros have encountered other Negros that come . . . because some have come from Ecuador, from Peru . . . mostly they have come from the United States, from different states, right? Cubans, also Africans, they have also come in recent times . . . and, well, from other places . . . from Haiti.

Many from within the Costa Chica region do not even know of the several other Black identified regions within the country. The encuentros demonstrate to Black Mexicans in the Costa Chica that the existence of Blackness is not limited to the coastal region of Mexico but is a global phenomenon.

Another core theme of the Carta Descriptiva document is simply labeled "Economía" (economy). This long and detailed section—two full pages and eleven subsections—is aimed at getting a sense of the economic activities that define the comunidades Negras of the Costa Chica region. The main goal of the section is to "detectar las formas de articulación de las unidades prodcutivas familiares en diversos aspectos" (recognize the forms of articulation between family productive units in several different aspects). The objective is to understand in what ways each community can be seen as an "unidad economica" (economic unit). The subsections within this core theme of economy include "agriculture, raising of livestock, forestry, fishing, salt mining, migration, government support," "festival cycles and seasonal production," "economic cooperation," and "market systems and forms of exchange." After reading the subsections of the document, one begins to get a sense that the intention of the core theme of economy is to outline the "traditional" ways in which the communities of the Costa Chica solve the common human problems of resource procurement and management. The document contextualizes these practices through the understanding of traditions in the same ways that Indigenous communities are seen to employ traditional trade and subsistence activities.

The location of a Black economy within the context of tradition is designed, whether intentionally or intuitively, to place the African-descendant population outside of the context of modernity, or at least modern capitalist production, and to situate Black communities within the realm of the peasantry and tradition, much in the same ways in which an anthropology of the mid-twentieth century attempted to situate Indigenous communities of Latin America and Africa (Hobsbawm and Ranger 1983; Trouillot 1984). The questions in the subsections of the document are interested in understanding the traditional forms of cultivation utilized in the communities and whether the introduction of new types of agricultural products have modified these traditional forms. Similar to the manner in which I was chasing Blackness, as outlined in chapter 1, the government approached the communities as if they have remained untouched and left to their own cultural production within their social isolation. The architects of the document overlook how African descendants arrived to the region in the first place, as part of the colonial project, through enslavement, and later capitalist reproduction through cattle ranching, cotton production, and agricultural development in the region (Vinson and Restall 2009; Guardino 1996; Chassen-López 1998). These connections to the state, as well as the cultural myths and norms of the nation, are sacrificed for the perception of the comunidades Negras as traditional and therefore potentially practicing quasi-Indigenous forms of economic production.

Lucila, an activist and key collaborator in this research, explained to me that the region surrounding the Lagunas de Chacahua was home to numerous plantations in the recent past. She remembers the Río Verde river at the outskirts of her town of Charco Redondo being used to move a number of agricultural products to the nearby town of El Azufre. The remains of the plantations are visible in the region, but the memory of the ways in which Black labor was manifested as the means of production within the capitalist economy of the region is less visible on a larger regional and national scale, as African-descendant communities have been excluded from larger contemporary formal economies. A convenient forgetting of the economic history of the region allows for the large-scale reinvention of the African-descendant population in the Costa Chica region through the lens of tradition and culture, rather than the more realistic context of the social and physical relations around modern and contemporary production.

The sub-questions of the CDI document go on to inquire: When and where do Black communities sell their agricultural and livestock goods? (¿En dónde se venden todos los productos agrícolas/cárnicos/lácteos]?) What market days do they utilize? (¿Qué día se realizan éstos [tianguies o mercados]?) And what types of collective work/organization exist in the communities? (¿Existen formas de trabajo colectivo?) Marcelo, a resident of the small town of La Pastoría (now deceased) and head of a local collective, explained to me how he and his collective were attempting to organize members of the community in order to run a pair of community owned, ecologically friendly cabañas and a restaurant on the banks of one of the Lagunas de Chacahua on which the community is situated. To reference the system of community labor needed for this project, Marcelo borrowed the term "tequio," a term used in Indigenous communities to refer to the system of collective labor organized around public works in Indigenous towns (Cohen 1999). Marcelo explained to me that the collective was having trouble getting the townspeople to recognize their obligations to the community project and to organize for tequio. During one of our conversations, we were continuously interrupted, as Marcelo had to make repeated phone calls and requests for an announcement over the town PA system for members of the collective to assemble for the day's tequio project: the cleaning of the new restaurant and cabañas designed to attract ecotourism to the town. The problem with organization meant that one could not rely on the cabañas to be available for rent or on the restaurant to be stocked and ready for any tourist groups that might happen to enter the community, announced or otherwise. African-descendant communities are relying on "non-traditional" forms in order to give the appearance of tradition within the communities as well as the political and social problems associated with this process of invention. The term "tequio" is also used within the Carta Descriptiva. The term is used in a way that establishes the perception of traditional forms of organization and commerce within the communities. This ultimately is part of the language necessary for recognition and the politics of cultural difference. Through this effort of recognizing

Black Mexicans, the Mexican government continues to perceive African-descendant communities as outside of the modern capitalist model. Trouillot's (1984) considerations of the Black peasantry as a product of modern capitalism, rather than a phenomenon prior to and outside of this mode of production (Robinson 1983, 2019; Du Bois 2007; Trouillot 1984, 1992), fall on deaf ears with regard to the invention of a modern Black peasantry in Mexico.

Within the basic subtext of the economy theme, the interest in cultural practices around production becomes clear. One of the sub-questions asks about "other activities," such as basic handicrafts. Unlike the Indigenous communities of the region, the Black communities within the Costa Chica were not known for traditional handicrafts, and no one with whom I spoke mentioned the production of traditional handicrafts as part of the cultural traditions within the region. Lucila mentioned to me that she was in the process, supported by Ecosta, of developing a women's co-op that produced products such as jams, salts, and oils that could be sold at regional tourist hot spots. However, these products were not perceived by Lucila, her collective, or the Costa Chica communities in general as traditional cultural handicrafts representative of the region or of Black women's traditional roles in the region, much less the traditions of African descendants in general. However, Lucila did express her belief in the need for such elements, as she understood that this was one of the successes of Indigenous communities in representing difference, and therefore value, within the context of the local tourist economy. On one occasion, Lucila and I spent the day scouring the region for material artifacts that would fit the bill for representing African-descendant difference in the region.

At one point, Lucila thought a local artist, known for manufacturing wooden jaguar heads, held the key. However, Lucila, as described in chapter 1, soon recognized the limits of the ability for the jaguar head to represent the Black communities of the Costa Chica. For some reason, neither Lucila, nor any of my other collaborators, mentioned the masks used in the many cultural dances celebrated in the region, such as the Danza de los Diablos, the Danza de los Toros, or the Danza de las Tortugas. Within the region, such dances utilize elaborate costumes that include masks and other props. However, these props are not yet mass produced as representative cultural artifacts of the region. This is evidence that the African-descendant communities of the Costa Chica have yet to begin to contextualize their own existence and presence in the region through the culture concept or within the economic logic of multiculturalism. That is to argue that in 2011 Black

Mexicans in the region had yet to become actual subjects of the culture concept. In a discussion about Black culture in the region, Sergio explained his thoughts on the reason for this lack of cultural contextualization:

> Well, I think that there is also a justification that explains that we are not at the same level of possibilities to show our culture of African descent. The Indigenous peoples, when the Spanish arrived, even if they were perceived as an object to work, they received a certain level of protection, through encomienda.[8] Moreover, they were taught professions, craftworks. And this way they had the opportunity to shape their culture so it could remain there. The Indigenous peoples were considered humans, even if at a much lower level in comparison with Spanish or Europeans. But the Negro was not even considered that, it was an animal, it had no soul, et cetera. And they [the Spanish] were so careful not to allow them [*Negros*] to shape their culture . . . no musical, or dance, or plastic expression [expressive material arts]. Nothing, because they were not even allowed to relate among themselves, not even people from the same community.

Sergio identifies a similar process of forgetting that I have mentioned previously and seems to suggest that the handicrafts that Indigenous communities are known for now are more of an invention of colonialism and Spanish-Indigenous relations than authentic cultural forms.[9] This shows a similar process of Indigeneity being perceived outside of the modern relations of production in order to craft a false sense of authenticity and tradition. Bulmaro, the activist mentioned in chapter 2, made a similar argument about what appears to be authentic Indigenous clothing in the region. Bulmaro explained, "the way they [Indigenous Mexicans] dress is not original from them, it was imposed on them. The colonial governments, in order to identify and distinguish among pueblos, they imposed certain clothes on them. With colors and all that, like the clothes of Amuzgos, Mixtecos, Tlapanecos, Nahuatl, Zapoteco, but they did not originate from them [Indigenous groups]. Others imposed that on them to be identifiable. But now they embrace them as their own." Bulmaro clearly recognizes the process of invention that comes along with the recognition of difference. This is directly in line with Knight's (1990) discussion of the early project of "creating the Indian" through conquest. This process appears to have been reproduced for Black Mexicans by the CDI and the use of the Carta Descriptiva. The Carta, as a constructed text (Mallon 1994), acts as a guide for collecting cultural traits that are conceived to be definitive of Black communities. The issue here, as discussed by Knight in the context of Indigeneity, is that these cultural traits and characteristics have been historically developed through dialogue and relationships with other non-Blacks. Ironically, then, as Black communities have not lived in true geographic isolation, the CDI is cataloging the historic process of Mexican cultural development rather than a supposed authentic "Black" culture. The historical process of forgetting or invisibilizing Blackness makes Blackness appear isolated and therefore "pure" as it is being "rediscovered." Ironically, the government's strategy of recognition attempted to put the process of cultural development on hold and tried to "fix" cultural traits as a strategy for fixing Black difference. In this way, the process of recognition is attempting to actually produce or invent the Black Mexican. Bulmaro seemed skeptical of the real possibilities for justice associated with the culture concept within a politics of difference.

The implications for social sciences such as anthropology, which become responsible for reproducing these processes and the notion of difference (Knight 1990, 77), are not lost on the activists and townspeople of the Costa Chica. Many of the activists I spoke with are learning how to play the game of cultural representation in order to better the lives of the community members within the region, even if these gains may ultimately be in the short term. The political and mutual aid organizations of the regions are clearly aware of the politics of difference necessary to facilitate a project of Black recognition. Sergio explained,

Mexico Negro, a civil organization, was the first civil organization constituted to fight for the constitutional recognition of the Black population of Mexico and to fight against all kinds of discrimination, and to reexamine the value of our identity, to strengthen our identity. Obviously, in order to achieve this, we had to develop certain activities, like painting classes focused on themes related to *Negros* [temática Negra], to people of African descent [Afrodescendientes], some painting contests, cultural programs where we could recover, spread and promote our cultural traditions, and, well . . . We do gastronomic shows, painting workshops, mask workshops [talleres de mascaras], among other workshops that we organize there. Finally, we also do an exhibition with all the products resulting from the workshops and, obviously, with some of the works that we have been making throughout the year, within the frame of the programmed activities.

Through the workshops and exhibitions, the Black activists of both Oaxaca and Guerrero are attempting to link cultural traditions to material artifacts in a way that is translatable to local and federal governments, as well as to a larger general Mestizo population. It will be partly through these material artifacts, and the production of meaning around and through these artifacts (Warren 2001), that the African-descendant population can become visible and consumable by the larger Mexican community.

One of the longer sections of the Carta Descriptiva discusses the theme of Identidad, Lengua, Indumentaria, Cultura, Culinaria, Arte, e Historia Colectiva (identity, language native/traditional dress, culture, culinary practices, art, and collective history). These points seemed to be addressed implicitly in several other sections of the document; however, this section attempts to address these core cultural elements directly. According to the document, the purpose of this section is "to define how common cultural practices, uses of language, collective historical and present memories, culinary practices, common dress, and shared health knowledge and practices, form a framework for a collective sense that distinguishes the community from other collectives . . . so the community can then be seen as a cultural unit." The research theme is designed according to a particular intuitive logic of difference between "us" and "them." This difference is ultimately necessary for the official recognition of the comunidades Negras as a legitimate pueblo or people. The key to this process is Black Mexicans' need to represent themselves as distinguishable from others yet simultaneously recognizable and claimable to a larger group. While this need for recognition is not a new phenomenon, the multicultural moment creates the potential for some modes of recognition to fail within the context of broader public/national recognition (Taylor 1994). For the Mestizo, the nation acts symbolically as the larger collective of which the individual is a part. Furthermore, individuality is afforded to the Mestizo through the nation in a way that is not accessible to the African descendant. Ironically, the main marker of difference, skin color, which I argue most importantly distinguishes Mexico's African descendants from the general Mestizo population, is not a part of the arithmetic or formula of acceptable recognition. However, a small section of the Carta Descriptiva, which I will discuss shortly, is dedicated to the issues of "Invisibility, Racism, and Discrimination."

The first question of the core theme focusing on culture and identity asks, "¿Que elementos culturales nos distinguen?" (What cultural characteristics distinguish us?) This question sets the stage for the recognition of a series of legitimate cultural features that will be used for the cultural demarcation of Mexico's African descendants in the future. Following this general inquiry is a series of questions on language and language use meant to identify local vocabulary and common oral expressions (*vocablos locales y expresiones orales*). Language continues to be one of the most widely accepted markers of racial and ethnic difference in Mexico, obeying a seemingly simple Spanish/Indigenous binary (Saldívar and Walsh 2014, 457; Telles and PERLA 2014, 31). Two questions stand out in this section. The first—"¿Cuáles son los vocablos propios que pensamos que forman parte de nuestra 'manera de ser'?" (What unique words do we think form part of our "way of being"?)—is meant to identify specific words that are unique to the African-descendant population of the Costa Chica. One problem with this question is that while the communities of the Costa Chica have been forgotten by the broader nation-state, they do not live in total geographic and social isolation. Lacking this isolation, the African-descendant communities of the Costa Chica, unlike the Indigenous groups of the region, do not speak an ancient dialect, or even a dialect much different from the Spanish dialect spoken generally throughout the coastal region.[10]

There are, however, a few distinct linguistic characteristics of the Spanish dialect spoken in the region, many of which rely on a specific accent or tone. For example, people of the region commonly agree that they "swallow" ending syllables of certain words. They also recognize that instead of using a hard S in the ending of words, the S in many words is formed by using an aspiration. These characteristics have become common to the Spanish speakers of the coastal region. While many African descendants and non-African descendants alike in the coastal communities use this form, some make a connection to this way of speaking and Blackness as a cultural and social identity. Much like Nestor's discussion of mistaken identity for lack of changing one's accent, Sergio explained to me the ways in which language usage and manner of speaking can be linked to stereotypes and discrimination. Sergio told me,

Now, if we go to those spaces where we, Negros, have to interact with indígenas, with Mestizos, right? Eh . . . they say: "Yeah, but you are Negro." Or . . . as we say, they attack us because they say we do not speak as they do, that we don't pronounce the S and for that reason, they laugh at us, they say we do not know how to express ourselves . . . and also the way we dress and all that, so . . . We need to see that apart from all the discrimination, socially, institutionally . . . we have the marginalization that comes from the ethnic groups we are part of.

Lucila also agreed that language was one of the traits that distinguished African descendants from Mestizos and Indigenous communities, but when I pushed her to identify words that were specific to the Black communities of the region, Lucila was hard-pressed to come up with very many words unique to the community. Lucila identified *cuculustre*, a word common in the region for referring to very curly hair, "very chino [curly] hair," as Nestor would explain, as being a word unique to the region. Another term related to me was the word *bajareque*. According to Lucila, *bajareque* is a word specific to Black communities within the region and is used to describe a temporary shelter or shack that could be taken down and rebuilt rather quickly somewhere else. After our initial discussion about the word, I could not escape the feeling that I had heard this word somewhere before. I thought that maybe I had heard it used in casual conversation in the region and figured it may have come up in one of the many conversations in which I negotiated lodging in one of the cabañas common in the area. However, a few years later, after rewatching the 1964 film *Soy Cuba*, it dawned on me that I had heard the term years before in that film.[11] At the very least, *bajareque* has been in use in Cuba since the production of that film. In the context of Black recognition in Mexico, this term is being utilized, by Lucila and others, as a way of establishing an authentic form of difference. The term may also be inadvertently creating a diasporic connection. Whether or not this term has links to the history of forced migration, and later more voluntary movement (Sue 2010), of African descendants between Cuba and Mexico is less relevant than the fact that it may be part of the new official myth of Blackness in the Costa Chica region, the writing or telling of which may serve to unite communities within the diaspora (Edwards 2003; Gordon and Anderson 1999).

Another question within the core theme of identity has to do with the preparation, consumption, and potentially the meaning, of food, discussed by the Carta Descriptiva as cultura culinaria (culinary practices). The questions in the subsection are: "What typical food dishes represent us in the community?"; "What ingredients do we use to prepare these dishes?"; and "In what moments do we prepare these dishes?" According to Brett, the very act of codification makes food appear exotic (2012, 161). Oaxaca, as a cultural region and longtime tourist destination, is seen as having a tradition of incorporating Indigenous flavors into the general diet popular within the region. Travelers to the region inevitably learn about the numerous ingredients in the seemingly simple cooking sauce *mole*—before they learn about a rich variety of moles, from brown (richly flavored with chocolate) to deep red (known as mole Colorado), to yellow, and even green. Each one of these sauces is said to have been developed to complement different proteins and is eaten at different times of year, depending upon the festival cycle and particular communities celebrating. On the tourist walk of Alcala in the city center of Oaxaca, numerous restaurants promote authentic dishes with names that speak to the long-standing Indigenous traditions of the regions. Restaurants and bars with names such as La Zanduga, Zapotec Mixology Bar, Itanoni ("corn flower" in the Mixtec language), and La Tlayuda are common in the city center, and speak to the ability to literally consume Indigeneity as part of the culinary tourist experience. La Tlayuda taps into this relationship of consumption quite literally, as the slogan for the restaurant is "Oaxaca entre por el estómago" (Oaxaca enters through the stomach). Indigeneity, through the exotification of food, is exploited as a means of developing the tourist economy within the city (Brett 2012, 161). This backdrop and the tradition of consuming Indigenous culture and tradition informs the CDI's questions about culinary culture in the context of Black Mexican recognition.

In 2015, I organized an anthropological field methods course to the Costa Chica supported by the Center for Latin American Studies at San Diego State University. In the course, we attempted to document the numerous recipes that are a part of the culinary repertoire of the communities in the region. Again, Lucila proved to be instrumental in this project, preparing several dishes for our group so that we could document the recipes and preparation of what we thought were locally specific dishes. For the most part, the dishes that Lucila prepared that afternoon and the others that she related to us orally (some thirty culinary and another twenty or so medicinal recipes) were familiar, in some form or another, to many of the non-Black Mexican American students, and to me, who had grown up in Mexico or in the US-Mexico border region. Lucila prepared several soups and simple mole dishes for us over the following week, all of which she explained were common in the region. The simple menus of some of the *comedores* (simple food stands and restaurants) in the regions confirmed that the dishes prepared by Lucila were indeed common to the area. But these dishes were not locally specific due to their preparation and the uniquely exotic pallet of the African descendants who prepared them. Rather, the substitution of common elements due to the availability and tastes of the communities in the region made these recipes familiar and recognizable as recipes common throughout Mexico. For example, because of local herb species and tastes, a Oaxacan might substitute *hierba santa* or *epazote* in their preparation of a dish that typically calls for cilantro in a more northern preparation of the dish.

Another factor associated with the culinary traditions in the region is poverty. Due to the limited incomes of many in the region, common consumption seems to be limited to locally caught fish, chiles, and tortillas. The staple ingredients in the dish, however, remain the same. In these recipes, the most common ingredients are onion, tomato, and a number of chiles, with fish and chicken being the most common proteins. From these recipes, those looking for the exotic flavors associated with cultural difference so commonly promoted in the city would ultimately be disappointed.

There were also several ingredients that might seem offensive to the collective Western palate. These ingredients include sea turtle, sea turtle eggs, iguana, and armadillo, which are rarely promoted as part of the Indigenous traditions so valued in the menus common in the city but seemed to be locally sourced staples in the Costa Chica. Bulmaro, when talking about culturally specific foods, places iguana and armadillo at the top of the list. At times identifying as "Afro-Mixteco"[12] due to his Black and Mixtec roots, Bulmaro explained, "Well, we have our diet, which is a distinctive feature. We normally eat armadillo; do you know armadillo? That one, indígenas; Negros, the iguana. If they serve you iguana for a meal, I mean, you can kidnap a Negro with iguana broth, with iguana mole. Yes, you can take him. And the Indian, with an armadillo. You can take the Indian with an armadillo too. But not the Negro. If you give him armadillo . . . he won't have it." Both iguana and armadillo are hunted locally within the communities of the Costa Chica.

The iguana, as well as the sea turtle, are governmentally protected animals within the region, which is intended to limit the consumption of these animals in the communities of the Costa Chica. There are no special provisions for African-descendant communities in the Costa Chica to capture and consume protected species. Rather, there seems to be a campaign to eliminate the iguana and sea turtle from the local diet altogether, which has gained some traction within local communities. For example, on one occasion I was sent by a friend and collaborator to purchase an iguana from a local relative who had recently been successful in capturing a large one. Not knowing of the governmental ban, I happily went on this errand. Upon returning to the community, with my iguana tied at the legs and arms and secured to my backpack, I was admonished and chided by some for carrying the creature, obviously with the intention of making a meal of the lizard. As I strolled through the small community, I was met with shouts of "es prohibido" (it is prohibited) from those whom I passed on my way back to the family who had originally sent me on the errand.

Once I returned to the family, the shouts of admonishment received from some turned to excitement by others, as my friend Jose got his instruments ready to prepare the animal for the cooking pot. I was told that killing the animal swiftly was an important part of the process, as it ensured that the meat would not be tough due to the stiffening of the muscles that would be a part of the trauma of a long and clumsy death. Lucila also shared a recipe for iguana, accompanied with the same directions for killing the animal. Several people in the region have discussed with me the idea of creating iguana farms and sanctuaries with the intention of harvesting the meat for a local market. However, as of yet, the few existing iguana sanctuaries are limited to the protection and propagation of the species for visual consumption on the part of tourists interested in getting a glimpse of the local wildlife, including the local species of caiman. While mole seemed to be a common culinary element in the region, even used to prepare iguana and sea turtle, I doubt that animal proteins such as iguana and sea turtle will be promoted as part of the unique cultural heritage and traditions of Black Mexicans anytime soon, at least within the context of tourist promotion to the region.

Two more subsections of the Carta Descriptiva within the core themes of identity and culture are examined here in order to convey the ways that culture is part of the common logic around a recipe for recognition within the context of Blackness in Mexico. As mentioned, Bulmaro understood that the distinct set of clothing supposedly unique to different Indigenous communities was more a colonial invention than a set of strict internal prescriptions set by communities themselves. Whether or not this is the case, Indigenous communities in Oaxaca have become recognizable by a set of weaving patterns and colors that are seen to correspond with different ethnic and regional Indigenous groups. This seems to be the case in many regions within the country as well as Latin America more broadly. The ability to recognize cultural groups based on their styles of dress has become so common that it has worked its way into the Carta Descriptiva used by the CDI. The theme of indumentaria (dress) asks a series of follow-up questions including, but not limited to, "How do we like to dress?"; "What colors do we prefer to dress in?"; and "In what ways does our form of dress distinguish us from others?" In asking these questions, the CDI is attempting to recognize the cultural uniform associated with traditional forms of Blackness within the region. The preferred uniform for many of the men in the region is a pair of board shorts and flip-flops that seem to represent their time spent on the *lancha* (small fishing boat equipped with an outboard motor) or *panga* (a human-powered canoe) and in the water fishing. Apart from this, men commonly wear jeans and untucked button-down shirts made of thin materials to keep cool in the hot weather. Women seem to be most comfortable in lightweight store-bought dresses, while younger women wear any number of fashionable items, such as knockoff designer jeans and miniskirts. I asked Bulmaro about the cultural connection between dress and Blackness, and he told me an interesting tale that seemed to act as a political statement on the articulation of colonization, sexual exploitation, and culture. Bulmaro explained,

> So, those who brought the first domestic workers here gave them uniforms, right? But those who worked on the fields, in other regions of the country, they gave them calzón [breeches]. And the dude [Spanish Creole] went to the palenques [settlements founded by escaped or freed slaves], the palenques were like spaces outside the hacienda [estate/farm/plantation] where the Negros messed around. When girls were sent to dance. And the damn Spanish went there to nose around and look at the Negra and [said to himself], "Damn it, she is hotter than my wife." They [Negros] used skimpy clothes, exotic clothes, in humid regions. So, suddenly, he left his wife and went to the palenques, and the Spanish woman was wearing buttons up to here [gesturing to the neck] and a long skirt. She did not show a thing. Then she accused the Negra of witchcraft. But the only witchcraft was that he took her to those places and that the Spanish guy liked her. He was a depraved bastard. But those ritual dances that Negros normally do were observed by the Spanish people in a different way, they went for the perverse [interpretation]. That was the problem. From there, they thought that the Negra was responsible for the spell on the Spanish women's husbands.

Bulmaro recognizes that the uniforms thought by the CDI to reference cultural uniqueness, if it ever existed, is more of a representation of colonial exploitation and perhaps enduring poverty than a true symbol of traditions and cultural authenticity. Currently, clothes such as elaborate dresses with vibrant colors are being used to popularly represent Blackness through social media and tourist media outlets. Similarly, representations of men in the Costa Chica dressed similarly to the Jarocho (a recognized African-descendant-influenced folk style in Veracruz), in a white shirt and pants with a red sash, can be found representing the Costa Chica on these same tourist and social media outlets. However, it is very rare to see this type of ethnic clothing worn in Black communities of the Costa Chica region. Contrary to earlier scholarly observations (Hoffman 2007; Sue 2010), it now appears that the increased presence of state institutions in the Costa Chica are having an impact on Black identity formation and the ways that Blackness can be ethnically represented within Mexico and beyond.

The question of origins plays a key role in this process of contemporary cultural invention. Another of the subsections of the Carta Descriptiva within the core theme of identity and culture is the question of "historia local—formación de la comunidad y hechos principales" (local history—formation of the community and founding events). The first question asks whether participants remember the origin of their community (¿recuerda el origen de esta comunidad?). Many Indigenous communities in the region continue to relate origin myths of the specific communities and their associated ethnic groups. Several of the Mixteco activists and language teachers with whom I have worked and studied, for example, share a common narrative of the town of Apoala as being the home of the first Mixtecos (see Troike 1978). According to the narrative, the mountains around Apoala are the site for the emergence of the first Mixteco, who descended from the clouds. A similar narrative focusing on Blackness and Black origins in the Costa Chica has yet to develop and does not appear to frame Black Mexicans' understandings of their own being in the region. Many of the people with whom I spoke shared the sense that African descendants had always occupied the communities in the Costa Chica. There were others who discussed the remains of a capsized ship in the region that was responsible for bringing the first Africans to the shores of the Costa Chica (see Lewis 2001).

However, historians are more convinced that African descendants were brought to the region to work in agricultural production and as ranch hands who eventually left these farms and ranches to make their own settlements (e.g., Lewis 2012; Castañeda 2012; Vinson 2001). A mural outside of the town of Corralero corroborates this history, stating that the town was founded in 1910 as an outgrowth of a ranch in the area located next to the lagoon with the same name. This mural connects Blackness to one of the key dates of Mexican history, the beginning of the Mexican Revolution.

Many people with whom I spoke made similar connections and spoke of many towns within the Costa Chica as being key locations within the revolution. Furthermore, many spoke of their ancestors' participation in the war. This local understanding of Blackness places African descendants as key conspirators in the history of the nation, as opposed to the government project of recognition that is attempting to frame Blackness as premodern and traditional. Bulmaro had some strong opinions on the intersection of Blackness and nation in Mexico, as well as the participation of key African-descendant figures in both the War for Independence and the Mexican Revolution. Bulmaro told me,

> I believe the government has a big debt with us in relation to the historical processes that we have here. We could talk about the process of independence, where a Negro was the main actor in that movement and this Negro is not recognized as such, Vicente Guerrero. So, they feel, or we feel, very proud: "Ah, Vicente Guerrero was also Negro." But who knows how he felt? Maybe he never knew he was Negro. We know it and we feel it as a symbol of participation of the Negros in the history of Mexico. It is a debt they owe us. You, assholes [Mexican historians], recognize that he was Negro and that he felt as a Negro. I mean, say it, but we are not very sure of that. In the process of the revolution, we had Emiliano Zapata, the greatest caudillo [military leader] of the Mexican Revolution, he was strong in this . . . in his ideology—"I want land and liberty for my people." And he died, but he kept saying, until the end, that the most important thing was that. And those who killed him were inside the revolution, but they were pursuing different goals. So, they became enemies within the revolution. So, what we need to rescue from Zapata is not so much the fact that he was Negro but his persisting way of thinking, and that was a conjugation of . . . of being Mexican and being Afro.

Bulmaro's identification of two key historical figures as Negro, even if they may have not recognized themselves as such, centers Blackness squarely within the historical national narrative rather than within the cultural margins. Furthermore, Bulmaro's recognition that the figures may not have felt Negro or identified as such shows that he is acutely aware of the produced or invented nature of a cultural Blackness and race within contemporary Mexico.

When pushed to further elaborate on Zapata as Negro, Bulmaro told me, "He was Negro, Afro-Mexican, he was. Now, did we ask Emiliano Zapata if he felt himself as a Negro? No, maybe he would feel ashamed if someone told him he was Negro. Because of what it meant, because of what Negros meant in Mexico, right?" This is what the project of Black recognition is up against in Oaxaca and Guerrero: a simultaneous embrace and disavowing of Blackness. While the communities and activists of the Costa Chica embrace their own being as products of Mexican history, those responsible for the facilitation of official recognition would rather reject the fact of Blackness as a historical racial experience and construct and can only embrace Blackness as an element of prenational authenticity and tradition for the invention of a new cultural landscape within the frame of the Mestizo nation-state (Saldívar 2014).

Conclusion

The process of making difference official is based on colonial conceptions of essential categorical difference. Rather than attempting to reconcile the tensions brought about by understandings of essential forms of difference, the project to make difference official, with the goal of state and federal recognition for African descendants, could very well serve to reinforce the tensions and forms of inequality that the project set out to displace. As African descendants in Mexico were simultaneously part and product of the colonial and later national process through their incorporation into the Spanish Republic of New Spain, African descendants may never be able to truly claim certain types of social or cultural difference in the same way that Indigenous communities can. In attempting to officialize difference without interrogating the continued colonial logics inherent in the practice and manifestations of current forms of difference and the ways in which these logics then produce Black (as well as Indigenous) subjectivities and realities, the process of Black Mexican recognition could very well be seen as a colonial project in and of itself. Furthermore, while the strategy for cultural recognition does create visibility for Black Mexicans within the cultural landscape of the nation, this visibility does little for issues of racism and discrimination since it fails to recognize the existence and historic role of a racially Black subject position within the nation.

Michaels argues, "Talk of culture is not (as Du Bois so often insisted) an alternative to talk of race, but a continuation of it by other means" (cited in Appiah and Gates 1995, 3). The process of making difference official that is underway in Mexico now relies partly on the conflation of race and culture in order to construct difference as part of a continued process of racialization. I am not arguing that this process cannot bring about some benefits for African descendants within the Costa Chica and Mexico more broadly. I do, however, suggest that we need to look more deeply into the process and interrogate what it is that the CDI, SAI, and the grassroots organizations are struggling to officially recognize, and that we take Michaels's warning/critique seriously when he argues that "the modern concept of culture is not, in other words, a critique of racism; it is a form of racism" (1992, 683). Perhaps rather than addressing anti-Black discrimination and racism, the project for official Black cultural recognition in Mexico has instead reproduced the social relations that historically facilitated both citizenship and Black exclusion.

4

Citizenship, Black Value, and the Production of the Black Subject in Mexico

The colonial conceptualization and utilization of Blackness represented a deeply entrenched racial ideology present at the time of the conception and invention of the nation in the Americas (Kazanjian 2003; Wynter 1984). Therefore, this racial ideology should be seen as one of the foundational building blocks for not only the nation in the Americas (Goldberg 2002) but also the conceptualization of the modern "American"[1] citizen. I argue that modern citizenship is a form of subject making (Balibar 2015, 2016), in which the nation is used as the mirror (Hernández Cuevas 2004; Taylor 1994; Handler 1988; Greene 2012; Telles and PERLA 2014) through which multiple subjects are produced and through which those privileged subjects who are allowed to recognize their own image within the national mirror (and therefore embody the nation) can therefore be perceived as the "norm-subject" (Wynter 2003). Rather than perceiving citizenship as an individual property constituted through an individual relationship with the nation-state in which citizens are deemed members through a bundle of entitlements (Hébert and Rosen 2007; Turner and Hamilton 1994), I suggest that we take a more critical approach to citizenship (Hébert and Rosen 2007; Turner and Hamilton 1994) in which it is approached as the relations between citizens and a by-product of the practical and material manifestation of our ideology around the actual social and political relations surrounding production (Kazanjian 2003; Greene 2012; Jerry 2018) within the modern nation. In this way, I argue that the process of recognizing African descendants in Mexico is simultaneously a project for the reproduction of the non-Black Mestizo nation/citizen. Focusing too sharply on the political by-product of Black exclusion and the existence of Black communities as communities apart (Hoffman 2014) has drawn our attention away from the reality of Black exclusion as an inherent part of the process of modern citizenship (Kazanjian 2003). As Kazanjian (2003) demonstrates, citizenship in the Americas has always been conceived through the exclusion/management (both ideological and physical) of Blackness within the nation (Moten 2003). For African descendants in the Americas, citizenship is experienced partly through that exclusion. Furthermore, it is that exclusion that facilitates the non-Black experience of citizenship in the Americas.

Williams argues that "when cultural distinctiveness becomes a criterion of group identity formation in a single political unit it is certainly a product of the power relations existing among citizens of that unit" (1989, 420). The recognition of African descendants in Mexico based on the conception of cultural difference does little to recognize the entanglements of Blackness with the historic production of the privileged non-Black (in many ways read as White) Mestizo citizen, nor the contemporary experience and political situation of African-descendant communities throughout the region. The approach to citizenship as a modern form of subjectivization by and through the nation holds the potential to offer a powerful tool to help disentangle the many relationships that rely on Blackness as a foundational oppositional condition by which the modern citizen/subject, always intuitively read as non-Black, is allowed to exist. Furthermore, taking a relational approach to citizenship shifts our attention from the single unit(s) of analysis and brings back a focus on the social relations in which the unit of analysis is allowed to take form or is given value (Williams 1989; Fields 1990, 2003).

Rather than focusing on citizenship as a direct relationship between individuals/communities and the nation-state, recently scholars have focused on how citizenship produces subjects (Balibar 2015, 2016), as well as citizenship as an actual relation of property among subjects (Shachar and Hirschl 2007) within a capitalist mode of production (Kazanjian 2003). The focus on the productive and relational nature of citizenship allows a sharper focus on the ways in which citizenship is used as a method of interpellation (Althusser 1984) of not one but all subjects in relation to the Subject, which in the context of citizenship and modern capitalism remains the nation. Shifting our attention to the relational nature of this process forces us to ask the question, what roles are particular citizen/subjects (Balibar 2016) expected to play within this relationship, and ultimately the reproduction of the nation itself? This recognition can be a powerful analytical tool, as it allows us to focus on the manner by which citizenship ultimately relies on the production and reproduction of multiple subject positions within the nation. This shifts the focus from identity politics to the business of locating and ethnographically elaborating on the sites for the reproduction of the mutually constituted subject positions that are ultimately relied upon for the reproduction of the nation itself. This shift allows us to focus less on how individuals identify and experience exclusions, and more on the social relations in which racial value is produced and the specific subject positions, whether acknowledged or not, that individuals and groups of peoples are expected to occupy and the role that these subject positions play in the overall experience of citizenship.

The Reproduction of the Black Subject as the Means for Reproducing Whiteness

Oliver describes the difference between subjectivity and subject position "as the difference between one's sense of oneself as a self with agency and one's historical and social position in one's culture" (2004, xiv). She goes on to argue that subject positions, "although mobile, are constituted in our social interactions and our positions within our culture and context; history and circumstance govern them" (xv). Oliver's focus on subject position and subjectivity, while mostly focusing on the individual, is helpful in thinking through how the subject is always a product of social relationships. Taking this argument one step further, we can focus not only on how the subject is produced but on how the reproduction of subjects is also used to reproduce the social relations around the subject. Historically, the Black subject was utilized as the means of production for modernity (Trouillot 1984; Du Bois 2007, 2014), as well as for the production of the privileged subject position, or norm-subject (Wynter 2003), within the nation. In other words, the multiple forms of Whiteness produced within the colonial moment in and through a relation to Blackness (Vinson 2005b, 61), which have therefore been continually reproduced henceforth, both mark and enable modernity's production (Kazanjian 2003). Oliver argues that subjectivity logically occurs prior to a subject position but that the two are always interconnected (2004, xv). While it would be impossible to argue against the interconnection and contextually constructed nature of subjectivity and subject position, with regard to the production of the modern Black subject, we must pause in the intuitive acceptance of a particular racial subjectivity as existing a priori to a subject position. The current project for the cultural and political production of the Black Mexican citizen helps to complicate this perception.

Another example, from my current research on youth citizenship in the US Southwest, helps concretely begin the conversation. Through my research on the production of racial geographies as the requisite real estate for claims to citizenship, I have begun to look at how the use of the racial epithet "nigger" acts as a methodology for continually reproducing both Black and non-Black subjects (Jerry 2018). This research reveals that many Black people in the United States are confronted with this word at an early age, oftentimes in elementary school. I focus on the imposition of the "nigger," not only as a moment of interpellation of a racialized subject but also as a critical methodology, or even technology, for the reproduction of a privileged White/non-Black subject, as well as the social relations in which the White subject continues to be normalized as the privileged subject. That is to say, the use of the word "nigger" as a racial epithet continues to be an important social technology for the reproduction of both White (indirectly) and Black (directly) subjects, based on a preexisting subject position, as well as the racial economy (Wilson 2009) in which these subjectivities continue to find meaning and value. This process highlights the limited publicly acceptable subject positions available to Black people within the United States and, as I will make clear, throughout the Americas—and more broadly on a global scale.

The subject position of the "nigger," along with the many undervalued social locations represented by the "nigger position" (Wynter 1984, 2003) within a larger hierarchy, exists before the actual material human manifestation of the "nigger," and more generally the Black subject, is ever hailed into being. This existence of the subject position before the existence of the subject would mean, then, and my research on the subject continues to support this hypothesis, that for some time within the early development of the Black racialized subject, there is a disconnect between the Black subject position and the subjectivities associated with Blackness that are undoubtedly later developed through a relentless process of socialization. In line with Althusser (1984), this process incorporates the Black body as the means of production for not only the production of a particular racial order but for the actual reproduction of Whiteness, and the White subject itself (Fanon 2008). Through a sanctioned process of exclusion, this ideological relationship—the social relations surrounding production (Kazanjian 2003, 20)—is one of the main theoretical underpinnings, as well as my working theoretical definition, of citizenship in this book.[2]

One of Oliver's main arguments in her *Colonization of Psychic Space* is that "without considering subject position, we assume that all subjects are alike, we level differences, or like traditional psychoanalysis, we develop a normative notion of subject formation based on one particular group, gender, or class of people" (2004, xvi). This leveling of difference allows for the utilization of ideal theories as a strategy for securing the ideal forms that are then seen to be the natural material manifestations of these ideal theories.[3] We thereby skew our analysis as we attempt to fit the experiences of our research subjects into theories rather than theorize around the experiences of our subjects—or even ourselves as subjects—within the many social relationships of the modern world. For example, it has become customary to discuss those on the margins of citizenship within the contexts and terms associated with the ideal citizen, as if those whose exclusion is used as a baseline for the definition of the norm-subject could ever occupy the position of ideal citizen. Thus, we accept the existence of a normative type of citizen and then theorize other forms of citizenship relative to the ideal in an attempt to maintain that ideal as an ultimately achievable and intact form. Rather than continuing to theorize multiple forms that inadvertently reify or maintain an ideal privileged form or type (the citizen), I argue that it is more productive to focus on the relational nature of citizenship, in which the privileged citizen/subject (White/Mestizo) is produced through the operation of marginalizing the "Other" (Mullen 1994, 73–74). That is, I propose we understand citizenship as a dialectic in and of itself. Drawing on Oliver, I suggest that in terms of recognizing citizenship as a methodology for producing the subject (subjectivization), we should start from the position of those who have been abjected and excluded by ideal theories of citizenship. As Oliver argues, "without a psychoanalytic theory for and revolving around those othered by the Freudian model subject, we continue to base our theories of subjectivity on the very norm that we are trying to overcome; in this way, our theories collaborate with the oppressive values that we are working against" (2004, xvi). Oliver's development of a psychoanalytic theory of oppression is useful for a focus on citizenship as a form of subjectivization. Instead of assuming that citizenship works on a hierarchical level and therefore that those on the margins can ultimately scale the ladder, the approach to citizenship as a dialectic recognizes how the other is positioned on the margins in order to reinforce the privileged subject at the center. Moten, drawing on Hartman (1997) and Butler (1997), elaborates on this dialectic and argues that "the call to subjectivity is understood also as a call to subjection and subjugation and appeals for redress or protection to the state or to the structure or idea of citizenship—as well as modes of radical performativity or subversive impersonation—are always already imbedded in the structure they would escape" (2003, 2).

Following Fanon (2008), Oliver writes that "the negative affects of the oppressors are 'deposited in the bones' of the oppressed. Affects move between bodies; colonization and oppression operate through depositing the unwanted affects of the dominant group onto those othered by that group in order to sustain its privileged position" (2004, xix). This process of depositing, also discussed by Césaire (1972) and Wynter (2003), is how Black and White become forever entangled in the Americas, one being the mirror image of the other; the subject being possessed by the object it possesses (Moten 2003, 1). Kazanjian cautions against the a priori existence of the norm-subject. He explains, "Existential or psychological theories of projection uninformed by psychoanalysis continue to use the model of a subject projecting onto the other that which it does not like about itself, without explaining the conditions of possibility for a subject who projects or likes or dislikes, or the historically specific conditions under which this general, projecting, liking, and disliking subject is active or inactive" (2003, 15). The question, then, is, How does the norm-subject come into being and reproduce itself? Wynter argues that in the Americas, "it was to be the peoples of Black African descent who would be constructed as the ultimate referent of the 'racially inferior' Human Other" (2003, 266). This demonstrates the mutually constituted nature of the Black and White subject positions and the process of producing a White subject position through the production of a Black subject position. It is important to recognize that this process is continually reenacted through mundane relations between citizens/ subjects.

In colonial Latin America, this situation might have been similar for Native Americans were it not for the church and its representatives such as Bartolomé de las Casas and the belief that the Indigenous of the Americas ultimately held the capacity for humanity and the recuperation of the "savage soul" (Heuman 2014; Wynter 2003). Wynter explains that de las Casas's proposal for the use of African slave labor in the Americas came not from a racist belief in the lack of African humanity and Africans' inherent suitability for slave labor, but rather his belief that Africans had "been enslaved and enserfed" within the "just title" terms of orthodox Christian theology at the time (2003, 293). However, by the time de las Casas realized that enslaved Africans had been acquired outside of the "just title" terms of Christian theology, the damage had already been done and "the mass slave trade from

Africa across the Atlantic that would give rise to today's transnational Black Diaspora had taken on a life and unstoppable dynamic of its own" (Wynter 2003, 293) The perceived possibility of Indigenous redemption outlined by de las Casas sets the potential for the Indigenous to occupy a place, or space, around the truth of cultural difference, rather than the truth of racial or species difference, which allowed for Indigeneity to be perceived as another form of the Human rather than beyond the bounds of humanity (Wynter 2003; Wilderson 2020). The humanity associated with colonial Indigeneity also created the possibility for publicly acceptable ways to express the affects of oppression (Oliver 2004) associated with being Indigenous. This possibility continues to be withheld from African descendants in Mexico, whose claims to racial difference position them within the nation as what Ng'weno (2007, 2012) describes as "'suspect citizens'; those whose tie to the land (and therefore to the nation) is continually questioned" (2012, 165).

The possibility for the expression, as well as the historic recognition and incorporation of the affects of Indigenous oppression into the national narrative, that allows for the subject position of Indigeneity to be expressed as an acceptable subjectivity is interpretable through a supposedly shared version of Mexican history. The imposition of this shared version creates an acceptable manner, such as the cultural recognition discussed in the previous chapter, by which the norm-subject is willing to accept any representation and social relation with the historically oppressed. Taylor suggests that a problem with recognition arises when the broader society does not mirror back to a group that which they see in themselves (1994, 25). The underlying tension between Black activists and the almost exclusively non-Black government organizations and employees implementing the project of Black recognition in Mexico is ultimately a by-product of the process of agreeing upon an acceptable way to represent the particular historical effects and affects of oppression associated with the Black experience in Mexico as well as the associated process of sublimation that comes with the invention of a people.[4] What is at stake in the project for African-descendant recognition in Mexico is access to the means of production of the public/political self. Sublimation and idealization are necessary for the development of psychic life as well as for transformative and restorative resistance to oppression. However, according to Oliver, "in an oppressive culture that abjects, excludes, or marginalizes certain groups or types of bodies, sublimation and idealization can become the privilege of dominant groups, and idealization can become a cruel, judging, superego" (2004, xx).

Oliver argues that "sublimation allows us to connect and communicate with others by making our bodies and experiences meaningful; we become beings who mean by sublimating our bodily drives and affects. Sublimation, then, is necessary for both subjectivity or individuality and community or sociality" (xx). The ideological and administrative trick of colonialism, a trick that continues to act as a real inheritance in the modern moment (Jerry 2021), was to withhold this ability to sublimate from the other, and then to exploit the other in the process of sublimation within the self of the privileged subject, or Subject (Althusser 1984). At first glance, this may appear to be akin to the concept of social death (Patterson 1982). However, I would argue against the perception that the idea of being socially dead had ever supremely permeated the rich cultural and social spaces of Black Mexicans. But the question remains, in what ways does the management of Blackness continue to facilitate the sublimation of both Black and non-Black (Mestizo/Indigenous) subjectivities? I agree with Vincent Brown (2009), that we should not over rely on the concept/framework put forth by Patterson of "social death as the basic condition of slavery" (1982, 1233), or even within a capitalist mode of production, discussed as racial capitalism by Robinson (1983) thereafter. However, it is important to take seriously the ways in which dominant non-Black society continues to conceive of the value of Black lives (that is, the potential for Black lives to produce value) and attempts to limit the range of subject positions available to Blackness in order to enact a material world based on Black value.

While the question of Black agency (Brown 2009) is an important one, a relational approach to citizenship helps illuminate the ways that, through restricted access to individuality and sublimation, at least in the context of a broader set of social and power relations, society continues to attempt to make Blackness a static position. Furthermore, it is Blackness as a static position that sets the stage for non-Black stability and social maneuverability. In this way, from the perspective of non-Black people, the Black subject position is imagined to operate as the means of production for not only the economy and broader nation but Whiteness itself. This is made possible by legal and customary strategies, such as legal recognition and mundane anti-Black discrimination, that attempt to make Blackness a static position through the maintenance of a historic Black subject position. The point here should not be to only discuss the condition of Blackness, but also to discuss the condition of the broader society that relies on a Black subject position, and the ways that societies continue to reinvest in the value (or disvalue) of Blackness as a relational subject position. In this way we avoid the potential to conceptualize the outcome of this relationship as a type of Black pathology. Rather, we can focus on the pathology of a society informed by White ideals. This is to accept the claims by scholars such as Du Bois and Wilderson that White society itself is pathological (Du Bois, cited in Wilderson 2020). This can be seen by continued attempts to incorporate Blackness into a White-centric world. This is the context in which negotiations around African-descendant recognition in Mexico become a terrain of struggle (McKittrick 2006).

The public perception of Whiteness as the privileged social category and position is not simply a natural state of public affairs. It must be constantly managed through representations and reproductions of the other, which then act as the potential foundation for the process of sublimation, at least in the sense of the public self, within both the privileged and racialized citizen. As discussed in the previous chapter, the current process of recognition of African descendants underway in Mexico is about managing and controlling the process of sublimation. The Mexican government is attempting to control the means of meaning-making for African descendants in Mexico as a way of transforming Black Mexicans into manageable multicultural subjects. Not only is this necessary for the operation of the economies of development and tourism within Mexico and Latin America more broadly (Saldaña-Portillo 2003), but it also reinforces a persistent system of racial (or ethnic) value (Comaroff and Comaroff 2009). Wade argues that elite representations of the other are not only representations of something "out-there" but are a strategy fundamental to the reproduction of their own position (2001, 855). In the terms laid out by Wynter, the power to represent the other is an "indispensable function of the inscripting and instituting of the norm subject" (2003, 309). Attempting to regulate Black sublimation, and therefore Black subjectivity, is a strategy to manage the possibility of a crisis of identity for the Mestizo (or Whiteness) in the multicultural Mexican nation brought about by the demands for Black recognition. Thus, the other on which the Subject (i.e., Whiteness and the ideological concept of the nation) depends for subjectivity is maintained, thereby maintaining the system of racial value. Simply put, the other continues to be exploited as the means of production for the reproduction of the Subject. This is a predatory relationship through which the other is consumed in multiple forms as a way of nourishing representations of the nation (Wade 2001; Taussig 1987, 1993) and the privileged national subject.

Clarifying the relational nature of sublimation and subjectivity allows us to avoid falling victim to the "all too popular discourse of autonomous self-governed individuals that covers over how that sense of autonomy, self-governance, and individuality was formed" (Oliver 2004, xxi). This is also key to uncovering the way in which the "ideal" appears to be achievable by all citizens, yet in reality is restricted by way of the mundane border inspections that are employed daily as a way of reproducing the "other" (Lugo 2000, 2008). The ideal citizen is the citizen for whom a sense of autonomy, self-governance, and individuality is never questioned, and for whom the actual process by which the achievement of this sense of autonomy, self-governance, and individuality is never laid bare. The ideal has the privilege to believe that their bodies and behaviors do not require interpretation and therefore can make that belief reality (Oliver 2004, xxii) partly by maintaining the power to interpret others. The commonly overlooked issue here is that it takes both ideological and material work to allow for the privileged unconscious to appear as the ideal. The process of cultural and political recognition for African descendants in Mexico serves as one example of this work, as the methodologies employed for recognition are intuitively aimed at maintaining the order of difference that is taken for granted. Instead of questioning the ways in which Black Mexicans have been excluded from the contemporary narrative of the origins of the Mexican people, the governmental approach to the project for African-descendant recognition contextualizes Blackness as a by-product of the multicultural politics of the present and uses the same strategies relevant to the present political climate of both mestizaje and multiculturalism.[5] In this way, the Afro-Mexican is allowed to take form without threatening the broader political philosophy of mestizaje, even though this same ideology was used to exclude Blackness from any association with the formal Mexican nation in the first place.

The strategy of Black cultural recognition does nothing to change the conditional nature of Black existence or the potential experiences of citizenship available to Black Mexicans. Moreover, incorporation in this fashion allows the "average" Mexican Mestizo to ignore the historical processes associated with their own being, as well as to ignore the by-product of these processes as it has manifested itself as Black exclusion. This manner of incorporation forces newly minted "Afro-Mexicanos" to become responsible for embracing a history that is singularly associated with their own Blackness (Fanon 2008), as well as the unique burden that is the historic inheritance of Black skin (James 2009, 33). This shifting of historical burdens acts as a mechanism for the nation and Mestizos to avoid any modern guilt or implication associated with the historic production of the Black subject and can also work to displace that guilt by shifting the burden of existence onto the re-racialized Black body.

Oliver argues that the thesis that alienation, guilt, and anxiety are inherent in the human condition, as put forth by philosophers of alienation, covers up the concrete guilt associated with the oppression and domination that guaranteed White privilege in the face of specific others against whom the White subject has constituted itself as privileged (2004, 2). Oliver's argument asks us to think of the ways that Whiteness as a privileged position is rationalized through philosophy, as well as concrete political and social projects masked as philanthropy, after its own constitution as the natural privileged subject, thus justifying its "natural" position within the system of racial value (Kazanjian 2003). This would suggest that Black exclusion is constitutive of citizenship (Kazanjian 2003, 59), and Blackness cannot be imagined occupying the position of citizen within the terms of our current order of knowledge, as Blackness is continually reproduced as the antithesis (Wynter 2005). However, this should not stop us from recognizing the ways in which Blackness is used to produce others who can exist as the norm-subject or privileged citizen. As I discuss in the conclusion of this book, my approach to the phenomenon of implication (2018) lays this process bare, as the struggle for Black rights and recognition in several social and political arenas breaks the silence around the broader processes of oppression and domination. The phenomenon of implication also implicates Whiteness in the process of subjectification of the other to the privileged White Subject, simply by publicly asking the question "How and why did we get here?" (see chapter 3). This process implicates those in the contemporary moment as keepers of the past as a strategy for solidifying and reproducing White/Mestizo privilege in the present.

If we take seriously the insights of postcolonial scholars such as C.L.R. James (1989, 2009), Fanon (2008), Robinson (1983, 2007, 2019), Trouillot (1984, 1992, 1995), and Kazanjian (2003), we see that slavery and colonization is the ideological environment in which citizenship in the Americas was conceived. The conception and theorizing of citizenship, as well as the nation, in the Americas was first and foremost a racial project (Goldberg 2002) that depended upon the preexisting racial value brought about by colonial social relations to produce the new nation. While the nation became the mechanism through which the White citizen/subject was alienated and othered, and therefore allowed to come into being, a Black subject position continued to be subordinated and relied upon as a means for producing the White citizen, and by proxy the nation. All the while Black subjects were excluded from capturing the value associated with their own bodies as the means of production. This oppression by way of exclusion from the "means of production of value" (Oliver 2004, 13) is important to the ideological and physical relationship that I highlight by using the term "racial economy." Within this racial economy the Black body is used as the means of production but excluded from the product of its own labor, and therefore excluded from owning the actual means of production and capturing the value associated with its own labor. This process is dialectical in nature as the Black body is inserted into a racial economy in a way that facilitates Black exclusion for the means of producing Whiteness and the nation-state overall.[6]

Culturalizing Blackness leaves the preexisting racial economy intact by avoiding the conversation of how it was that Whiteness was ever privileged in the social relations of mestizaje (and therefore Blackness excluded) in the first place. The main argument of this book and the bulk of its ethnographic material attempts to elaborate on this process by focusing on how, by way of cultural recognition, Blackness is being incorporated into the preexisting schema of mestizaje in a way that utilizes Blackness as the means of production for Whiteness/Mestizoness, and the now multicultural state,[7] while simultaneously reproducing the perceived mutual exclusivity of Black and Mexican (Sue 2010; Jones 2018). In this way, the strategy for Black recognition in Mexico continues to reproduce the social relations of production through which modern citizenship has always been conceived (Kazanjian 2003).

Citizenship as a Methodology for Interpreting the Black Experience in Mexico

Currently, popular/public discourses on citizenship approach citizenship as a personal possession or property in the "simple" sense of the word (Shachar and Hirschl 2007). Harris complicates this simplified approach to property and reminds her readers that "although by popular usage property describes 'things' owned by persons, or the rights of persons with respect to a thing, the concept of property prevalent among most theorists, even prior to the twentieth century, is that property may consist of rights in 'things' that are intangible. Property is thus said to be a right, not a thing, characterized as metaphysical, not physical" (1993, 1725). Harris goes on to argue, drawing on Macpherson (1978), that property is a right or a claim that one anticipates or excepts will be enforced by others (1993, 1730). The perception of citizenship as a "thing," and by extension personal property in the simple sense, allows one to sidestep the actual relational nature of citizenship as a theoretical concept. Focusing on citizenship in the simple "thingified" sense and avoiding the relational nature of citizenship (Ignatieff 1995) allows for one to posit different forms or types of citizenship that are applicable to specific individuals (or groups), most commonly manifesting as conditional forms that are then interpreted through an experience of a type of hierarchical or "second-class" citizenship. This in turn allows for the perception of a hierarchical relationship in which "first-class" citizenship as an ideal is hypothetically attainable by those on the lower rungs of the citizenship hierarchy. The hierarchical class-based approach (first class, second class, etc.) to citizenship overlooks the actual roots of our modern capitalist form of citizenship itself and the ways in which modern citizenship as an ideology for inclusion of the ideal type is based on the subjugation of one class or classes over the other, all within a system in which the most important marker of class inclusion is the condition of Blackness or non-Blackness (Kazanjian 2003; Hall 1980). This has allowed for Blackness to be intuitively associated with a particular condition/position (exclusion) within the relations of citizenship. Perhaps better said, drawing on Hall's (1980) insights on race and class, race and the perceived condition of Black or non-Black becomes a mode by which citizenship is experienced. This insight allows us to see that the only way to accurately apply citizenship as a hierarchical relationship in which those on the bottom can eventually obtain the ideal form of citizenship at the top of this hierarchy is by excluding the Black experience from our theorizing around citizenship altogether.

Approaching citizenship as a hierarchy or set of vertical relations (Telles 2004), or as multiple forms, reifies citizenship as an ideal form of, or as simply a synonym for, belonging. Dixon and Burdick, for example, explain that "citizenship construction is the process by which the excluded build a legal and social framework that recognizes and accepts them, transforming them from noncitizens into citizens. This political transformation is rooted in concepts such as cultural citizenship, new citizenship, and active citizenship, each of which offer legitimation to claims of rights, space, and belonging in the dominant society" (2012, 10). While rights-based struggles have produced some real material gains for African descendants, these struggles have not been able to address the dialectical nature of citizenship and have therefore been unsuccessful overall in dealing with White supremacy and incorporating Blackness into the ideal image of the nation.

Dixon and Burdick see this as being especially true with state-inscribed strategies, arguing that "state initiatives simultaneously open up new spaces from which to challenge White/mixed supremacy while actually working in more or less invisible ways to reinscribe it" (2012, 13). I suggest a productive way to deal with this issue is by looking at citizenship, at least in the Americas, as a dialectic based on a colonial dichotomy between "us" and "them" or "we" and "the other." This allows for the recognition that citizenship has always imagined an "other," whose purpose was explicitly to work as a material agent for the production of citizenship and inclusion for the accepted/privileged norm-subject. As the Black body was never imagined to be able to transition into the ideal citizen, later political inclusions of Black people into the citizenry may be better seen as ways of officially institutionalizing this ontological position of the "other" (Wynter 1984, 2003; Wilderson 2020) associated with the Black subject position.

Applying current conceptions of hierarchical citizenship or citizenship as forms, seen as a type of qualified citizenship by Kallhoff (2013), fails to take seriously the ways in which the process of utilizing the other as the means of producing the privileged citizen is first and foremost a racial project. Rather than looking at Blackness through the lens of second-class citizenship, I suggest a deeper look at the role of the Black subject position in the relations of citizenship—that is, a foundational element necessary for citizenship (as an organizing principle and a form of modern subjectivization) to exist in the first place. If we accept that modern citizenship was theorized from the very beginning to be exclusive, then we may see that using it as a mechanism for inclusivity ignores the systematic work that has been done to exclude Blackness from the principle concept of modern citizenship (Kazanjian 2003), and continues to be a strategy for governing the ways in which we allow particular groups to access Whiteness while simultaneously reinforcing Blackness as the baseline by which the other is measured.[8] As Harris argues, "the fundamental precept of whiteness—the core of its value—is its exclusivity. But exclusivity is predicated not on any intrinsic characteristic, but on the existence of the symbolic 'other'" (1993, 1790).

This relationship rests on what I refer to as a persistent racial economy, as the colonial logics of value placed upon racial subjects, specifically the Black subject, are continually called upon to make the whole system work. This system of racial value is a necessary foundation for a wider political economy in which racialized subjects fit within particular economic niches and facilitate the experience of citizenship enjoyed by those seen to be potentially acceptable and includable subjects of the nation. In other words, I argue that there exists only one form of citizenship within our current capitalist mode of production.[9] The question then becomes: how does Blackness determine how people can experience modern citizenship? An analysis of the political project of recognition aimed at African descendants in Mexico demonstrates that focusing on the productive and consumptive aspects of citizenship—its relational or dialectic nature—must act as the starting point in theoretically and ethnographically approaching this question.

A relational approach to citizenship calls attention to the legacy of modern citizenship as a dialectic of simultaneous inclusion and exclusion and reminds us that citizenship is not simply a position bestowed upon a citizen/subject; it is an actual ontological relationship that theorizes a dynamic entanglement between difference within the modern nation. The conception of "Black modernity" as counterculture put forth by Paul Gilroy (1993); the notion of vernacularism as discussed by Homi Bhabha (1996), Anthony Kwame Appiah (2005), Charles Briggs (2005), and Jason McGraw (2014); the "vernacular modernities" put forth by Napolitano (2002); and the conception of "racial time" as theorized by Michael Hanchard (1999) and Charles W. Mills (2014) are all useful concepts here. They allow for the perception or theorization of multiple experiences of the same phenomenon simultaneously in the present by different groups. As Wade (2010) argues, it is necessary to see Black peoples, Indigenous peoples, and the nation as mutually constitutive cultural categories in which the nation feeds on the power of Black and Indigenous peoples in the same way that they feed on the nation (111). Therefore, the question is not what type of citizen individuals are, but how an experience of citizenship is overdetermined by the historical construction and reproduction of otherness as well as the historical relationship between otherness and the nation.

Popular approaches that perceive citizenship through the conception of multiple forms intuitively overlook this insight, as distinct forms of citizenship are seen to apply only to a nation's population of "people of color" or those citizens who are perceived to be marginalized in some form or another.[10] For example, within multiculturalist regimes, people seen as culturally, ethnically, and racially different are allowed to participate as citizens within the parameters of difference mainly with the requirement that they add something new or desirable to the overall citizenry. These "forms" neglect the ideal experience (see Sue 2013) as those who are allowed to occupy the space of the ideal are simply conceived of as citizens or the norm-subject. Instead, these different forms of citizenship are commonly used to create theoretical and analytical frameworks of belonging representative of a given political moment.

Rather than asking what forms of citizenship exist within a mode of production, a more productive approach is to focus on the enduring social relations that continue to facilitate the mode of governance associated with a particular mode of production. As opposed to different forms of citizenship, the citizenship experiences of the other are simply vernacular experiences of the same form of citizenship in which particular brands of "others" are used as the means for reproducing the privileged citizen and the broader nation-state. This relationship creates a dialectic of belonging, a relationship between citizens, where individuals' experiences of belonging are facilitated by, and dependent on, others' experience of belonging. The ways in which Black Mexicans' belonging to the nation is regularly questioned and inspected at social, cultural, and geographical borders is a stark example. Lucila's experience, as well as my own, outlined in chapters 1 and 5, demonstrates how Blackness is allowed to cross such borders and is afforded reentry only after the mutual exclusivity of Black and Mexican is reestablished. Hidden within this process of Black exclusion is the way that the inspections of Black Mexicans at the internal and external borders of the nation also facilitate the reproduction of the non-Black Mestizo norm-subject.

Black cultural recognition facilitates this process and reproduces the relations of citizenship within Mexico by reproducing a Black subject position that does not threaten the privileged position of the non-Black Mestizo. In this way, even as Black Mexicans are incorporated into the multicultural nation, the underlying value associated with Blackness and the Black subject position remains intact. Focusing on the actual process of Black cultural recognition in Mexico, rather than Black Mexican culture, sheds light on the broader social relations in which race is replicated and employed for the reproduction of the nation. I argue that the social relations in which race is continually put to work is essentially what we mean to capture by the modern use of citizenship. That is, citizenship, in modern times, has always been a way to operationalize our theorizing of the social relations around production (Kazanjian 2003; Jerry 2018), as well as to solidify these relations through a racialized system in which particular bodies are imagined operating as the means for producing the nation and the privileged citizen therein.

Black Value and the Production of the Nation

Harris argues that "the description of symbolic relations as 'economies' has become a cliché in cultural studies" (1993, 2). However, in the context of color discrimination, Harris finds the metaphor appropriate, as it "highlights the mobile and dynamic quality of color, as well as its complexity" (2). Scholars have made it clear that for Black people, our being has always been (and continues to be) an economic issue. I use the phrase "racial economy" to highlight the way that Black value is produced, reproduced, and put to work, and in some cases even traded, in society. By using the phrase, I also mean to question the ways in which Black people can access the value created by their own labor and being, as well as the mechanisms that are put in place to limit this self-access to Black value. The commensuration of race and ethnicity into value acts as a hegemonic mechanism that defines individuals,' as well as entire populations,' place within regional and national economies.

An NPR story entitled "Demographic Changes Spark Debate Over Immigration in Nevada" outlines the general logic by which communities of color are perceived as the means for reproducing Whiteness and the products for the act of consumption that then defines Whiteness (Wade 2001).[11] When the interviewer asks a White American woman in Reno, Nevada, about the city's changing demographics as a result of Mexican immigrants, the woman explains, "We can all enjoy each other's multicultures [sic], and, like, we all like Mexican food, or we like, you know, all different kinds of food and things, but don't come here and take. And that's what I think I'm seeing, like a lot of people are coming and taking."[12] She later claims that immigrants "are taking work from native-born citizens"—where "native-born citizens" acts as a politically correct nonracial code for Anglo Whiteness. The woman also seems to blame her husband's inability to receive disability for his back problems on the "fact" that "immigrants are using up" all the resources. In this woman's mind, if Mexicans—in this case, Mexican immigrants—add to the value of her life through the production of things that she enjoys consuming (e.g., Mexican food), then Mexicans are tolerable. However, when those Mexicans demand access to the nation and consume those things that the country has to offer—jobs, social services, and so on—then they are seen as threatening. In this way, the other is positioned to act as the means of production. In the most recent multicultural iteration, communities of color are expected to produce multicultural products (food, entertainment, leisure activities) to nourish the nation (Wade 2001), or they serve as resources for exploitation in larger-scale development projects, producing those things that add value to the everyday experience of Whiteness. As the above-cited example reveals, when this relationship is turned upside down, the "natural" order is disrupted. We can see a similar position for Indigeneity within the racial economy that operates within Mexico.

Indigeneity, and the many associated cultural aesthetics, have become a defining factor of the state of Oaxaca. In the city center of Oaxaca, one can find any number of cultural elements being exploited by Indigenous and Mestizos alike. In many cases, the most successful of these ventures appear to be taken on by Mestizo individuals who have the capital to start or continue businesses initiated by previous generations. Many of these businesses sell "authentic" wares produced in the many Indigenous communities that surround the city proper. Other businesses, such as the numerous restaurants that line the main tourist walks surrounding the Zocalo, promote authentic cuisine but are owned and operated by Mestizo individuals. Any number of these restaurants can be seen promoting their fusion cuisines through imagery that invokes authentic Mixtec, Zapotec, or some other culinary culture. At the same time, one can see Indigenous panhandlers on the same streets in which their culture is being promoted to tourists by Mestizo restaurateurs. In the cultural and racial economy of Oaxaca, the value of Indigeneity is more easily captured by Mestizos with the capital to enter the vibrant tourist economy that has come to define the region. On the other hand, Indigeneity is less exploitable for those who are forced to carry the actual social burdens associated with Indigeneity. This relationship is one of the key aspects of a racial economy, an economy in which the value of race and ethnicity can be captured and traded in limited ways by those who represent the categories of race and ethnicity.

The racial economy of mestizaje in Mexico allows for the value of Indigeneity to be more easily captured and put to work by non-Indigenous people in order to exploit a cultural tourism market that relies on the historic conceptualization of southern Mexico as the Indigenous region within the country. This is partly possible through the incorporation of Indigeneity in the form of culture into the fabric of the nation. This means that average Mestizos can claim Indigenous culture as their own, and therefore capture the value that Indigenous culture represents in the nation. This economic relationship is in line with the symbolic use of Indigeneity by the Creole elite as the means for producing the Mestizo Mexican nation, as well as the Mestizo itself, at the beginning of the nineteenth century. A key difference here is the way in which Indigenous communities are not divorced from their cultural property as a by-product of this process. The fact that Indigenous communities are able to maintain partial ownership rights of their culture creates the possibility for them to capture the value associated with Indigeneity. While limited access to capital makes this process more difficult, as the Zapatista strategy discussed in chapter 2 demonstrates, the ability to make claims to the nation through the foundational inclusion of an Indigenous subject position has been an important strategy for Indigenous struggles throughout Latin America.

The current project for the multicultural recognition of Black Mexicans is attempting to insert Black Mexicans into a similar, if not the same, role occupied by Indigeneity within Mexico's racial economy. However, the project for Black recognition within Mexico has failed to recognize the different roles that Black and Indigenous value has historically played in the Mexican racial economy and the production of the nation. Knight argues that in Mexico, "the conflict between racial ideology and sociopolitical circumstances leaves Indians—still the victims of externally imposed categories—caught in a dilemma. Official ideology proclaims their worth, even their superiority (hence the phenomenon of instrumental indigenismo); but sociopolitical circumstances repeatedly display the reality of prejudice" (1990, 101). The racial and ethnic value of both Indigenous and Black Mexicans has been appropriated and put to work to produce the Mestizo and the Mexican nation. This logic of racial value, and the ability to extract value from the other, seems to be the continuity between the colonial, independence, revolutionary, and multicultural eras in Mexico. The question is, What role do Black and Indigenous peoples play in this relationship and the differing impacts that this relationship continues to have on the material reality of Indigenous and Black communities? While both Black and Indigenous communities are affected, they are affected in profoundly different ways.

The fact that Indigeneity has been explicitly incorporated into the historic foundation of the Mestizo nation creates the potential for Indigenous Mexicans to capture the value associated with Indigeneity in a way that may not be possible for Black Mexicans. That is to argue that Black Mexicans have been completely alienated from the value, or "color capital" (Mullen 1994), that they create in Mexican society. Hernández Cuevas's (2004, viv, 32) recognition of the ways in which African ethnic contributions were plagiarized by the Creole elite and then ascribed to Spanish and Indigenous origins alone is important here. The contemporary outcome of this has meant that Black Mexicans have been divorced (alienated) from the cultural property that was historically used to produce and represent the nation and are therefore unable to capture the value of Black culture through claims to the nation. In this way, Black Mexican cultural claims continue to locate Blackness beyond the nation. Because Black Mexicans are limited from capturing the value that they create in society, Black value continues to be employed for the direct benefit of non-Blacks. This means that Black people remain the "instruments for," rather than "beneficiaries of," the production of value (Wilderson 2020, 13). The fact that Black people have been restricted from capturing the value associated with their being is the key distinction between the use of Indigeneity as the symbolic means for producing the Mexican nation (and the ideal national Mestizo citizen/subject) and the use of Blackness as the actual means of production.

For the sake of an efficiently functioning colonial bureaucracy, the Spanish created two separate republics, one Spanish and one Indigenous (Lomnitz-Adler 1992; Menchaca 2001; Poole 2004). This system left many of the preexisting Indigenous forms of governance intact in the interest of facilitating a well-oiled bureaucratic tribute machine. This tribute system facilitated the efficient extraction of resources from Indigenous communities, using the preexisting Indigenous noble class as the new foremen and overseers of Indigenous labor. Within this system, Africans and their descendants were seen as a separate class of slave labor within the Spanish republic to be wielded by Spanish hands. This class was seen not to merit its own republic and therefore remained intimately tied to the Spanish republic. Lomnitz-Adler argues that "although Africans too were thought of as a nación (a community of blood), the Spaniards tried to block the existence of a slave society" (1992, 267). This blocking of a slave society was the practical work of maintaining a dialectic in which Blackness allowed for the reproduction of Spanishness/Whiteness. This created an intimate symbolic relationship that did not exist between Indigeneity and Spanishness that allowed African descendants to act as a distorted mirror of sorts in which Blackness was reflected to recognize what Spanish was not. What is it that the vampire sees in the mirror when they do not see themselves? The answer to this question must be more than nothing. Rather, the vampire sees the world as it is by being allowed to not see the messiness that is represented by their own presence. Free of this messiness, the vampire, and in this case Whiteness, is/was free from feeling the social weight of its own presence and therefore free to perceive the world within the context of the ideal—a condition never afforded to Blackness.

In order to be put to work within the colonies, the condition of the ideal was actively solidified through the reproduction of ideology and withheld from the Black body. When de las Casas declares in 1511 that Africans and their descendants, due to their perceived physical robustness (Aguirre Beltrán 1989), are needed to replace the Indigenous as labor for the colonial project, the concretization of Black people as the preferred source of labor power was not the only by-product (Ramsay 2016; Lomnitz 2001; Harris 1993; Harrison 1995). Even though recanted several years later, this decree, within the context of colonialism as both an economic project and a project of administration within the context of a proto-capitalist mode of production, enabled the development of an ideology of anti-Blackness that would become important for facilitating the production of the Mexican nation from that moment forward (Harris 1993). Furthermore, this ideology allowed for the development of a racial economy in which Blackness was, and still is, commensurable and afforded a particular value that would set the stage for all other social, cultural, political, and economic exchanges within the viceroyalty of New Spain, as well as the future Mexican nation itself.

The actual legal-cum-cultural work of de las Casas's edict that Indigenous souls and bodies were ultimately salvageable places Black people at the bottom of the social, political, and legal hierarchy. This edict also sets the foundation for an ideological system of value in which Blackness would stand as the baseline antagonist for determining the multiple degrees of non-Spanishness. Even as the edict was later retracted, the ideological work the system of value was founded upon had already been used to create a static variable around which the colonial, and later national, system would all be organized (Harris 1993). In this way, we see the development of a pernicious and persistent racial economy that would allow for Blackness to act as the means of production (both physical and ideological) for the colonial order. The only way to counteract this relationship in the later national period was to simply omit Blackness from the practical and ideological production of the new national figure, the Mestizo as *the* quintessential Mexican citizen.

While the Black body became invisible within the new Mestizo nation by way of incorporation of the Indigenous as the symbolic means for producing the nation in addition to the physical and rhetorical isolation and exclusion of Black people in the nineteenth century and beyond (Vinson

2005a, 2005b), the threat of Blackness continued to operate as a ghost in Mexican society, which in turn allowed for the maintenance of the colonial racial economy. This can be seen not only in the literally eugenic writings of José Vasconcelos during the Mexican Revolution (the second major national period in Mexican history), but also in the more mundane mechanisms through which Blackness continued to operate as the baseline for Whiteness in Mexico. Examples include any number of ways in which popular Mexican music derides Blackness; popular jokes and sayings such as "trabajar como Negro para vivir como Blanco" (working like a Black to live like a White) (Cerón-Anaya 2019; Sue 2010, 2013); the lingering figure of Memín Penguín (Moreno Figueroa and Saldívar Tanaka 2016); and the recently made over "negrito" pastry, now simply "nito," made popular by the Grupo Bimbo company. These last examples were utilized in the early and mid-twentieth century to do the work of minstrelsy, a way of allowing the public to create a positive identity in opposition to Blackness (Harris 1993, 1743; Wynter 1979). Sue recognizes that this tradition was very much alive even until 2010 when a group of broadcasters appeared on Mexican television in "Blackface" in order to represent a "South African Theme" during the coverage of the 2010 World Cup matches (2013, 191).

Castañeda examines the use of similar caricatures to represent Blackness in the National Folkloric Ballet in Veracruz and argues that such images continue to reflect the political and social realities as well as the local and national discourses on Blackness in Mexico (Shay 2002, 83, 225, cited in Castañeda 2012, 103). I witnessed a similar media representation of Blackness in the broadcast of the 2007 Under 20 World Cup while in Oaxaca, Mexico. During a national broadcast, as the Mexican sub-20 team geared up to play the Democratic Republic of the Congo on July 7, replays of the Mexican team scoring goals were intercut with scenes from the 1995 movie *Congo*. In the montage, every time the Mexican team was shown scoring a goal, the imagery would cut to scenes from *Congo* in which crumbling ruins could be seen falling onto the heads of panicking gorillas. This powerful representation of the Mexican media's prediction of the winner of the game demonstrates the underlying value of an enduring Black subject position in Mexico.

Williams argues that "not all individuals have equal power to fix the coordinates of self-other identity formation. Nor are individuals equally empowered to opt out of the labeling process, to become the invisible against which others' visibility is measured" (1989, 420). In the context of ethnic identity, Williams sees this as a relation between the subject and the object.

For Africans in colonial Mexico, being Black meant being simultaneously Spanish and non-Spanish: Spanish in the sense that Black was related to a broader Spanish system through the position of servitude and slave labor, and non-Spanish in the sense that to be Black meant that an individual was socially everything that Spanish was not. In the context of the developing Mexican nation and ideal citizen, this subject/object relationship between Spanish and Black meant that Mestizo or Mexican popular forms of music, food, and dance would systematically omit their Africanness and "rather claim to be expressions of Spanish and Amerindian origins" (Hernández Cuevas 2004, 32). In the language of Fanon (2008) and Althusser (1984), this is better represented as a dialectic of belonging, and later citizenship, as Blackness was subjected to Whiteness; the possessed object of the Spanish, and later Mexican, subject (Williams 1989). A foundational dialectic was constructed in which the racial position of Black helped define the racial position and social location of Spanish. The intrinsic value of race (in this case Black) became relational when placed within a broader social system. The legacy of this system can be seen in the manifestation of the racial economy that currently operates throughout Latin America.

An Ethnographic Example

My ethnographic research within the Los Angeles, California, area demonstrates the impact of this racial economy on Black Mexicans and their limited ability to capture the value associated with Blackness. Due to the increasing number of Indigenous Oaxacan migrants within the region, several ethnic grocery stores and markets have been established within the area. At the 2009 Guelaguetza Popular, sponsored by the Los Angeles–based organization Organización Regional de Oaxaca, several different ethnic commodities were available for consumption. In fact, a rather large commercial flier entitled "Guía Commercial-Los Angeles-Oaxaca" was produced for the event in order to highlight the numerous Indigenous and Mestizo merchants in the area who cater to the growing Oaxacan population. This guide included everything from authentic Oaxacan cheeses (queso Oaxaca and Quesillo) to money-wiring services. Because Indigenous groups are allowed to maintain partial ownership of what is perceived to be a common Mexican cultural property, the Indigenous communities within the region can also limitedly capture some of the positive value associated with Indigeneity and can convert this value into real social, cultural, and economic capital within an economy that thrives on the consumption of difference.

For Indigenous Oaxacans, the shared meaning of Indigeneity within the broader ethnoracial social relations of both Mexico and the United States has allowed for the development of what Kearney has labeled "OaxaCalifornia" (2000, 177; Stephen 2007; Ramirez Rios 2019), a transnational social, cultural, and political space. This space allows for the conceptualization of continuity between Indigenous struggles between Oaxaca, Baja California, and the United States (Kearney 2000) and sets the potential for Indigeneity to be put to work in similar ways between the two countries. In this way, shared conceptualizations of both Indigeneity and Mexicanness create the possibility for a cultural space that supports the development of Oaxacan Indigenous communities and allows them to capture the value of Indigeneity. This is not the case for Black Mexicans whose Blackness is illegible within current conceptions of Mexicanness, Indigeneity (Vasquez 2010), and American Blackness (Jones 2013, 1575) on the US-Mexico border. Moreover, the fact that the racial categories of Black and Latino are seen as mutually exclusive (Jones 2018, 570; Sue 2013) (on both sides of the border) allows Blackness to be excluded from the cultural spaces of both Mexicanness in its multiple forms and Oaxacan Indigeneity.

The Guelaguetza, named for a Zapotec term referencing reciprocity and hospitality, is an event that is organized to highlight the many cultural and geographical regions within the state of Oaxaca. These cultural regions include La Región de Valles Centrales (Central Valleys), La Región de La Sierra Norte (Northern Highlands), La Región de La Mixteca (Mixtec Region), and La Región de La Costa (Northwestern Coastal Region), to name a few. The Guelaguetza uses music, dance, and other cultural attributes to reinforce the notion of distinct cultural groups and to consolidate cultural identities around these groups and their associated geographic regions (Hoffman and Rinaudo 2014). While the Guelaguetza is a site of cultural transmission and transformation among the community, this event fits into a lager set of social relations dictated by a contemporary form of multicultural politics where the broadcasting of an Indigenous identity is seen to create a certain type of social, cultural, and economic capital. The Guelaguetza does indeed bring the broader Los Angeles "Oaxacan community" together. But in highlighting a contemporary Indigenous identity, the Guelaguetza serves as a sign to the larger region and state that an active Indigenous population exists within this community. This Indigenous identity fits within a larger multicultural politic that values Indigeneity in several different ways, particularly within Mexico but also in the United States, and reinforces the development of Mexican Indigenous identities over a general Mestizo or White identity (Stephen 2007). The Guelaguetza, in both Los Angeles and Oaxaca, also creates a mechanism for harnessing Indigenous value and transforming it into capital for Indigenous communities.

According to Smith, "the word value . . . has two different meanings, and sometimes expresses the utility of some particular object, and sometimes the power of purchasing other goods which the possession of that object conveys" (2000, 41). Therefore, value can mean both "use-value" and "exchange-value." To understand the meaning of "value," we must understand its place in a larger system (Graeber 2001, 14). And, to understand how race becomes valuable within a larger system of social relations, we must also think about the process of commensuration, the comparison of different entities according to a common metric (Espeland and Stevens 1998, 313). According to Espeland and Stevens, "commensuration is no mere technical process but a fundamental feature of social life. Commensuration as a practical task requires enormous organization and discipline, in a Foucauldian sense, that has become largely invisible to us. Commensuration is often so taken for granted that we forget the work it requires and the assumptions that surround its use . . . It is symbolic, inherently interpretive, deeply political" (1998, 315).

It is beyond argument that the work, discipline, and assumptions at play within the contemporary commensuration of Blackness have their roots within the modern era of slavery and the contact period with the "New World" in the sixteenth century, where racial ideologies and practices were experimented with and later solidified. Kazanjian (2003) offers an example through his analysis of the narrative of Venture Smith, *A Narrative of the Life and Adventures of Venture, a Native of Africa*. In the narrative, Smith explains that he got his name after being purchased by a ship's steward for "four gallons of rum, and a piece of calico" (60–61) and was called Venture on account of being purchased with the steward's own private "venture." Kazanjian argues that this monetary and linguistic transaction "aims to transform Smith into a generic sign of commercial speculation and capitalist exchange, to abstract his very being into the formal logic of value" (60–61). This logic of value creates an economy in which Black value is literally commensurable and exchangeable ("four gallons of rum, and a piece of calico") (see also Derby 2003, 34). Limiting Black people from tapping into this value also ensures that Blackness remains at the level of means of production, as Black people are never realized as "an equal in exchange" (Kazanjian 2003, 63) and can never capture the value created by a broader

Black subject position. The work and discipline at play within the process of commensuration is constantly being done. For Indigenous people, the fact that an Indigenous subject position has been positively worked into the conception of the ideal within Mexicanness allows Indigenous ethnic groups to capture the value of Indigeneity and extract economic value by "transforming social networks and culture into value" (Elyachar 2005, 9). The Guelaguetza festival in both Los Angeles and Oaxacan communities plays an important role in this process. However, the social relations around Black value limit the ways in which Blackness can be similarly transformed and put to different work.

The coastal region of Oaxaca has long been a racially and ethnically diverse region. However, because the region is home to a large population of Black Mexicans, nearly five hundred thousand, according to the 2015 Mexican inter-census, the region is often referred to as a "Black" region within Mexico and is quickly becoming famous within many circles such as academics interested in Mexico's racial history, and ecotourists. Arguably, the Black Lives Matter movement in the United States has also generated interest in Black Mexican communities among Mexican Americans, who are now paying more attention to developments in the region. The Guelaguetza Popular highlights the Costa Chica region simply as La Costa. This is true in both the Guelaguetza festival in the city of Oaxaca, as well as the Guelaguetza festivals organized in Los Angeles. The performance of the Guelaguetza demonstrates the limits for transforming Black value within a larger racial and ethnic hierarchy.

Within the Guelaguetza, the dances of La Costa are highlighted as being culturally representative of the region. One dance that is performed in the Guelaguetza festival is the Danza de Los Diablos. Many Black communities in the coastal region practice this dance, and many residents describe it as being representative of an African (even if only by way of the Black body) heritage. While the dance is often presented within the festival as representative of the coast and of Blackness within the region, the physical representation of Blackness is often absent within the festival. Talking with Martin, a former Los Angeles resident who has since returned to his Costa Chica community of Morelos, I found out that a folkloric performance group of Mestizos from the town of Pinotepa Nacional, rather than Black performers, regularly performs the dance in the official state Guelaguetza celebration in Oaxaca City. While Blackness is symbolically represented as an ethnic element within the national landscape, its physical representation was still undervalued as represented by a conspicuous absence in the performances. In this way, the Guelaguetza plays a double role, recognizing the history of Oaxaca and the historical presence of African descendants while simultaneously rendering the contemporary presence of Black Mexicans invisible within the state. Paschel's (2016) work demonstrates a similar example of how Carnival in Brazil uses many Black images to represent the national form. However, participation of Black people in the Carnival is limited, therefore limiting the ways that Black Brazilians can represent the nation through the national form of Carnival. Blackness in Oaxaca, then, is put to work through the Guelaguetza festival for the benefit and reproduction of Indigeneity and the non-Black Mestizo nation, while simultaneously limiting Black Mexican's access to the value they add to the process.

Hoffman argues that there is "objectively no advantage—political, ideological, or material—in 'being' (becoming, claiming to be) black" in Mexico (2014, 87). While this might be true in the context of individual value for Black Mexicans, we should not allow this reality about the state of identity politics in Mexico to lead to the conclusion that there is no value in Blackness. The actual value of Blackness in Mexico is to be found in the power of production and can easily be harnessed by non-Blacks. Rinaudo (2014), speaking with a young non-Black Mestizo man who played drums in the public bus stations of Veracruz in order to make a few bucks, offers a salient example of how Blackness is put to work by non-Blacks. Rinaudo explains the conversation in the following way:

> Respondent: I really enjoy coming here to El Portal in the late evening when there is a special atmosphere, and everyone joins a little in the fun of what's Black in you (laughs).
> Rinaudo: Do you define yourself as Black?
> Respondent: No, not at all, but we all have some Black ancestors, don't we? So, when you hear this music and you're plunged in this ambience, you can't help but start moving in a certain way . . .
> Rinaudo: Just how? Could you be more explicit?
> Respondent: Not really. I don't see myself . . . But if you take my buddies, like Ricardo: he feels it more like a Jamaican, you see, reggae man, easy . . . While Fallo'll really be influenced by the rap movement, hip hop and all that. Sara, my girlfriend, lets loose with African dance. You see, that's really another style . . . (155).

This demonstrates how Blackness gets appropriated and becomes an aesthetic that non-Blacks can tap into and employ as a strategy for earning a few dollars on the streets. However, this strategy does not change the value of Blackness as it applies to Black Mexicans and the way that being Black is experienced by everyday Black Mexicans in Veracruz or in Mexico as a whole, as the literature on color prejudice and stereotypes shows. Black value here is literally productive both economically and ideologically and allows for the production of non-Black countercultural identities, referred to by Rinaudo as *callejera* (street) culture (157). This is an example of how the value of Blackness can be utilized by others yet restricted from benefiting Black people.

This same strategy is put to work through the Guelaguetza festival in Oaxaca and Los Angeles. At the Guelaguetza Popular in Los Angeles, the coastal region is also represented, complete with the familiar appropriation of Blackness. Martin is part of a dance group that practices the Danza de Los Diablos in Los Angeles. While Martin's own physical appearance potentially allows for his racial/ethnic identity to be more fluid than some, he told me that he does identify as "Negro," and that many of his family members are perceived as Black or "Negro" in both the United States and Mexico. While Martin's group was not invited to perform the Danza de Los Diablos at the Los Angeles Guelaguetza, Blackness was symbolically present, if physically absent (Telles and PERLA 2014). Between dance performances, the folkloric groups perform skits that are supposed to be representative of the common cultural gendered exchanges that take place within the different regions. In one skit, a man tried to convince a potential lover that he was sexually potent and would be a good romantic partner. The young woman responded by saying that the only thing his penis was good for was urinating. This "burn" was well received by the attending Oaxacan immigrants and the larger crowd in general. Within the skit, the young man referred to the young woman as "mi prieta" (my dark one), and she referred to him as "mi Negro" (my Black one). Some might argue that these terms have been adopted into a common Mexican parlance and are therefore regularly used by most Mexicans, even as terms of endearment, in several different regions, as well as in popular media. But in the regional context of La Costa within the Guelaguetza celebration, these terms take on a conspicuous racial connotation. In this way, Blackness is represented and becomes visible at the Guelaguetza. However, the presence of Blackness is put to work to add value and to serve the purposes of the Indigenous community. All the performers in this particular festival were of "Indigenous" descent, and the performances of these Indigenous bodies reinforced the contemporary notion of Oaxaca as "the Indigenous state" within Mexico and allowed the Oaxacan community in Los Angeles to exploit this perception.[13]

Martin keeps track of these cultural events. Martin is the secretary of an organization created in the early 2000s by Oaxacans from the Costa Chica region of Mexico, by the name of Organización Afro-Mexicana. Individuals from the Costa Chica created the organization in order to provide support for those who remain in the Costa Chica. The organization, I was told, has 501(c)3 nonprofit status and was imagined, for the time being, as strictly a US organization. German Acevedo, the then president of the organization, told me that they were attempting to supply their home communities with medical attention and resources that the government does not provide. The organization itself provides insight into the way in which groups negotiate a contemporary racial economy. In a conversation with German, I asked him: Why organize as a "Black" organization? German responded that their original intent was not to organize around the idea of race but instead to organize around a regional identity. After conversations with Padre Glynn Jemmott Nelson, a priest, political organizer, and member of the Oaxaca-based group Mexico Negro living in Oaxaca for the last twenty years, the founders decided to name the organization Organización Afro-Mexicana.[14] While not all of the members would identify as Afro-Mexican or "Negro," the naming of the organization points to an attempt to exploit a particular multicultural moment in which race/ethnicity is given a particular value and invokes a particular type of capital. This strategy is a direct response to the success of Indigenous organizing around ethnicity in creating visibility for Indigenous issues within Mexico during the past decades. The Organización Afro-Mexicana group and others like it in Mexico demonstrate how the contemporary value of Blackness within Mexico is being challenged within the boundaries of the United States and is now in the process of being reimagined.

While I did not get an opportunity to sufficiently explore how racial experiences within the United States and interaction with US Blacks are changing Afro-Mexicans' conceptions of race, the question is important to thinking through alternative national and regional economies of race. In crossing the physical border between Mexico and the United States, migrants also cross several ideological borders and boundaries (Lugo 2000, 2008; Stephen 2007). Local and regional histories and national identities make for differing values of race and ethnicity within different locations, defining different parameters and possibilities of racial exchange. The organizing strategies adopted by both Indigenous and Black Mexicans in Los Angeles are developed within Mexico due to particular forms of multicultural politics within the nation, specifically the state of Oaxaca. The possibilities open to these strategies may vary in the United States due to differing racial histories and discourses. The shared meaning and value of Indigeneity between Mexican communities in Mexico and Mexican American communities in the United States may potentially work in favor of Indigenous Oaxaqueños[15] and help develop transnational ties that rely on similarities between US and Mexican racial economies (Ramirez Rios and Jerry 2020). However, for Black Mexicans, organizing around their Mexican Blackness requires that they simultaneously make distinctions between US Mexican and Black Americans. This strategy may only alienate Black Mexicans from both groups.

Conclusion

Within this chapter I have attempted to provide a framework for approaching citizenship beyond democratic practices for inclusion and a synonym for belonging. I argue that citizenship is a privileged form of belonging reinforced by specific and deliberate forms of exclusion. However, those who are excluded should not be perceived as outside the realm of citizenship, or "non-citizens." Rather, those on the margins are a necessary feature for the existence of the core (Das and Poole 2004), and exclusion is always a methodology for a particular form of inclusion. Therefore, I argue that citizenship is fundamentally a relation between citizens in which particular subjects are used as the means for reproducing the nation for the benefit of those who are ultimately positioned, at least potentially, to embody the nation and capture the value that the nation represents.

The notion of citizenship is best perceived as the physical manifestation or realization of our theorizing on the relations surrounding production (Kazanjian 2003; Jerry 2021) in a modern capitalist mode of production. Looking at citizenship as the social relations of production and the Black body as continuing to represent the means of production within that relation allows us to recognize the ways that Black Mexicans—and African descendants in general—are afforded limited access to the means of representing their own Blackness and the value produced by an enduring Black subject position. Ultimately, drawing from Hall's observations on class, I argue that Blackness is a modality through which citizenship is experienced. Thinking of the Black body as the means of production, both materially within an economy of development and symbolically in terms of the ideological building blocks of the multicultural nation-state, is a means of identifying the ways in which the current Mexican strategy for recognition is truly limited with regard to citizenship and the possibility of equal participation. Through the Mexican approach to recognition, the desire to do right by a historically marginalized community in Mexico is ultimately turned upside down as the Black body is rearticulated within a historic set of relations within a preexisting racial economy.

5

A Black Subject Position and Narrative
Representations of Blackness
in the Costa Chica

Estás trabajando como Negro para vivir como Blanco.

(You are working like a "Negro" to live like a White.)

This ethnographic chapter focuses on the way that some African descendants in Mexico experience a Black subject position and tell the story of what it means to be them. It is recognizably impossible to paint a picture of every individual experience and expression of Blackness by local Costa Chica residents. But a snapshot of these experiences and expressions helps demonstrate the existence of a Black subject position and how this subject position frames subjectivities that may be common to many Black Mexicans. These perceived commonalities are explicitly drawn upon by both Black and non-Black Mexicans as part of the conscious racial project that informs the political process of recognition.

This chapter touches upon a number of different narratives in order to create a composite snapshot. However, the chapter focuses mainly on three distinct examples, ranging from how one woman is attempting to create, or remember, a distinct cultural identity through the promotion of a cultural narrative surrounding Blackness in the Costa Chica (as well as the larger nation and Latin American region); the ways that Black activists are attempting to incorporate their communities into the global ecotourism industry (based on their understanding of a unique culture, history, and life ways, to self-professed definitions, and representations); and, last, conceptions of Blackness through artwork that has gained international attention. These narratives demonstrate the stakes of the cultural and political project currently taking place within the Costa Chica. They both contradict and reinforce negative stereotypes, and they shed light on activists' feelings and beliefs about the broader racial and political project of Blackness in the Costa Chica, as well as the social locations available to Black subjects in Mexico.

I begin by briefly presenting a few shorter narratives, distinct in their form and function, to provide context and nuance for the three central narratives. First, these brief narratives were not relayed to me as part of a larger political narrative or as representative of a larger group identity. In fact, they were not related to me as narratives per se, but rather emerged as I inquired about personal knowledge and experiences in the Costa Chica and the communities of the region. These personal narratives express experiences and communicate qualities that bind individuals together through the region, serving as a foundation or platform from, and through, which larger political narratives are created and contextualized. These narratives should be read as representative of experiences and identities that are always in process. And as such, they represent methodologies for the telling of a particular present as a way of imagining multiple futures.

The first narratives are mainly personal stories that shed light on the ways in which people "inject" themselves into space and place as they retell stories of past experiences. These narratives help us understand how people relate their own experiences to a racialized and cultural Blackness. In contrast, the three central narratives reflect personal and group projects that were conceived of as intentional Black Mexican political projects. These political projects explicitly rely on Blackness as a basis for their conceptualization and presentation. Some of these narratives can be seen simply as reflections on past experiences, while the main narratives show the actual process behind the construction of a narrative of self and a people as the activists engage with the art of crafting narratives of self and community.

Three Personal Narratives of Self

Getsemani

Getsemani and the following narrative from Liliana offer two different perspectives, one positive and the other less so, on the issues of ideological and physical Blackness. I met twenty-year-old Getsemani in Chacahua. She is originally from another part of the Costa Chica but was in Chacahua working with relatives who owned and operated a small restaurant and several humble cabanas (simple cabins). This work allowed Getsemani the ability to leave her smaller town in the Lagunas de Chacahua National Park.

However, her work at the small business did not offer her the opportunity to earn a significant amount of money, especially when compared to opportunities further beyond the region in destinations such as Acapulco, Mexico City, or the United States. Although Getsemani was only moderately interested in my research on the current Black project for constitutional recognition, our initial conversation opened another, more profound conversation regarding her personal feelings about her own Blackness.

Getsemani explained to me that she did not "like" her color. When I asked her why, she found it difficult to explain and could not really offer a concrete answer. She suggested that it was easier to be "Blanco que Negro"[1] (White rather than Black: speaking of skin color), and then reiterated that she did not like her color and stayed out of the sun so that she would not get darker. It is ironic that Getsemani avoids the sun in Chacahua, as tourists generally come to Chacahua for the sun, surf, and the activities promoted through the ecotourism industry. Chacahua is quickly becoming known within surfing circles for a gentler surf than the beaches in the nearby professional surf beach of Puerto Escondido, and therefore surfers are becoming more regular tourists as they take advantage of the low-cost, low-frills amenities.[2] I could not get Getsemani to talk much about the subject of skin color, as she seemed to be embarrassed about talking about her own dark brown skin. Plenty of African descendants in Chacahua are quick to identify as Black (Negro), regularly identifying with the term "Negro" in my presence. However, lacking a political identity to support this racial identification, there were many, such as Getsemani, who continued to self-discriminate. Lucila Mariche Magadán (discussed below) is one of several activists in Chacahua attempting to change this. But for now, even as a cultural identity is beginning to emerge, the true political manifestation of a Black identity has yet to be realized.

While Getsemani did tell me that she did not like her skin color and "no me gusta meterme en el sol, porque no quiero quemarme más" (I don't like to go out into the sun because I don't want to darken myself more), she also told me that she defended her people (*gente*) from discrimination. She related to me an experience she had in middle school in Puebla, where she lived for several years. As Jones demonstrates, because of the urban invisibility of Blackness in Mexico, Black Mexicans' first experiences of discrimination and marginalization often come when they travel to urban spaces for school, work, or business (2013, 1571; Lara 2014, 125). When her class discussed African descendants in Mexico, in a context that she did not elaborate on, many students had negative things to say about Negros.

Getsemani, according to her story, defended Negros from her classmates' accusations by telling them that those negative things were not true and that modern-day "negros also had White blood [*sangre Blanco*] while Whites shared Black blood [*sangre Negro*]." Clearly, Getsemani was referring to the common unions of darker- and lighter-skinned individuals within the region and the broader recognition of Mexico as a nation of Mestizos.[3] While Getsemani would not give me any specific examples of the things her classmates said, her response demonstrates the way in which her defense of Blackness does not rely on a positive construction or promotion of cultural or racial elements. Rather, her defensive strategy relies on the idea, somewhat underdeveloped, of mestizaje. Part of the problem for Getsemani is that she does not have a foundation—historical, cultural, or political—to draw upon and with which she could then defend her gente. Instead, she can only combat racism with the old notion, the national notion, that "we are the same." The idea of "Blackness" on the coast is intuitively, and often explicitly, used as a baseline by which positive social value is created and measured.

Getsemani's narrative demonstrates how the use of racial terms for "White" reference physical or class characteristics such as beauty or wealth (Sue 2013; Lugo 2008). Sue (2013) discusses the use of these terms as a type of slippage, as people in everyday conversation unconsciously insert these terms into everyday conversation without intentionally attempting to shift meaning. This demonstrates a popular intuitive and unconscious connection with the racial term *Blanco* and social class and positive aesthetics. This also demonstrates how Blackness operates as a dark matter in order to give other terms multiple meanings, and suggests that in Mexico, class terms are always racial terms. This allows people to effortlessly, and often unconsciously, switch between terms while maintaining the same racial meaning (Sue 2013). This process relies on the anchoring of a Black subject position within the broader set of social relations as a mechanism for creating value around other subject positions and subjects.

Sue (2013) provides a good example in her discussion about how employers convey ideas about an ideal employee and employability in the city of Veracruz. She uses the concept of being "presentable" to explain how race gets coded within job advertisements. She explains that "job seekers need to be able to determine whether they are acceptable candidates for an advertised position. If good presentation is listed as a desired or required characteristic, potential employees need to be able to decipher what the employer means by this seemingly vague term" (Sue 2013, 44). In this example, "good presentation" acts as an antonym for the perceived negative aesthetics associated with racial Blackness. In contrast, the term "bad presentation" is used as a direct synonym for dark skin (2013, 45). While some will automatically know that they need not apply based on the color of their skin, others will be able to trade their phenotype for better employment. Sue's work in Veracruz and Getsemani's experience in Puebla demonstrate how a Black subject position is used to reproduce a baseline for exclusion in Mexican social and economic relations. In this way, non-Black inclusion is dependent on reproducing strategies for Black exclusion. This, I would argue, is at the heart of the relationship we refer to as modern citizenship.

The colonial roots of the Mexican nation, apart from a general recognition of Indigeneity as being pre-national, are lacking in popular narratives of the nation, which ultimately start with the independence era and the development of the new national subject, the Mestizo. Sergio, an activist from Cuajinicuilapa mentioned earlier, explained that this might be because "the institutional, governmental party, I think it has . . . an intentional discourse, a very intentional discourse. Firstly, they wanted to hide from us, reasons . . . , not to recognize the economic, cultural, and social contributions of slavery, of Negros, of slaves, right? And to say, well, in Mexico there was no slavery. I mean, to convince them." Sergio also believed that this strategy was also visible in government activities promoting visibility. For this reason, Getsemani's classmates were not able to access an acceptable historical framework through which to interpret Blackness, much less Getsemani's modern appearance in a majority-White classroom in Puebla.

Getsemani told me that it was hard for her to be in Puebla because "most of the people in Puebla are White [Blanca]." While Getsemani relied on the historic notion of mestizaje to defend "her people," her narrative clearly shows that she also relies on the notion of racial difference to tell her story and to construct her own self-image. Due to the positive value that she accords to Blanco, Getsemani finds it hard to take very much pride in her "color." Therefore, she continues to place negative value on her own Black skin, as the colonial connection between decency and beauty (Lugo 2008, 142) continues to position Getsemani's Black body as the magic mirror (Hernández Cuevas 2004) through which the value associated with the positive aesthetics of non-Black Mestizos are reproduced. Getsemani has internalized the popular conceptions about color and Black value and therefore her attempts to defend her gente must rely on the prevailing racial economy and social framework of mestizaje—the mixing of sangre Blanco y Negro and racial redemption through Whitening—rather than more substantial elements of Blackness shared by African descendants within the region. There is an interesting contradiction at play here. While the popular narrative of race privileges Whiteness, local narratives seem to value Blackness within the context of local communities and histories (Jones 2013). However, when Blackness is contextualized within the frame of the nation, the local privileging of Blackness loses out to Whiteness in the context of the broader racial economy of mestizaje. The racial triangle here seems to spin like a compass searching for magnetic north until a particular context allows for the extraction of racial value within any social or political situation.

Liliana

Shortly after speaking with Getsemani, I had a casual conversation with Liliana, a resident of Chacahua, while we shared a *camioneta* (small, covered truck transport) ride from Chacahua to the launch landing heading toward the small Costa Chica town of Zapotalito outside of the commercial center of Río Grande. Liliana told me of a "ciclo de video" (film festival) by the name of Identidad Negra, which was being promoted that spring (2011) within the immediate communities surrounding the Lagunas de Chacahua. The ciclo de video, according to the official advertisement, tackled the history of slavery (*historia de esclavismo*), Black identity (*identidad Negra*), racism and discrimination (*racismo y discriminación*), and Black movements (*movimientos Negros*). I found out later that this ciclo de video was sponsored by the ecological organization Ecosta Yutu Cuii and facilitated by local activist Lucila Mariche Magadán. The festival was scheduled over a period of four weeks and included the local towns of Chacahua, Charco Redondo, El Azufre, La Pastoría, Lagartero, and Cerro Hermoso, all within the Lagunas de Chacahua National Park.

After telling me of the ciclo de video, Liliana explained to me that many people do not know any history about where Black Mexicans are from or how they got to the coast. This is partly because unlike Indigenous communities—who have been folklorized within primary education as a vestige of Mexico's glorious past and whose cultural elements are shown to be important to the Mestizo identity as a national standard (Telles and PERLA 2014, 46)—the history of slavery and the historic contributions of Black people in Mexico are simply not taught in Mexican schools (Lewis 2012, 4). Liliana informed me that she herself had been to the United States and was surprised to see Black people there, as she had thought that there were only Black people in Chacahua and the surrounding area. Liliana was about forty years old or so, and her age and lack of knowledge about the "African diaspora" shed some light on the relative age of the new cultural and political movement represented by local projects such as the Identidad Negra film festival and on how this movement had yet to really take effect within smaller communities.

In fact, the larger official Mexican project of Afro-Mexican recognition seemed to have done little to combat racism and develop a strong social foundation, as witnessed by Getsemani's narrative of her own lack of self-esteem. The fact that some of the institutional projects of recognition, such as the Tercera Raíz Project, a campaign to recognize the colonial contributions of African descendants, come from places and institutions such as UNAM in Mexico City and the Instituto Veracruzano de la Cultura also testifies to these projects' lack of impact.[4] Discussions like these with Liliana and Getsemani make clear that recognition does not necessarily facilitate equality or even a general attitude of anti-racism, as the multicultural model supports the values inherent to mestizaje (Hale 2002; Telles and PERLA 2014; Telles and Garcia 2013; Wade 2001) and allows for the use of Black communities to act as the means for producing the Mestizo, rather than as true subjects on par with Mestizos. Historically, this can be seen with Indigenous communities, as Indigenous recognition was the historical mechanism by which to produce the Mestizo as the subject of the new Mexican nation. However, the explicit use of Indigeneity within the narrative of the nation and the ideal subject creates the actual potential for a change in the value associated with Indigeneity. The project of Black recognition seems to make it easier for Mestizos to reconcile the existence of Blackness in the nation, rather than making it easier to be Black in Mexico.

Liliana had no problem referring to Blacks as "Negras" or "Negros." She herself was quite dark in complexion and self-identified as Negra. The younger Getsemani, on the other hand, told me that for the most part "Negro" is a negative term. My experience with this term through countless conversations is that the value associated with it depends upon context and upon who is using the term and when it is being used. Liliana, for example, used the term to mark inclusivity and refer to the larger group with which she also identified, while Getsemani had encountered and internalized the term in a negative way. Getsemani may not have been able to use or even hear the word without putting it into a Black/White dichotomy and then imparting a negative social value to the term within a racial hierarchy.

Informed by the arithmetic of the broader racial economy, *Negra/o* for Getsemani is always the negative counterpart of *Blanco*.

Bulmaro, an activist from the town of Cuajinicuilapa, also recognized this dialectic in which Blackness is used as a means for reproducing and stabilizing Whiteness. In discussing the broader conception of Blackness in Mexico, he explained,

> Negros are slaves. They are useful to dance, to kill and do other things . . . The chingones [cool ones], the intellectuals, "they are White." The revolution was led by Mr. So and So. Even if they struggle to recognize Emiliano Zapata . . . we have always been in the fucked-up part. So, our people should be recognized by our people. We are not some pendejos [jerks], as they want us to believe. They have made us think like that for all our damn life. And we need to find a way to transmit that revindication to our people. You need to feel you rock, you are not a birdbrain, you are a person of sciences, of arts . . . I mean, we do not know our own history. So, we live in the "latent life" [vida latente], and in that sense the state owes a great debt to us.

Bulmaro speaks of a social reality in which Blackness, historical and modern, is used to contextualize Whiteness (read as modernity) rather than as a legitimate position unto itself. By referencing some of the heroes of the Mexican Revolution as Black, Bulmaro is attempting to embody mestizaje (Wade 2005). While there may not be any historical proof of Zapata being identified or identifying as Black, the fact of mestizaje should make this assertion theoretically possible. However, because Bulmaro cannot claim "substantive" or "personal" authority (Flathman 1995, 112) through the physical embodiment of the nation as a Black person, his strategy of giving Zapata a history of Blackness may potentially incorporate Black individuals into the nation on a theoretical level. But the strategy is less successful in changing the fundamental truths of the nation and stops short of creating the possibility for others to see the nation within Bulmaro's Black face.

Paolo

A conversation I had with Paolo helps illustrate the point of context. Paolo, now deceased, was a resident of Chacahua, where he and his wife ran a small but successful cabana and restaurant business. Trying to get a sense of generational linkages to Chacahua, I asked Paolo if his great-grandfather was also from Chacahua. He explained that he did not know his great-grandfather but that he thought that he might have been from Africa. He said that he might have arrived in the Costa Chica as well with his grandfather. Paolo explained that a ship landed at Puerto Miniso, a small beach a few kilometers outside of Collantes, and from this port, "los Negros desembarcaron" (the Blacks landed) and began to mix with the Indigenous in the Costa Chica.[5]

Paolo told me that the Negros were well received by the Indigenous, and he elaborated this point by relating an anecdote from his youth. When he was eighteen, Paolo explained, he went to an Indigenous pueblo to trade and sell fish, where he was welcomed by the Indigenous community, "especially the women." He told me and the group that had become his captive audience that the women were enamored by his hair and skin color, and rubbed his hair, saying "ven acá, morenito" (come here, little dark one). I asked whether Negros were still well received in the Indigenous communities of the coast, and he responded, "Yes." In a later interview, Bulmaro corroborated Paolo's story. Bulmaro explained,

> Through time, history has told us that we have had relations [with Indigenous people] in every sense. Even sexual relations with indígenas. Then, we do not know what we are. Some identify us by our color, others because we dance as Afros, others because we play Afro music. But sometimes the features are very light and that is why cultures are mixed. And at the level of the comunidad, we do things as the indígenas do and the indígenas do things as the Negros do.

Paolo's response about being well received in Indigenous communities contradicted a past conversation in which he told me that there were often tensions between Negros and Indigenous on the coast. However, our previous conversation was within the context of a different type of commerce. Many locals in Chacahua consume marijuana, but the actual marijuana trade can bring trouble, and there is some shared animosity toward those who make it their business to sell drugs. The trouble may also come from the competition between communities to capitalize on the tourist market and the demand for marijuana. In this way, local growers may be seen as competition as this system then gets racialized. Cocaine, in its processed street form, complicates this relationship even more, as the coast is becoming well known for narco trafficking and the business provides opportunities for many young people on the coast, both in the Black towns of the Costa Chica and the non-Black communities in the Isthmus region. For example, upon my arrival to Chacahua I looked forward to reconnecting with a friend I had made during several previous trips. While catching up with Paolo, he explained that our mutual friend had been murdered twenty days prior. When I asked why, Paolo responded by simply saying "por sus cosas" (for his stuff), which undoubtedly meant his involvement in the illicit marijuana and cocaine trade.

Paolo's narrative of his own Blackness walked the line between positive and negative value. While he may not have internalized the negative value in the way that Getsemani had in creating her own self-image, Paolo was aware of the ways in which Blackness could be simultaneously anchored to a number of positions within the continuum of social value. He found a way to involve Africa in his narrative. Africa as a trope for a distant homeland (Gohar 2008 Harris 2009; Howe 1998; Mirmotahari 2012; Shavit 2001; Walters 1993) can anchor those who feel as if they have no officially recognized claim to the local lands that they inhabit, in effect allowing diaspora to operate as a kind of marronage (Bucknor 2012; Cummings 2010). But Paolo's invocation of Africa seems to serve another purpose, especially as he is relatively successful in the small town. His invocation seems to be a way to make a family connection that eluded him through his lack of knowledge about his grandfathers. Paolo did not lay claim to a distant homeland but rather laid claim to a genealogy that allowed him to connect to past unknown generations. This sheds light on the influence that local activists, as well as the impact that narratives of "roots," have on the general population and social/cultural memory.

The idea of "roots" is also something that can potentially have contradictory effects. For example, the official rhetoric of recognition offered by the federal government includes "Afro-Mexicanos" as "the third root" of the nation (la tercera raíz). While this rhetoric reinforces mestizaje, it also superficially recognizes African descendants within the actual production of the Mexican nation. At the same time, some activists and most official organelles promote Africa as the place from which Negros in the Costa Chica originated. At first glance, this seems to be a contradiction, but the narrative of Africa as a point of origin does not necessarily have to counteract the national rhetoric of the third root. Getsemani unknowingly clarified this for me. I asked her about her thoughts on the idea of La Tercera Raíz. Among other points, Getsemani explained to me that raíz is often used as a synonym for "race," and at times raíz is better understood as "roots." When some people say somos raíz, they mean quite literally that "they were sown here" (the Costa Chica) and are continuing the process of growth and development on the coast that was started by their Black ancestors. Through this strategy, African descendants in the Costa Chica can lay claim to difference without relinquishing claims of autochthony.

Africa has even sparked the imagination of the younger generations, as illustrated by the following example. I asked Paolo where I could try the local preparation of iguana. He explained to me that if I went to see some of his in-laws in the small town of Charco Redondo, they would sell me a live iguana, which I should bring back so that Paolo's wife could prepare it in a traditional red mole sauce. After securing my prize in the town of Charco Redondo, I decided to walk to the edge of town and wait for the *colectivo* (taxi with a fixed price and route) that would take me back to Chacahua. On my way through the town, I met Dalia, a sixteen-year-old girl who worked at her father's small *miscelánea* (convenience store) located in their home. As I sat unsuccessfully trying to cool off with a cold drink, I struck up a conversation with Dalia about the town and those passing by. Dalia asked me of my profession and where I originated. She was shocked to hear that I was from California. Interested in her perception of me, I asked her where she thought I was from. To my surprise she responded, "Africa." I told her that I had never been to Africa, and that I had lived in California for most of my life. She asked if I spoke English, and I responded with a few sentences in the English language. Still unconvinced, like my experience in the Isthmus as outlined in chapter 1, she told me that I must have been from Africa because there were no Blacks in the United States. Although it penetrates the imagination of many in the Costa Chica, Africa is often used to reference local racial origins but does not seem to be commonly understood as a diasporic center. As I sat drinking an orange soda and attempting to avoid some of the hottest weather of the year, Africa, at least in the mind of Dalia, arrived in Charco Redondo. In this case Africa and my presence did not signify the mythical homeland of the Black diaspora but the very real homeland of present-day Africans (whoever they may be), and a Blackness that may be unique to Africa, similar, yet not the same, to a Blackness found in Charco Redondo. More and more folks in the Costa Chica are becoming familiar with Africa, not as a historical place but in a more contemporary context, as Black Africans continue to visit the Costa Chica, often as participants in the Encuentro de los Pueblos Negros (meetings of the Black towns) and other political gatherings sponsored by the many grassroots organizations in the region, one of which was being held in the small town of Charco during my trip in 2011. It was in Charco Redondo that I would eventually meet local activist Lucila Mariche Magadán.

Three Narratives of Cultural and Political Activism

Lucila

Lucila Mariche Magadán is a local activist and advocate for Black recognition and rights. She was born and raised in the town of Charco Redondo. She works part-time for, and in collaboration with, Heladio Reyes and the ecological organization Ecosta Yutu Cuii.[6] This distinction between "working for" and "in collaboration with" is important to Lucila, as she works on several projects directly supported by Ecosta but brings an energy and politics to the organization that is all her own. Through Ecosta Yutu Cuii, Lucila has been able to attend several symposia, both locally and internationally, focusing on rights and issues related to African descendants in Latin America and the diaspora worldwide. If the resources of Ecosta Yutu Cuii were not available to Lucila, she would continue to work in the Costa Chica, informing other residents of forgotten local histories and the importance of self-esteem and self-identification (auto-identificación),[7] something for which she is often negatively judged by non-Black residents.

Lucila's own personal project combines the importance of cultural recognition with a strong focus on local and institutional recognition of processes of racialization, anti-Black racism, and discriminatory practices. Because of Lucila's own experience of Blackness, her political work is both professional and personal. This work has a fire and sense of immediacy that makes many Black and non-Black activists in the region uncomfortable. This tendency to make people nervous comes from her style of direct engagement and her desire to unhinge historically accepted discourses about Blackness and Black value. While Lucila herself may not explicitly articulate these discourses, she is nonetheless aware of them, as partly evidenced by her frustration and passion for her work. I spent quite a bit of time with Lucila during my research trip in 2011, as well as subsequent follow-up trips, traveling and talking with her while she conducted her work. Lucila is not traditionally or formally university educated, yet she has a sense of intuition and motivation for change that makes her a true "organic intellectual."

I asked Lucila about the need to promote a Black identity. I explained that I did not quite understand the need to promote such a racialized identity if African descendants on the coast already had access to locally understood identities such as costeño or moreno (often *morenito*, a common reference used by non-Blacks from other parts of Oaxaca, Guerrero, and

Mexico).[8] Simply put, I asked Lucila, "Why identify oneself as Negro [in its racially understood form]? Why use that identity?" Lucila explained to me that for her "it's an honor to be Black, to know that my race and ancestry is Black." Lucila also elaborated on some of the benefits, not simply material, that could come with racially identifying as Black. I asked Lucila whether the government would respond positively to organizing around cultural difference (cultural Blackness) in a manner similar to the political organizing of Indigenous groups. Lucila explained,

> Well, that's what we want . . . just like the Indigenous group has recognition, has help and support through many resources that the government offers . . . we also want that here. The Black race does not have that here. The Black race does not have that. We want for one to be able to say, "I am Black, and I need support in this project," and for the government to follow through with the petition. And that they do not say, "Well you are Black but in Mexico there are no Blacks." But the reality is something else.

Lucila's response is telling in a few ways. While she acknowledged that resources are an important part of the demands of activists, she is also aware that other benefits can come from identification as Black—or Indigenous, for that matter. All communities of the Costa Chica sorely need resources, as necessities such as basic health care, education, and building materials are scarce. But Lucila's response also highlights the symbolic benefits of identification and government recognition. Lucila is aware of the potential for recognition to counteract the effects of invisibility and the potential impacts on discrimination and racism that recognition could offer. Potentially, recognition would allow for Black Mexicans in the Costa Chica to make real connections between their lived realities and the historical processes that have created these realities, beyond the subscription to the naturalness of Black inferiority in the popular discourse that circulates through the nation.

Through her own self-education and interaction with local activists, Lucila is aware of the history of African slavery in Mexico.[9] I asked Lucila how Blacks got to the Costa Chica, and she explained that Blacks were brought as slaves, "with their hands and feet tied up. They came from the African continent. They came as a form of merchandise to perform intense labor work that the Indigenous could not perform. They were brought in as an exportation material . . . to this continent. In this way, we learn that our ancestors did not come of their own will but were forced to come."

This information is partially consistent with the propaganda presented by the Museo de Las Culturas Afro-Mestizas in Cuajinicuilapa. The museum, inaugurated in 1995, is part of a larger wave of nationwide community museums created with the support of institutions like the National Institute for Anthropology and History (INAH) (Hoffman 2014). The museum highlights the Middle Passage (*travesía*) and the areas of Africa from which most Africans were extracted, but it stops short of presenting any actual information about slavery as a mode of production, or the role that Africans and their descendants played in the construction of the Mexican nation. The museum approaches "African cultures" as cultural elements unto themselves, rather than one of the building blocks of a broader Mexican culture (Hernández Cuevas 2004)—and the modern experience of the "Americas"—and one of the components of La Tercera Raíz. The museum also presents several supposed African cultural survivals such as the roundhouse (rare if not extinct in the region), the practice of carrying babies on the hip, and the carrying of any number of items on the head as representative of the African cultural traits remaining in the region.

Lucila drew upon some of this rhetoric to tell the story of "her ancestors," but she used her personal knowledge of local history to fill in some of the gaps between the Middle Passage and the present. I asked Lucila about the ship that landed in Puerto Miniso. Lucila explained,

> It's believed that there are still remains of the ship . . . they came from there and a lot of the people from that area . . . I remember my grandmother would tell me that they would call them the abajeños, because they came from the lower area towards here. So, in my community, Charco Redondo, cotton used to be cultivated and they would export it through boats. From my community, they would export it through boats, and then embark it to the port of Acapulco. Back then there were no roads. So, they would travel through boats.

In Lucila's narrative, the African continent, as a symbol, plays a role but does not take center stage. Nor is the continent in some ahistorical limbo awaiting the return of its long-lost children. To avoid this trap, Lucila turned her narrative to local histories of production in the Costa Chica, specifically in the community of Charco Redondo. Lucila's discursive move allows for a focus on the present and a connection to the past to fill in the gap between the Middle Passage and the present multicultural political era, of which the Black movement in the Costa Chica and more broadly Mexico is a part. The ship plays a role as an artifact in the collective conscience of many Blacks in the Costa Chica, but the ship's ruins may be a metaphorical way to suggest the severed connection between continents while helping to maintain a sense of history or rootedness within the region.

Lucila's narrative of the production of cotton within the region helps reinforce this rootedness, and it helps make a historic claim to the region, one that may date back to a time before the invention of the national body. She explained to me that she did not know in which year the town was established, but that she knew that it was an old town with a history of cotton production (Chassen-López 1998, 104). In fact, she physically took me to the outskirts of the town to show me the remains of the plantation, or "cotton factory" as she explained it. She explained that this was the site where local Blacks would work the cotton, which was later taken to the ports along with chickens, pigs, and cows. She tried to take me into the plantation for a tour, but the whole area was sectioned off by barbed wire. When we knocked at the gate of the current owners to explain our interest, we were turned away.

Lucila's narrative counters a popular understanding, or denial, of Black existence in Mexico. Her narrative not only brings attention to the existence of a Black community (or communities), but it also makes explicit connections between the past and present. These temporal connections serve to anchor the community and draw attention to the historic processes of which they are a part. This anchoring provides locals some context for the official project of government recognition, and it brings some of the power back to the local people by allowing them to situate themselves within the process of recognition. Lucila is aware of this, as her personal project for the Costa Chica does not stop with state recognition. Rather, she wants to make people aware of the real products of processes such as historic invisibility, racism, and discrimination, processes that are perceived as somewhat paradoxical in practice due to the impact of the mestizaje ideology yet still define the lived experiences of Blacks within the Costa Chica communities.

I asked Lucila about her overall political goals and about one of her current social projects that she has undertaken with the support of Ecosta Yutu Cuii. Lucila explained that because "some of us have internalized discrimination" (auto-discriminación), she wants the individual to take "conscience, to accept oneself." She explained that low self-esteem relied on stereotypes perpetuated by Blacks within their own communities. She explained, "We say, 'not you because you are Black, lazy, and do not want to work . . . you don't work, you like to party.' This is a despicable lie . . . because as Blacks . . . if we propose to finish a job, we accomplish it. In my personal life, I like to be responsible . . . to show the opposite of what Black is thought to be." Another woman I spoke with countered, in an interesting way, this stereotype of African descendants as being lazy and not wanting to work. She explained that many men must wake up very early in the morning in order to work with the tides and the natural rhythm of fishing life. This means that in the middle of the day, many men lay around in hammocks and appear to be lazily wasting the day away. According to this woman, however, this is a misunderstanding, as the men have been working all night and into the early morning. A standard clock to understand the daily rhythm of fishing life does not apply in the Costa Chica and can lead to misunderstandings that produce and reinforce stereotypes of laziness and frivolity (Rosaldo 1974).

Lucila's work adds a grassroots element to the project of Black recognition that would be lost through simple state recognition of the cultural existence of Black communities. Lucila's work with local communities through her ciclo de video project is a good example of this. Lucila explains that she shows videos to Black communities that tell people that they should accept themselves and "say proudly, 'I am Black, and I deserve respect' . . . to be able to live and not feel more or less than others . . . because we are Black people." While Lucila is very active in issues of self-esteem and cultural promotion, she is also aware of the need for official state and federal recognition. Lucila explained that within the government, "there is no recognition that they [Negros] exist, they are important because of their culture, traditions . . . it would be good that the government shows interest by asking where these communities are located, what they do, and what they want." Lucila continued by expressing her frustration with the current lack of general recognition of Mexico's Black population. She explained that the "government people [officials] assume that there are only Black people in Central America, Haiti, and other countries. This is a despicable lie because they know that many were stolen from Africa. There are many Black settlements in the Pacific coast. I don't know if they really don't know about it, or they choose to ignore it." As I discussed in the opening chapter, Lucila has firsthand experience with this historic exclusion from the popular imagination and representation of the Mexican citizenry, as she is often accused of being from Central America when she travels outside the coastal region. Because of the perceived mutual exclusivity between Black and Mexican (Sue 2010), the experience of being told that one is a foreigner is common to many Black people in Mexico (Sue 2010; Hoffman and Rinaudo 2014;

Jones 2013, Cerón-Anaya 2019). Lucila was hesitant to explicitly accuse the government of some heinous plot/conspiracy, but her frustrations show that she saw the government as somewhat culpable, as well as part of the potential solution to the injustice that comes along with official invisibility.

Regarding the government, Lucila explained that officials had projects of recognition for the Indigenous communities. She claimed that the government argued that Indigenous people are very important because they have "culture, tradition, and an identity." Lucila emphasized that Blacks in the Costa Chica need resources in order to help build physical infrastructure within the region. She explained that "in the cultural as well as economic aspect, we do not have any support from the state nor the national government. The Indigenous have a lot of resources and probably more support . . . in our Black population we do not have that. It's one of the privileges that as the third-root race we do not have. The government does not say that this project is specifically for the Black community." Lucila is right on track with her analysis of the situation. While the 1998 Indigenous law of Oaxaca (Ley de Derechos de los Pueblos y Comunidades Indígenas del Estado de Oaxaca) mentions "Pueblos Negros" (Black towns), their presence in the official document is an afterthought, a recognition of generic difference rather than a full recognition of a region of Black communities. This generic recognition is also characteristic of much of the literature on race in Mexico.

Lucila's grassroots level work within her community of Charco Redondo and the surrounding communities within the Costa Chica opposes this generic inclusion. Lucila understands that government recognition does not automatically equate to social and economic equality, so she attempts to promote the cultural aspects of Blackness through her work collecting recipes, poems, unique language, and local narratives from the surrounding communities. Lucila and other activists' grassroots work complements the project of state and local recognition by adding a component that the government project, based on a neoliberal logic of difference (Hale 2005; Postero 2007), overlooks. Lucila attempts a holistic approach to difference that may counteract some tendencies to self-identify simply for the possibility of "social welfare." This holistic approach allows for a complexity to be associated with Blackness that is undertheorized and simply overlooked by official recognition and narratives of Blackness in the region.

Marcelo

Marcelo Garcia Zagilon, Don Marcelo, had firsthand experience with how a political identity works for the economic gain of communities. However, Don Marcelo, and his larger collective in the lagoon town of La Pastoría, found that identity and a larger politics of difference still had to compete with the discourses of conservation and sustainability currently influencing state and federal approaches to the region. The Lagunas de Chacahua, and the surrounding forested area, are federally recognized as a national forest preserve. As such, Don Marcelo's organizing around Black identity had to compete with a larger Mexican economic project of ecotourism. Don Marcelo and his collective are forced to perform a certain type of authenticity within political and geographic space in order to capitalize on the trend and opportunities afforded to communities through ecotourism (Cotton and Jerry 2013; Grieves, Adler, and King 2014). Tourists arrive in the Costa Chica in search of some unspoiled wilderness, complete with all the wildlife that this wilderness supports. The danger here is that local people without economic and political capital (Bourdieu 1986) easily become trapped by the broader economic potentials that are created by ecotourism and the discourses of "untouched wildernesses" and conservation that comes with this economic strategy (Nixon 2005). This is doubly problematic when combined with nationally recognized wild lands and national parks.

Don Marcelo's commentary offers one example of the ways that groups can get trapped within geographical conceptions of space and the real potential—or lack thereof—for self-sustainability offered to the residents of the small communities within the Lagunas de Chacahua National Forest Preserve. The preserve is located within the geographic region of the Costa Chica and is an important resource for the many fishing communities that depend on the coastal resources for their livelihood. These communities depend on the resources that come directly from the lagoons and surrounding ocean, as well as the salt that is mined from the lands nearby. Don Marcelo, a fisherman and *minero de sal* (salt miner), makes it clear that while surrounded by an abundance of resources, the potential to capitalize on these resources is less abundant, as local communities are officially limited by the ways in which they can interact with the environment.[10]

Don Marcelo explained that he and some of his ecological collective were considering the development of a fish farm in the community of La Pastoría, on the shores of the main lagoon in the Lagunas de Chacahua system. This fish farm was conceived by his local collective to raise the economic potential of the Lagunas de Chacahua towns by capitalizing on the tourist industry's need for fresh, local seafood. As it is, the communities of the Lagunas de Chacahua find a market for their products in local urban centers such as Puerto Escondido and Pinotepa Nacional. However, the competition is intense as fishing is the main economic strategy within the coastal towns, and there do not seem to be any serious organized unions of local fisherman in the Black towns. The transactions often take place through middlemen who bring the product of the coast to surrounding mountainous and Indigenous communities as well as the commercial centers further into the interior, including Oaxaca City.

In La Pastoría, Don Marcelo explained that when they brought the proposal of a large fish farm to economically support their local communities to the Mexican government Marcelo and his collective were told that the land was strictly for use as a national park and that the development of the fish farm would be a violation of national park regulations. The national park is currently promoted, nationally and internationally, as an ecotourism destination where visitors can see several species of local birds, caiman, turtles, iguanas, and other sea species. There is even a crocodile preserve/farm on the northern side of the community of Chacahua, which is part of a larger Mexican academic biology program, complete with several apartments built to house the biologists when in residence. The people who live within this national park can unconsciously become a part of the natural landscape, even though they are simultaneously excluded from fully capitalizing on the bounty of the region, which in turn severely limits their ability to maintain any local autonomy. As the national park becomes a preserve for wildlife and the natural (traditional and authentic) lifestyles that it supports, it also becomes a trap of poverty in which residents are subsumed as a local resource within the ecotourism industry. This all seems to be in line with the prevailing logic of utilizing marginalized ethnic/racial communities as the means of production within the multicultural state. Ecotourism creates the very limited potential for local communities to capitalize on tourists' desires to experience untouched and preserved wildlife, as the revenues generated from ecotourism primarily benefit those beyond the communities in which ecotourism projects are undertaken (Grieves, Adler, and King 2014, 85).

One of the issues that comes out of this example is the difference between communal lands, occupied by many Indigenous communities through the ejido system (governmentally recognized communal lands), and the noncommunal lands, occupied by many African descendants in this section of the Costa Chica. Further down the southern coast of Oaxaca in the Isthmus region lies La Barra, a small town popular for its right-point surf break. Less popular for surf tourists is the fish farm maintained by the local Indigenous community. This fish farm gives residents the ability to purchase affordable fish and is maintained by the local community. It is not clear if the community has incorporated their operation into a larger-scale economic enterprise, but the ability to create such an operation shows the difference in potential available to Indigenous communities who can support claims to autonomy through access to land rights (Wade 2010). Currently, Black Mexicans lack what Wade describes as accepted "customary territories" (Wade 2010). This means that Black Mexicans' imaginings of new ways to engage with lands are limited, especially when they fall into the category of national parks.

Don Marcelo's fish farm would not only support the local community through affordable access to a variety of popular fish; it would also create the potential for a degree of autonomy by developing local infrastructure (e.g., roads, clinics, schools) through the farm's profits. Even while Marcelo's group was thinking of the farming strategy as a way to generate surplus, the farming project might be considered a noncapitalist enterprise in that the focus of the project was on equitable distribution of surplus (Escobar 2008, 73) rather than generating profits for specific individuals. When asked about the effect that the fish farm might have on the local fishing industry, Marcelo explained that the market for the fish farm would not only be local families and individuals within the community. Rather, the fish farm would focus largely on the tourist industry within the popular destinations of the Costa Chica and further up and down the coast.

Marcelo's collective and the national government are both focusing on the same ecotourism market. However, due to the prevailing historical logic of social relations and differing perspectives on ecotourism and sustainability, the fish farm project falls beyond the purview of the Mexican government's intended use of the national forest space. In fact, the intentions of Don Marcelo's project could quite possibly be seen as contradictory to the development logics that perceive ethnic/racial communities as sustainable resource managers (Escobar 2008), which allow for the governmental conception of Black people's role in the national forest project in the first place. What's more, the park was only declared a national forest in 1937, long after the lands of the coastal lagoons were occupied by its current African-descendant communities. However, as African descendants were not intended to benefit from the postrevolutionary land reforms that allowed for Indigenous collective land rights through the ejido system, African descendants exist as renters rather than owners of their "traditional" cultural geographies (Joseph and Buchenau 2013, 94; Chassen-López 1998, 104).[11] Without legitimate properties through which practices and claims to citizenship can be made and interpreted, African descendants' access to development strategies are severely limited.

As discussed earlier, the process of making difference official racializes space through both official and unofficial apparatuses. This racialization of space can work for or against local communities' interests, depending upon the ways in which local projects articulate with state and federal government projects. Organizing around difference, as Don Marcelo and his cohort have attempted to do, can have positive and negative outcomes, depending upon the wider field of politics that the project is forced to become a part of. These webs of relations and the underlying accepted "natural order of things" structure the ways that narratives of self are spun, maintained, and interpreted, as they situate local communities in larger social and economic projects and discourses. These projects also become a part of the process and methodology of racialization.

Don Marcelo's personal narratives of Blackness alternated between popular Black Mexican stereotypes (Hernández Cuevas 2004) and a genuine understanding of the history and processes behind these stereotypes. Marcelo's use of stereotypes demonstrates that Black Mexicans have a limited range of narrative tropes from which to draw in order to tell the story of their Blackness (Cox 2015, 147). This highlights the complexities involved in a political identification that revolves around Blackness, as well as some Black Mexicans' resistance to identify with the term "Negro" in the Costa Chica. This resistance is always context dependent, but it presents a real issue in terms of cultural and political organization. Don Marcelo's stereotypes, which he drew upon to clarify a popular understanding of Blackness, exacerbate this resistance. Don Marcelo explained to me that "Blacks like to party; this they really enjoy. Be careful with the party and the hammock [la hamaca]." As a trope, la hamaca connects el Negro and el flojero (lazy one)—the quintessential lazy peasant. La hamaca can be seen as almost synonymous with el Negro in the stereotype, as stereotypes suggest that you might be hard-pressed to find one without the other; that is, you may be hard-pressed to find an empty hammock in any Costa Chica town. As I discussed above, this stereotype completely mischaracterizes the actual rhythm of a life dependent upon the bounty of the ocean and the tides. Nonetheless, the stereotype is ubiquitous around the Costa Chica.[12]

Don Marcelo continued with the popular stereotypes, explaining that "the Black is very happy even if they have nothing to eat. That is, the other races worry more about having food, that their family is doing well and all that, and the Black not so much . . ." Don Marcelo thought that maybe this was the reason that the Spanish chose to enslave the Africans and send them to Mexico. He acknowledged the *fuerza* (strength) that was natural to Blacks, a strength that is commonly cited as a reason for the Spanish preference for African slaves in comparison to Indigenous peoples. Don Marcelo explained, "Strength, yes we have that, but few like to study." Part of the reason for Don Marcelo's embrace of such stereotypes may be due to personal experience. For example, the Oaxacan government, in the name of the then governor, chose Don Marcelo's son to receive one of two full scholarships to cover the living expenses associated with attending UNAM in Mexico City. This scholarship would have afforded his son the opportunity to study in Mexico City with little to no living expenses, but it was said that Don Marcelo's son declined the scholarship.

The stereotype mentioned by Don Marcelo may not accurately account for his son's resistance to education, even when presented with the opportunity of a full scholarship. Another way to interpret his son's resistance is to recognize that the twelve- to fourteen-hour bus ride to the capital city was in effect a sentence of exile in an oasis of non-Blackness and racial discrimination. Don Marcelo's son declined to speak with me, even after much prodding from his father, but it is worth considering that the lack of national recognition and the state-promoted connection between race and place, combined with the discrimination documented in this and previous chapters, could have likely played a significant role in Don Marcelo's son's resistance to receiving an education outside of the Costa Chica. This is the problem with the geographic location and situation of race and culture. It creates a situation where one is only allowed to exist (if existence is predicated on racial/cultural being) within specific, sanctioned geographic locations. Jones quotes one of her respondents from the Costa Chica who went to an urban university as explaining that he rarely leaves the Costa Chica because of his experience of being ridiculed regularly about his skin color and therefore his inability to make many friends (2013, 1571). Villareal (2010, 666) also explains that skin color plays a significant role in the attainment of education in Mexico. Because of the invisibility associated with Blackness in Mexico's urban centers (Jones 2013, 1571; Huet 2014), attending university in the nation's capital, for Marcelo's son, would at the very least be an excruciatingly lonely several years.

Don Marcelo's commentary on the likes and proclivities of los Negros relies on several preexisting stereotypes, reinforced by his own experience in the Costa Chica and his personal experience with the next generation, to make sense of the Black experience in the Costa Chica. However, Don Marcelo's personal actions, as well as those of most people around him, do not fit with the overall "social facts" that these stereotypes draw upon or perpetuate. As witnessed by the local and federal governments' resistance to Don Marcelo's community fish farm project, attempts to politically and economically organize against marginalization frequently fail as those efforts do not jibe with the larger webs of relations in which they must be articulated. The racial and cultural stereotypes may be the only lens through which the Black experience in the Costa Chica can be perceived, even by those who continuously attempt to break out of their typecast social and economic racial scripts (Molina 2010).

At the time of writing this book, Don Marcelo's fish farm remained unrealized, but the Mexican government did support another strategy focused on ecotourism in the community. Wade (2010) explains how rural Afro-Colombians have historically been viewed in three ways within government-supported projects of development. Speaking specifically of the Plan Biopacífico (Bio Pacific Development Plan) project in Colombia, Wade argues that rural Black communities have been perceived as either utilizing practices that are destructive to the environment, through the lens of "stewardship" (Hébert and Rosen 2007, 35), or Black Colombians were seen in need of training on how to sustainably interact with their environment (Wade 2010). The Mexican government has been directly employing this last approach by training local communities on how to "sustainably engage" with the ecotourism economy. Rather than support the collective's fish farm, the Mexican government helped build a restaurant and two "ecofriendly" cabanas in the small town of La Pastoría. This support also included training from local organizations on how to cater to the gastronomic tastes and desires, as well as the sensibilities around the service industry, of foreign tourists. This is a strategy that has become popular in the region. For example, the government has contracted people with experience in tourism and hospitality management to hold workshops in the town of Chacahua for local cabana and restaurant owners on how to mix classic alcoholic cocktails such as margaritas and piña coladas.

In the town of La Pastoría, organizing local labor in order to meet the limited demands of local tourists created a new headache for Marcelo and his collective. The cultural entrepreneurial operation (Dawson 2014) is situated on the bank of one of the Lagoons in the national park, at the edge of the community, away from the already limited resources of the town. The location of the enterprise created staffing, supply, and safety issues. There was even a man, said to be the "local drunk," who would often cruise the area hoping to interact with the few tourists and guests who reserved the cabanas. When I arrived with a small group of students, the cabanas and restaurant appeared to be practically abandoned, and getting a group of men and women together to clean and prepare the cabanas—including allocating at least an hour to locate the keys and get the restaurant ready for food preparation—was almost more than my students were willing to tolerate.

Grieves, Adler, and King demonstrate that such projects often require at least five individuals working on related activities (2014, 97). Most large projects also require a host of other smaller auxiliary projects in order to support the larger economic scheme (2014, 101). Moreover, the labor for most of these related projects is unpaid (2014, 101). Another issue with these projects is that they require a host of professionals with skilled labor and specific knowledge. These professionals can be hard to find in the local communities. In the future, the communities might rely on young people within the community to become these professionals. However, this re-quires that communities convince these young people to go to universities or vocational schools. As Don Marcelo's son's experience demonstrates, this can be hard to do. Therefore, the highest-paying jobs associated with these schemes regularly benefit professionals from beyond the community.

The strategy of conservation through ecotourism is a trap (Wade 2010) that confines local community's abilities rather than a viable strategy for semi-autonomy. This trap attempts to convert those in the Costa Chica who have a strong tradition of self-sufficiency and self-reliance into the unfamiliar position of labor for the growing tourist market in the region. Hébert and Rosen (2007, 17), speaking specifically of community forestry projects in Oaxaca, demonstrate how community enterprises, such as the fish farm in the community of La Barra, grant communities a certain amount of autonomy. While this autonomy is still limited by government involvement through the issuing of permits and land leases, such projects can help finance schools, health clinics, ambulances, non-emergency trans-portation services, and other community infrastructure, as well as jobs that pay beyond the local minimum wage (Hébert and Rosen 2007, 25; Grieves, Adler, and King 2014, 85). Indigenous communities in Mexico have been better positioned to take advantage of these types of programs. However, the government is not ready to collaborate on these types of projects with the Black residents of the Lagunas de Chacahua region and has preferred to utilize the problematic strategy of ecotourism.

Aydée Rodríguez López

Aydée Rodríguez López, originally from one of the smaller towns surrounding the Oaxaca-Guerrero border, currently lives in the local market town of Cuajinicuilapa. She is the owner of a small restaurant as well as a painter who works with the themes of Blackness, history, and culture. Padre Glynn Jemmott Nelson introduced me to Aydée after discussing a local project that he was associated with.[13] Padre Glyn explained to me that Aydée was very active in the local art scene and used her talents to help promote African-descendant history and identity within local communities by participating in painting workshops for local youth. By the time I arrived in the Costa Chica, I was already familiar with Aydée's work, as she was featured in a 2009 exhibit at the California African American Museum in Los Angeles, California.[14] I remember looking at the exhibit and thinking how interesting it was that this work had found a place at the African American Museum in LA, while the Guelaguetza celebration that same year at MacArthur Park organized by Mestizo and Indigenous Oaxaca immigrants (also in Los Angeles) sidestepped the issue of Blackness. As seen by Aydée's exhibition in Los Angeles, Blackness is subject to translation when crossing the border as it is takes on a new value and meaning within the context of the US racial economy and racial relations. Therefore, in the United States, Aydée's work seemed a better fit for the African American Museum rather than a venue focused on Mexican American or Chicanx history. Aydée's work and her specific narrative of Blackness lies somewhere between these discourses of Blackness and Mexicanness, as she attempts to promote a positive perception of African descendants in the Costa Chica.

When I asked Aydée why she works with the theme of Black culture (La cultura Negra), Aydée proposed that "Black culture . . . in the state of Guerrero is forgotten [esta olvidada]." According to Aydée, in the small community where she was born, all the dances and traditions were preserved from the time when Blacks arrived in the Costa Chica, and she had grown up participating in this culture as a young child. This culture was the impetus for her wanting to paint. "Seeing all of this, and playing, and so when I began to paint, I said I'm going to recover [rescatar] all that is Black culture [la cultura Negra], and I'm going to fill the house with it until there is no empty space in the house. That is, I'm going to recover all that is Black culture, all the history . . . and yes, this is what I have been doing."

I found the idea of forgotten-ness interesting, as Cuajinicuilapa is one of the more recognizable Black towns of the Costa Chica. The town is located on the main highway that connects Acapulco to Puerto Escondido and is within the main route for Autobuses de Oriente buses making the journey from Mexico City and Acapulco to Puerto Escondido. The town, referred to by locals as Cuaji, was popularized by Gonzalo Aguirre Beltrán's anthropological work, *Cuijla: Esbozo Etnográfico de un Pueblo Negro* (Cuijla: Ethnographic sketch of a Black town), and the majority of the population is visually of African descent. It is this climate in which the forgotten-ness mentioned by Aydée was seen to exist. I asked Aydée how Black culture could be forgotten when there are gente Negra (Black people) in every corner of town. Aydée made it clear that biology and culture did not have to go hand in hand (see Michaels 1992). She explained that within a local context, the culture was forgotten, not the people. This idea of forgotten culture, often translated as a lack of culture, makes it possible for African descendants in Mexico to be overlooked within the project of multiculturalism while they are simultaneously racialized and excluded from the Mestizo ideal. As African descendants' cultural contributions to a broader national culture have been credited to the Spanish and Indigenous components of mestizaje (Hernández Cuevas 2004), Black Mexicans have been, until recently, forgotten and invisible within the rhetoric of multicultural politics. However, African descendants are still physically visible and susceptible to the real processes of racial discrimination that exist within the Costa Chica, as well as the broader nation, when they happen to venture out of the region. What have also been forgotten are the historical processes and discrimination that have been responsible for the creation and exclusion of African-descendant communities within Mexico.[15] Aydée's artistic work attempts to counteract this invisibility and forgotten-ness.

I asked Aydée why it was important to recover Black culture in the Costa Chica and Mexico. Rather than focusing on the resources and support that could come from multicultural recognition, Aydée's response was more in line with the potential for positive self-esteem and grounding that could come from embracing Black culture. Aydée argued, "It's important because it's always beautiful to conserve that of our ancestors. That is, ours is a historic culture. And for me, it's personally important. And I tell you, I carry this inside so that the kids and young adults can see the paintings and see the culture that our ancestors have left us as an inheritance, and so they go on forming the idea to conserve the culture as well. This stays in their little heads, that we have inherited a beautiful culture, and we must conserve this so that it is not lost." Aydée went on to explain that there is some success in this project, as she gives painting courses to youth on their school vacations. Aydée is aware of the need for, and value of, "rescuing Black culture" (rescatando la cultura Negra) in the current cultural and political climate. Her sense of the actual value of cultural revitalization and the potential that this revitalization has for youth empowerment finds expression through her art and her own brand of activism.

Although she has sold several of her pieces locally and abroad, it was never Aydée's intention to generate income from her art or to capitalize on the broader theme of Black culture and history. Originally, she had the idea of simply filling her house with beautiful art. Aydée explained, "I had the idea to fill my house with my paintings, because it's my house. But I never had the idea to show it because everyone laughed at my work. Everyone would say, 'How horrible you paint . . . your Negros are so ugly.'" However, due to a fortuitous meeting with Padre Glyn, Aydée's paintings received some international attention and now provide a modest income as well as generate interest within Mexico. Aydée told me that she could not believe that there was interest in her paintings. She explained, "I couldn't believe it, because people would always say such ugly things about my paintings, and it saddened me. But I said to myself, 'No, I have to continue painting.' And now I have sold a few and there are people interested in my work." The international interest in Aydée's paintings motivated her to keep painting, not only for her personal enjoyment but also as part of her larger personal political project. When I asked Aydée why local people would make fun of the paintings when they are so successful in other venues, Aydée thought that maybe it could be explained by the fact that "while Cuaji is a town where the majority of the population is Black, I think they know little about history, and at times the people of Cuaji don't accept being Black." Aydée's paintings were perceived through the local popular context of anti-Blackness, a context that frames much of the perception of local Blackness and a context in which local activists find themselves submerged.

International interest gave Aydée confidence in her own political project, as well as her artistic talent, but Aydée could not travel with her work to the United States because of the many problems that she had with her visa and her official voter identification/registration card (*credencial de elector*). She explained that "they" (local government officials) wrote her name with one *e*—as "Aide," rather than "Aydée." Because her paperwork did not match, her voter identification acted as a checkpoint (Jeganathan 2004; Lugo 2008), raising suspicion about Aydée's legal status, rather than a marker of legal citizenship. What's more, she had trouble acquiring her visa for the United States. She told me that "getting the passport is easy. The hard part is the visa for the US." Because of her difficulty acquiring a visa for the US and the illegibility issues (Das 2004) with her Mexican credentials, Aydée's paintings had to travel to the showing at the California African American Museum unaccompanied by the physical representation of the subject of and through which they were conceived. While the representation of Blackness could cross borders, Aydée's physical body, much like Esperanza in Ruth Behar's classic anthropological text *Translated Woman* (1993), remained trapped within the Costa Chica.

Conclusion

Within this chapter I have highlighted some of the narratives of Blackness within the Costa Chica and the political movement that continues to gain steam within the region. I have chosen to dedicate the focus here to three narratives, as they highlight the different approaches to the project of Black recognition, rights, and identity from below. While all three main narratives focus on different aspects of Blackness, they are all tied to the same overall political project. This highlights the complexities involved with the process of recognition, a complexity that does not exist, at least explicitly, within the official multicultural government strategy of recognition and making difference official.

I recognize that the narratives here may not be narratives of identity as such, but they are the narratives of the process of constructing a Black identity that is underway and continuing to develop within the Costa Chica. These narratives give us a glimpse of the processes surrounding difference that is currently underway in the Costa Chica as well as the ways that this process must engage with a preexisting Black subject position and the role that this subject position plays in the broader set of social relations. These narratives demonstrate the actual process of creating a foundation for the political project of Blackness (or at least the attempt to lay a foundation for this project) through the negotiation of the racialization process. This foundation is the first necessary building block, and it will be the platform upon which the narratives of future generations can be built. Through this project we can see the actual process, facilitated by a concurrent government sponsored project, of racial and cultural reproduction. This project emerges from a concrete if dispersed political awareness. Several of the people I spoke with referred to stories and traditions handed down from previous generations. Yet, due to the lack of historic recognition and the process of invisibility facilitated by a larger official project of mestizaje, the narratives are read not within the context of the nation but within the context of the Costa Chica region; they are forced to be read within the context of the present and the contemporary political fashion that gives these narratives meaning in the current economic and multicultural climate. This also means that these narratives draw on potentials and possibilities that may not have been available in the past to African descendants within the region. The art of producing narratives of Blackness comes through local invention based on the outcomes that local racial identities are utilized to bring about in addition to the specific roles and meanings that these identities can have within the context of the present.

Aydée, for example, painted a scene of the shipwreck (*naufragio*). The shipwreck, specifically the shipwreck in Puerto Miniso, is a way to speak to the origins of African descent in the region. In the current moment, the shipwreck is a trope to talk about Black existence in the Costa Chica rather than the diasporic trope of the Middle Passage. The current approach to recognition by local activists locates Blackness within the Mexican nation and therefore demands recognition based on Blacks' historic participation in the nation rather than the "prehistoric" (read pre-colonial and pre-national) existence. This strategy highlights the sense of autochthony that African descendants in the Costa Chica feel and changes the stakes of political recognition within Mexico.

On the one hand, the lack of locally and nationally recognized texts historicizing the presence and experience of African descendants and their role in the nation (whether racist, erroneous, or otherwise) creates a void that needs to be filled before many will really venture to bet on the actual potentials of a multicultural politics—a bet that may only yield returns for a limited time. On the other hand, this lack of "history" presents a unique space for invention. It is within this space that activists, artists, and educators such as Lucila, Aydée, Don Marcelo, Nestor, Sergio, Bulmaro, and others are becoming the authors of the modern-day narratives that will one day be the histories and documentation of histories that are so sorely lacking in Mexico's forgotten Black regions such as the Costa Chica.

Conclusion

Black Visibility and the Limits of Black Recognition in Mexico

Black Mexicans in the Costa Chica are weaving their present-day narratives about what it means to be Black in Mexico into the broader historical narrative about Blackness in the region and the nation. These narratives provide a testimony (Roque Ramirez 2003, 2005, 2007) about Blackness and the Black Mexican experience that in many ways is contrary to the popular narratives about Blackness that circulate in the nation and continue to frame the government's approach to Black recognition. Trouillot argues that "human beings participate in history as both actors and as narrators" (1995, 2). This double position creates a generative tension (Dawson 2014) within official projects of recognition. I argue that the self-positioning of local communities as narrators of regional and racial histories within projects of recognition can also be read as a struggle over the means of representation (and reproduction) of history and the nation (Trouillot 1995). As outlined throughout this book, the process of officializing difference has been conceived through, and continues to rely on, the nation's assumed monopoly on the means of representation of Blackness.

However, Black activists and the communities within the Costa Chica have challenged this monopoly over the means of representing Blackness to the nation, as well as the larger global community. One important example comes through the contestation over the process of officially naming Black Mexicans as multicultural subjects. In 2011, the CDI presented the plan for Black recognition to activists and representatives of the Black communities in the town of Jamiltepec, located on the racial and ethnic border between the coastal plain that is home to the Black communities of the Costa Chica and the Indigenous communities of the coastal mountainous region. In a small conference room, the non-Black Mestizo representatives of the CDI, from both the local and federal offices, emphasized the importance of "Afro-Mexican" recognition and their excitement to get the process underway that year. However, the meeting was never really able to get underway, as Black activists immediately took issue with the use of the term "Afro-Mexicano." The activists explained to the CDI representatives that they were, in fact, not Afro-Mexicanos, but rather they identified as "Negros." Such a casual and direct use of the term "Negro" in a public setting made several of the non-Black CDI representatives visibly uncomfortable. In response, one of the Mestizo representatives politely interrupted the activists and commented that "Negro" was a negative term and that it would therefore be in poor taste to use the term as one that represented the group as a whole within the project for official government recognition. The Black activists took offense to this explanation and continued to protest, while one Black woman in the group explained to the CDI representatives that it was "Blancos" who felt that "Negro" was a negative term. After an intense debate over the value of the term, the issue was tabled so that the more practical issues of the recognition process could be discussed.

The arguments over naming are not simply arguments over politically correct nomenclature. More importantly, they can and should be read as struggles over the power of self-representation and the process of sublimation (Oliver 2004). Activists' frustrations with the terms preferred by the CDI (terms such as "Afro-Mexicano" and "Afro-Mestizo") show that many locals' preference for "Negro" is an attempt to ground present conceptions of Blackness in the context of the historical construction of the category.[1] This connection to the historical production and experience of Black communities and the present condition of Blackness roots Blackness within the nation. It also makes the dialectical relationship between Whiteness and Blackness, Mestizos and Morenos, explicitly visible by forcing non-Black Mestizos to reckon with the role that the Black subject position has played in the production of the nation as well as the privileged Mexican citizen, the Mestizo.

Creating visibility around an enduring Black subject position was beyond the intentions of the multicultural recognition efforts of the Mexican state, as represented by the meeting in Jamiltepec that day in 2011. The state's recognition efforts are definitely aimed at a historically marginalized group. However, state officials fall short in their willingness to recognize the historical processes responsible for Black marginalization (Hale 2002). Instead, the state attempts to maintain its monopoly over the means of producing national history by using terms such as *Afro-Mexicano/a* or *Afro-Mestizo/a* that are seemingly aimed at inclusion and the eradication of contemporary discrimination. The state's continued monopoly on the means of representation allows any future narratives to continue operating around the accepted "order of things" and upon preexisting bundles of silences (Trouillot 1995, 27), bundles constructed and packaged within the context of state projects. These bundles of silences operate as rhetorical tools that allow for the interpretation of Mexicanness through a particular lens and are then themselves manifested as methodological tools for recognition while simultaneously allowing for the continued silencing of the history of the Black experience in the present.

Implication plays a major part in bringing this dialectical relationship sharply into view.[2] The activists' demand for the use of the term "Negro" within a broader set of social relations that associates the term with negative stereotypes allows the racial term "Negro" to act as a mnemonic device (Jerry 2018), which then has the ability to implicate multiple subjects in the historical process of racial subject-making. Negro as a mnemonic device implicates Black and non-Black subject positions as ontological positions produced within a broader power dynamic in which value is ascribed to at least two subject positions (Black and non-Black) through the use of the term "Negro," while the term itself is only applied to one of those subject positions. This is the moment when the invisible becomes visible. This is the moment when Whiteness becomes implicated in the social process responsible for the construction of Blackness and the interpellation of Black Mexicans through the use of the word "Negro." Depending upon the subject's position, this process implicates individuals as either raced or racist.[3] By attempting to force the CDI to use the term "Negro" as a term for official recognition, the Black activists at the meeting were attempting to force the CDI to recognize not only Black Mexicans as a group but also the history of Blackness in the nation and the historic conditions by which Black Mexicans were excluded in the first place. Therefore, contestations over naming, through the phenomenon of implication, threaten to unravel the bundles of silences that Trouillot argues are a part of any historical narrative (1995, 27).

Trouillot explains that "narratives are occasionally evoked as illustrations or, at best, deciphered as texts, but the process of their production rarely constitutes the object of study" (1995, 22). Trouillot's argument asks us to take seriously the power dynamics and the context in which narratives of Blackness (by both Black and non-Black Mexicans) are invented, told, refashioned, and eventually presented. This is an important task with regard to the ways in which African descendants tell the tales of what it means to be Black in the Costa Chica, as well as for thinking about the productive power that these narratives are afforded within the context of the contemporary cultural and political climate. Thinking about the process of these narratives' production allows us to make visible the power struggles that are a part of the racialization process underway in Mexico, and how this process impacts both Black and non-Black Mexicans.

Narratives of and about Blackness are not only historical representations and anecdotes about the people who physically represent Blackness. These narratives potentially have the power to shake up the normative discourses through which they have been produced. In effect, these narratives have the power to implicate—if not indict—the larger public as they make audible the silences around the dialectical relationships between perceived dichotomies such as White/Black, Mestizo/Indigenous, modern/traditional, rich/poor, urban/rural, and so on. Therefore, narratives of Blackness are not simply confessions or statements based on normative values and ideals (Ferguson 2004) of what it means to be Black; rather, they should be read as testimonials (Roque Ramirez 2005) of the lived experience of a broader racial economy that operates within the nation. These narratives help fill in the gap between the past and present with regard to the enduring role of a Black subject position within Mexico. Roque Ramirez argues that "to connect the past to the present, to make a history a collective process of human signification where all of us become agents for its production, is to be 'testifying'" (2005, 119). Testifying has the power to extract narratives of Black exclusion and marginalization from the context of Black history, and transplant it, or reinsert it, into the context of the history of the nation. However, the ways that these narratives will ultimately reach the ears of the nation, and the subjects who are allowed to embody the nation, depends on their translation within the discourses of race/nation and past/present as well as the racial economy in which the narratives are employed.

Roque Ramirez goes on to explain that "for marginalized communities involved in struggles for visibility, political identity, and space . . . testimonies about their existence are critical acts of documentation" (2005, 116). For communities whose narratives—or even existence, as is the case of African descendants in the Costa Chica—have been excluded from officially recognized histories, the "historical and evidentiary meanings of [their] existence prove to be an indispensable archive in the community and beyond" (Roque Ramirez 2005, 116). In this way, the communities of the Costa Chica are a living archive (Hall 2001; Roque Ramirez 2005), providing evidence of their will and ability to survive the silences of official narratives and histories. However, state projects of official recognition, as well as popular representations, complicate the potential power and effectiveness of this archive in some dangerous ways.

For example, the issue of Blackness in Mexico is becoming more visible in media and social media. Part of this visibility is a direct outcome of the Mexican government's recent efforts to count the country's population of African descendants, beginning with the 2015 Mexican inter-census. While these efforts have brought visibility to Mexico's Black population, the underlying intuitions around the mutual exclusivity of Blackness and Mexicanness continue to frame the limited ways in which Blackness in Mexico can be represented through popular media and social media. The Mexican government's efforts to recognize Black Mexicans as a cultural group seem to have had a major impact on broader representations of Black Mexicans, which largely rely on the folklorization of Blackness to tell the current story of Blackness in Mexico. This has meant that Black Mexican activists, as well as less politically active Black Mexicans, have also had to engage this strategy of folklorization. One telling example comes from a 2016 video on YouTube shot by Gustavo Mora for AJ+, an online news and current events channel run by Al Jazeera Media Network (www.ajplus.net). The video focuses on a Black Mexican dance troupe by the name of "Obatala" from the Costa Chica town of Collantes. In the video the group is seen performing African-inspired dances accompanied by the fast rhythm of "African-style" drumming. A member of the group explains that they chose to focus on dances from northern Africa after conducting internet research that revealed that the large majority of enslaved Africans who were brought to the region were in fact from parts of northern Africa. The dancers in the Obatala group studied videos on YouTube in order to incorporate these steps into their performances.

The cultural recognition of Black Mexicans as "Afro-Mexican" has required that Black Mexicans learn the language of culture in order to represent their difference to the nation and to the world. This has required a cultural invention of sorts, as Black Mexicans build a cultural repertoire that is aligned with broader popular intuitions and representations of their cultural difference. This has also meant that currently diaspora, specifically the African diaspora, is playing a larger role in representations of Blackness in Mexico, as Black Mexicans are looking more and more to Africa rather than the nation to create meaning around their Blackness (Gordon and Anderson 1999; Gordon 1998). This process has impacted the language that Black activists in the region, many of which were present at the

CDI meeting mentioned previously, are currently using to represent their struggle to the public and the Mexican government. In fact, many Black Mexican activists have incorporated the term "Afro-Mexican" into their political lexicon and have accepted the strategy of folklorization as a way of bringing visibility to the social issues that Black Mexicans continue to face in the nation. This strategy reinforces the historic social relations around citizenship in Mexico.

Godreau (2002) demonstrates how the folklorization of "Black" culture in Puerto Rico reinforces a national project of blanqueamiento, rather than subverting the historic effects of racism and marginalization on Black communities. The inclusion of Blackness into the national Mexican narrative has repositioned Blackness as one of the Mestizo-izing elements of the national citizenry. However, this inclusion relies upon some of the same ideological principles that relegate Blackness to the imagined margins of the nation (Godreau 2002, 282). This is one of the tricks of multicultural recognition, as it positions "cultural" populations as distinct from the general national citizenry (Godreau 2002; Goett 2011) through a narrative of discrete genesis. Through this sleight of hand, Blackness in Mexico continues to be perceived as extranational rather than playing a major part in the genesis of the nation. In this way, Black communities are being recognized and celebrated for maintaining an "African-derived culture" in spite of mestizaje. The folklorization of Black culture works to maintain the silences through which narratives of the nation operate (Godreau 2002; Trouillot 1995). This is what is at stake for Black communities of the Costa Chica and other regions of Mexico as the government institutes Black incorporation through the lenses of ethnicity and cultural difference. Black Mexican activists' attempts to negotiate with local, state, and federal governments over representation uncover the logics of race and the social relations around citizenship that these logics continue to reproduce within Mexico.

The fact that multicultural politics in Mexico is opening up a space for dialogue has created the potential for visibility around the role that a Black subject position plays in the traditional modes of incorporation and access to citizenship in Mexico. And even though the logic and rhetoric of mestizaje continue to inform the ways that culture and ethnicity can be interpreted, it cannot be denied that new possibilities of being for African descendants have been introduced. These new possibilities ask African descendants to reimagine the ways in which they conceive of themselves in relation to the broader citizenry and the nation. However, it appears that an enduring Black subject position in Mexico has created the potential for an equilibrium in which the process for Black recognition does not necessarily change the ways in which the nation and the broader citizenry see themselves in relation to Black Mexicans. What will be important for future work on Blackness and racial subject-making in Mexico is for researchers to recognize and take seriously the impacts of the historical production of Black cultural difference and a Black cultural subject. Focusing on the contemporary process of Black cultural recognition underway in Mexico might help understand the broader role that a Black subject position continues to play in the social relations around citizenship and the reproduction of the nation as well as the modern Mexican Mestizo.

Notes

Introduction: Citizenship and Black Recognition in Mexico

1. Several scholars have discussed Black Mexican migration to both the West and East Coasts of the United States (Lewis 2001; Vaughn 2001, 2005b). However, this migration, while growing, seems yet to have impacted the ways in which rural Black Mexicans in the Costa Chica imagine themselves as being connected to other US Black communities or even their general perception of the United States as a "White" nation.

2. *La tercera raíz* literally translates as "the third root" and is often popularly referred to as "the third race." Hoffman and Rinaudo explain that the "third root" rhetoric was popularized in 1987 as "Our Third Root" by the Dirección General de Culturas Populares. The project aimed to recognize the Latin American world's African cultural heritage and originated from an academic and political focus on the history of slavery (2014, 145).

3. Author's translation.

4. Interestingly, as discussed in later chapters, Lucila Mariche Magadán, an activist from the town of Charco Redondo, was at the time engaged in a project of documenting and inventing a number of "authentic cultural forms" that would provide towns recognition based on cultural products. For example, Santa Maria Atzompa would be recognized for its green glazed pottery, or the town of San Antonio Arrazola, which has become internationally known, would be recognized for its Alebrije figurines made of copal wood. Lucila believed that this was one path to recognition and success utilized by Indigenous groups that was currently out of the reach of coastal Negro/Black communities.

5. I later elaborate on my understanding of mestizaje as an acceptable form of Whiteness in Mexico and Latin America more broadly. The development of the ideology of mestizaje was ultimately used to create a new position within the spectrum of Whiteness while simultaneously distancing the Spanish Creole from the peninsular Spanish, but never truly adopting Indigenous nor Black as an acceptable racial position.

Chapter 1. Chasing Blackness: Racial Geography and a Methodology for Locating Blackness in Mexico

1. See Cotton and Jerry (2013) for considerations on how mapping is used in the region in order to racialize space and reinforce notions of race and difference.

2. According to the Migration Policy Institute (https://www.migrationpolicy.org/article/central-american-immigrants-united-states) as of 2015, 3.4 million Central Americans resided in the United States, a large majority of whom were from the northern triangle formed by El Salvador, Honduras, and Guatemala. At this time, Central Americans accounted for 8 percent of the 43.3 million immigrants in the United States.

3. See Goett (2011) for a discussion of how narcotics trafficking is seized upon to apply a discourse of illegality to Blacks in Central America.

4. A number of local dance traditions highlight this process; see Vaughn (2001) for one example. Shared culinary tastes may be recognized as another form of tradition. However, many of these aspects are also shared with Mestizo and Indigenous communities in the region and making any direct claims to these elements as specific to Black communities is debatable.

5. I acknowledge that the process of "becoming" is one that remains in motion, but it is important to consider that this process leads in a number of directions (perhaps infinite) depending upon the reference point upon which the process draws. This means that the directions for development depend upon the foundations from which they draw support. Tracing the process of becoming requires recognizing a particular foundation and context for the process of becoming. While the context of becoming within the push for political Blackness in Mexico is clear, the foundations that this process will draw upon are less clear and complicate issues of methodologies for tracing the process and future possibilities in the Mexican case.

6. Now renamed Seretaría de Pueblos Indígenas y Afromexicano (Secretary of Indigenous and Afromexican Affairs).

7. At the time of this research, the SAI was simply the Secretaría de Pueblos Indígenas. According to their website, the SAI has since become the Secretaría de Pueblos Indígenas y Afromexicanos. It should be noted that the word *Pueblo* in this context refers to the notion of a people, and therefore applies to the plural *Indígenas* (Indigenous) and singular *Afromexicano* (Afromexican). The abbreviation has yet to change and remains SAI.

Chapter 2. Dark Matter, Ideology, and Blackness in the Conceptualization of Mestizaje

1. The "Negrito" caricature was given a makeover in the early 2000s when the treat was renamed "nito." The character is still obviously of phenotypic African descent but now in a style more representative of the mulatto and the stereotypes of Afro-Latinidad, rather than the direct relation to a perceived Black Africanness.

2. See Falola and Childs (2004) for examples among the Yoruba diaspora in the Americas.

3. This project may be impossible based on the analysis of archival records in a moment where identity politics had yet to become the preferred method of political organization and resistance.

4. See Chasteen (2011) for similar approaches in countries such as Argentina, Brazil, and Uruguay during the same period in the second half of the nineteenth century.

5. There is also another side to this story, where family ties help create an identity of "Negro," even among those who would not socially feel the imposition of the racialized term. Martin, an activist discussed in another chapter, personifies this possibility, as he himself identifies with "Negro" even as his own phenotype often times avoids racial scrutiny thereby escaping the imposition of Blackness from without. This strategy can be capitalized on by different individuals, depending upon the context, but does not preclude racial affinity or the perception of one's self as "Negro."

6. The term "Afro" is now being used by some to reference their own ancestral connection to African descent while still allowing for distance from the racial implications of the terms "Black" or "Negro." For example, during a workshop in 2022 at the University of California, San Diego, an activist from the Costa Chica explained to our group that they identified as Afro based on cultural and familial descent but would not define themselves as Black based on their lighter skin color.

7. See Aguirre Beltrán (1958) for discussion of "traditional" African round house supposedly once common to the region.

8. UNESCO (2014).

9. This is potentially a perilous endeavor in itself. See Comaroff (2006) for an example of the dangers of the rearticulation of history within contemporary narratives of the nation in South Africa.

Chapter 3. Recognizing Culture and Making Difference Official

1. http://www.un.org/en/events/iypad2011/

2. African descendants are mentioned in the Oaxacan state constitution, but this mention is hardly an official recognition and is better seen as an afterthought as part of the general recognition of multicultural difference in the state and more specifically the recognition of Indigenous communities. In this regard, Guerrero is ahead of the state of Oaxaca in recognizing the existence of African descendants, perhaps because of the visibility of communities such as Cuajinicuilapa through the work of Aguirre Gonzalo Beltrán.

3. *Pueblo* is often used in Spanish to connote a people and not simply a geographic site or location as the literal translation, "town," would suggest.

4. I am not arguing that the Indigenous community is any less of a colonial "invention" than the Black community. However, due to the inability of Black colonial subjects to create their own separate sanctioned colonial communities, the intricacies involved in

the processes of colonial relations between the Indigenous and Spanish are fundamentally different than the dialectic involved with the development of Black and Spanish as distinct social and racial locations.

5. In 2015, Heladio had just been reelected for a second term as mayor, his first being several years prior.

6. Eric Wolf's (1982) work takes a similar approach to Indigenous peoples in general.

7. The political geography in the Costa Chica, just like that of Mexico overall, is broken down into a political hierarchy. The municipality (*municipio*) can be seen as the actual county in which a town is geographically located. However, *la cabecera* is the town by which the larger county derives its name. So, while the smaller towns of Chacahua, Charco Redondo, and Azufre, for example, are located in the municipality of Tututepec, the actual town of Tututepec is where all official business is conducted. In the case of Tututepec, the town is recognized as an Indigenous town, complete with an Indigenous cultural museum (Yuku Saa) in the town center, focusing on the Mixtec, or Nuu Savi, of the region. The terms used to reference Black communities and individuals are still under debate. This means that several terms are used interchangeably to describe Black towns and individuals. In the context of the Carta Descriptiva questions, *Moreno* should be read as "Black" and not simply as "darker-skinned" or "mixed with Black and Indigenous."

8. *Encomienda* here refers to the Spanish colonial system of assigning territory, and the Indigenous occupants of that territory, to Spanish landlords as a way of managing the extraction of "tribute" in the form of raw natural resources from Indigenous communities.

9. The *alebrije* (brightly colored wooden folk art sculptures) in Oaxaca might lend some truth to this argument, as the modern alibrije is known, however unpopularly, to be an invention of the twentieth century rather than a traditional cultural art form (Chibnik 2003).

10. Even the Indigenous dialects of the region have had to incorporate a number of *préstamos* (borrowed words) from Spanish in order to communicate particular concepts and processes that did not exist prior to the contact period. African descendants, like all in the area, have also borrowed a few terms from the different Indigenous groups in the region.

11. In the film, when Pedro's young daughter puts a coin in the jukebox and plays the song "Vamanos, ven guajira" by Carlos Farina and Enrique Pineda Barnett, the viewer hears the term *bajareque*. The song's use is similar to Lucila's. The lyrics are: "A mi, me gusta el guateque y echarle a mi gallo ron. La jamaca en el bajareque y tu cintura con son. La jamaca en el bajareque y tu cintura con son" (I like parties and bathing my rooster in rum. The hammock in the bajareque and your waist with son music. The hammock in the bajareque and your waist with son music). I have not been able to ask Lucila if she is familiar with the song's lyrics.

12. Bulmaro's self-identification as Afro-Mixteco should not be confused with an understanding of Blackness as Indigenous. Rather, Bulmaro's mention of an Afro-Mixteco identity references a racial mixing through the separate and distinct racial locations of his parents. This is similar to the racial reality expressed through a "Blaxican" identity

that is becoming common in Southern California, in which "Blaxican" refers to a person of Black and Mexican (mutually exclusive) descent rather than Black Mexican (or Afro-Mexican) descent.

Chapter 4. Citizenship, Black Value, and the Production of the Black Subject in Mexico

1. This conceptualization of the "American" should be read in the context of the greater Americas rather than in the context of the United States.

2. Although the two are undoubtedly related, "the social relations surrounding the means of production" as a concept should not be confused with the "relations to the means of production," which is responsible for the reproduction of a classed system.

3. See Mills (2014) for an in-depth discussion of ideal theory.

4. I recognize that the use of the term "invention," as applied to a living group of people, is problematic. However, I argue that this term is an appropriate way to discuss the strategy that the Mexican government is employing to make visible a preexisting group of people through the already accepted paradigms of mestizaje and multiculturalism. This term is also important for the recognition of the use of colonial racial ideologies, even as applied to the postcolony, as technologies for the reproduction or invention of particular subjects in order to materialize the ideal theories on which the modern nation-state continues to depend.

5. The positioning of mestizaje and multiculturalism as competing political forms is, as this book shows, overstated, as the Mexican brand of multiculturalism is really an attempt to reinforce the common narrative of mestizaje. This can easily be seen by attempts to incorporate Blackness into the model simply by using the term "Afro-Mestizo."

6. Interestingly, this relationship also helps explain how it is that Black cultural forms get "Whitewashed" and then appropriated as national forms in many nations within the Americas. See Jonathan Ritter's (2011) work in Ecuador for one example.

7. The term "pluri-cultural" is the Mexican government's preferred terminology for the overall ethnic/racial composition of the Mexican state.

8. This includes a material framework utilized to support the ideology of citizenship and all its associated codes.

9. This insight also applies to the different political economic developments within this mode of production, namely neoliberalism.

10. This oversight is a by-product of the acceptance of identity politics as the preferred method for political action in the contemporary world. However, this leaves the troubling question of what form of citizenship is afforded to the demonized White male and how we go about justifying the pursuit of that ideal form by any number of marginalized groups.

11. *All Things Considered* program on KCRW radio on Tuesday, October 18, 2017, http://www.npr.org/programs/all-things-considered/.

12. Whiteness is essentially a privileged position of consumption. This would explain how tensions between upper- and lower-class Whites are framed not within a framework

of race but as issues of access, while Black groups struggling with internal tensions continue to frame success in terms of Whiteness or a lack of authentic Blackness.

13. All but two, that is, who visually appeared to be of Asian descent. These two children were later confirmed to be of Korean ancestry. Their presence may be explained by the value given to multicultural education in the United States.

14. Padre Glyn himself interpreted this discussion in a dissimilar manner as we spoke in Huaxpaltepec later in 2011. According to Padre Glyn, it was German and Martin who were responsible for naming the organization Organización Afro-Mexicana.

15. See Stephen (2007) for a counterexample.

Chapter 5. A Black Subject Position and Narrative Representations of Blackness in the Costa Chica

1. The binary of *Blanco que Negro* (White rather than Black) is a binary important to race relations on the coast and should not be read as a translation or import on the part of the researcher.

2. The residents of Chacahua have been surfing their own beach for years now. In fact, several locals have been recognized through their success in national and international surf competitions at the nearby beaches of Zicatela, in Puerto Escondido, and others such as Roca Blanca along the coast.

3. It is interesting here that the racial binary of Black and White seems to be out of context for a conversation on Mexico. However, focusing on Blackness quickly reveals that this binary is an important racial frame in Mexico that is allowed to be ignored in the absence of actual Black bodies.

4. During the 2011 "Festival MA(yo)" (May 2–15, 2011), UNAM sponsored a conference focusing on Afro-Latino issues. This conference did not feature any presentations by local activists working in the Costa Chica region, but a book, *Afro America: La Tercera Raíz*, which presented the African presence in Mexico, was available for sale at the conference. This book was published by UNAM in Veracruz and offered much of the same information focusing on routes and early African cultural forms or contributions as available at the Museo in Cuajinicuilapa, within the context of the broader region of Latin America.

5. See Lewis (2001) for other examples of a similar narrative of "the ship" in the Costa Chica.

6. Lucila's arrangement with Ecosta Yutu Cuii is project based and does not constitute employment in the sense that she is officially and gainfully employed with the nonprofit organization. Ecosta Yutu Cuii itself has very limited resources and officially employs only a handful of local residents. The organization relies heavily on volunteer labor.

7. This term, "auto-identificación," is not common among local residents. However, I have heard a number of local residents use the term in conjunction with "self-esteem" and the perceived importance of a strong racial, ethnic, and cultural self-identification.

8. *Moreno* (brown-skinned) is often a term applied to Costeños. This term is difficult to pin down, as sometimes it refers to race, explicitly referencing people of African de-

scent, while other times it refers to people of the coast in general and the effect that the ever-present sun has on skin color. This term can simultaneously include and exclude. For example, it can reference a particular rootedness within the coastal region but can also deflect race, depending upon the situation and the racial location of the person in question. There is a real distinction made by people between *moreno por el sol, o por la sangre*, and it can even be used in multiple cultural contexts.

9. I spoke with one activist and middle school teacher who explained to me that while his own political project was working toward the promotion of the historical presence of Blacks in Mexico, his official position did not allow him to incorporate this history into his rhetoric and writing curriculum as it did not fit into the recognized general curriculum approved by the state. Two women in Chacahua explained that much of the education in the small towns comes through *telesecundarias*, which utilize prerecorded video lessons that come from somewhere outside of the Costa Chica and do not offer locally relevant content such as local Indigenous and Black history. This partly explains Lucila's need to educate herself on these issues.

10. See Nixon (2005) for examples of the ways that Western conceptions of ecology and environmentalism can impose strategies of conservation that neglect Indigenous histories of land use and disregard Indigenous people's claims to land and its resources.

11. Lewis (2012, 43) demonstrates that the Costa Chica town of San Nicolas was granted an ejido in 1933. However, she explains that loose rules governing the usage of ejido land meant that larger families with more resources were able to monopolize ejido land. Therefore, despite being *ejidatarios* (belonging to ejidos and having communal land rights) many moreno farmers were unable to subsist on their own land and were forced to sell their labor to other non-Black landowners and local businessmen.

12. This stereotype is very often applied to Mexicans from the perspective of the United States, as the once-popular image of the dozing or drunk Mexican under the safety of his large sombrero next to a fence or tree or Saguaro cactus attests.

13. Padre Glyn is credited for organizing the birth of the grassroots organization Mexico Negro in the early 1990s. Originally from the Island of Trinidad, Padre Glyn had worked in the Costa Chica region for over twenty years on issues of African-descendant economic, political, and cultural empowerment.

14. Aydée Rodríguez, "Inside My Head," California African American Museum, May 7–September 27, 2009.

15. The Black movement in Mexico threatens to expose the historical processes surrounding racialization and the marginalization or exclusion of Black communities. This visibility would explicitly undermine the rhetoric of mixing and racial equality in Mexico and, in the process, implicate Mestizos and Whites in the maintenance and perpetuation of these processes. This is what is at stake in the contests between state and federal governments and local activists represented as the official consultas that were conducted during 2011. This implication is also the reason that naming, a major issue of the consultas, becomes so very important. While different signifiers may be used to refer to the same racial/ethnic group, very few have the power to implicate Whiteness—that is, to make White privilege and White supremacy hyper-visible (West 2002)—in a way similar to the racial signifier "Negro."

Conclusion: Black Visibility and the Limits of Black Recognition in Mexico

1. The state attempted to sidestep this process in the 2015 inter-census by adding several terms (*Afromexicana* and *Afrodescendiente*) as a gloss for "Black." The question reads: "According to your culture, history, and traditions, do you consider yourself to be *Negra*, that is to say Afro-Mexican [Afromexicana], or Afro-descendant [Afrodescendiente]" (author's translation)? The question asks for a yes or no answer, rather than probing to find out about preferable nomenclature. A similar version of the question was also included in the 2020 census.

2. While I have not found a philosophical treatment of the phenomenon as I discuss it here, after reflecting on the term I began to see that several authors point to "implication" as having the power to make something visible that has been taken for granted. See Ferguson (2003) and Gupta (1995) for brief examples.

3. For example, during an interview for an ongoing project, the "Youth Citizenship Narrative Project," about when people first heard and made sense of the "N-word," an African American respondent told me that he had first heard the word as a small child on US television while watching a then-popular Western. He explained that a White character had directed the word toward one of the Black characters. The respondent went on to explain that, while he did not really understand what the word meant, he felt implicated by the word because it had been directed at one of the Black characters and therefore could possibly be used to reference him as well.

References

Aguirre Beltrán, G. 1958. *Cuijla: Esbozo Etnográfico de un Pueblo Negro*. Mexico: Fondo de Cultura Economica.

Aguirre Beltrán, G. 1989. *La Población Negra de México. Estudio Etnohistórico*, 3rd edition. Mexico City: Fondo de Cultura Económica.

Althusser, Louis. 1984. *Essays on Ideology*. London: Verso.

Anderson, Mark. 2007. "When Afro Becomes (Like) Indigenous: Garifuna and Afro-Indigenous Politics in Honduras." *Journal of Latin American and Caribbean Anthropology* 12(2): 384–413.

Anderson, Mark D. 2009. *Black and Indigenous: Garifuna Activism and Consumer Culture in Honduras*. Minneapolis: University of Minnesota Press.

Andrews, George Ried. 2004. *Afro-Latin America 1800–2000*. New York: Oxford University Press.

Aparicio, Ana. 2006. *Dominican-Americans and the Politics of Empowerment*. Gainesville: University Press of Florida.

Appiah, Anthony K. 1994. "Identity, Authenticity, Survival: Multicultural Societies and Social Reproduction." In *Multiculturalism: Examining the Politics of Recognition*, edited by Amy Gutmann and Charles Taylor, 149–164. Princeton, NJ: Princeton University Press.

Appiah, Anthony K. 2005. *The Ethics of Identity*. Princeton, NJ: Princeton University Press.

Appiah, Anthony Kwame, and Henry Louis Gates Jr. 1995. *Identities*. Chicago: University of Chicago Press.

Arce, B. Christine. 2017. *México's Nobodies: The Cultural Legacy of the Soldadera and Afro-Mexican Women*. Albany: State University of New York Press.

Arocha, Jaime. 1998. "Inclusion of Afro-Colombians: Unreachable National Goal?" *Latin American Perspectives* 25(3): 70–89.

Arrizón, Alicia. 2017. "Mestizaje." In *Key Words for Latina/o Studies*, edited by Deborah R. Vargas, Nancy Raquel Mirabal, and Lawrence La Fountain-Stokes, 133–136. New York: NYU Press.

Asher, Kirin. 2009. *Black and Green: Afro-Colombians, Development, and Nature in the Pacific Lowlands*. Durham, NC: Duke University Press.

Baca, G. 2008. Neoliberalism and Stories of Racial Redemption." *Dialectical Anthropology* 32(3): 219–241.

Balibar, Étienne. 2015. *Citizenship*. Cambridge: Polity Press.

Balibar, Étienne. 2016. *Citizen Subject: Foundations for Philosophical Anthropology*. New York: Fordham University Press.

Beiner, Ronald. 1995. "Introduction: Why Citizenship Constitutes a Theoretical Problem in the Last Decade of the Twentieth Century." In *Theorizing Citizenship*, edited by Ronald Beiner, 1–28. Albany: State University of New York Press.

Beaucage, Pierre. 1994. "The Opossum and the Coyote: Ethnic Identity and Ethnohistory in the Sierra Norte de Puebla (Mexico)." In *Latin American Identity and Constructions of Difference*, edited by Amaryll Chanady, 149–186. Minneapolis: University of Minnesota Press.

Behar, Ruth. 1993. *Translated Woman: Crossing the Border with Esperanza's Story*. Boston: Beacon Press.

Bejarano, Cristina. 2017. "Unruly Genomes: Proliferations of Meanings, Effects, and Affects Produced by the Idea of a National Genome in Mexico." Unpublished Talk Delivered at UC Riverside.

Bennett, Herman L. 2003. *Africans in Colonial Mexico Absolutism, Christianity, and Afro-Creole Consciousness*. Bloomington: Indiana University Press.

Berger, Mark T. 2001. "Romancing the Zapatistas: International Intellectuals and the Chiapas Rebellion." *Latin American Perspectives* 28(2): 149–170.

Bhabha, Homi K. 1994. *The Location of Culture*. London: Routledge.

Bhabha, Homi. 1996. "Unsatisfied: Notes on Vernacular Cosmopolitanism." In *Text and Nation: Cross-Disciplinary Essays on Cultural and National Identities*, edited by Peter C. Pfeiffer and Laura García-Moreno, 191–207. Columbia: Camden House.

Bhabha, Homi. K. 2002. "Of Mimicry and Man: The Ambivalence of Colonial Discourse." In *Race Critical Theories: Text and Context*, edited by Philomena Essed and David Theo Goldberg, 113–122. Malden, MA: Blackwell Publishers.

Blanchard, Sarah, Erin R. Hamilton, Nestor Rodríguez, and Hirotoshi Yoshioka. 2011. "Shifting Trends in Central American Migration: A Demographic Examination of Increasing Honduran-U.S. Immigration and Deportation." *Latin Americanist* 55(4): 61–84.

Bourdieu, Pierre. 1986. "The Forms of Capital." In *Handbook of Theory and Research for the Sociology of Education*, edited by John Richardson, 241–258. New York: Greenwood.

Brett, Joén. 2012. "Conclusions: Culture, Tradition, and Political Economy." In *Reimagining Marginalized Foods*, edited by Elizabeth Finnis, 156–166. Tucson: University of Arizona Press.

Briggs, Charles. L. 2005. "Genealogies of Race and Culture and the Failure of Vernacular Cosmopolitanisms: Rereading Franz Boas and W.E.B. Du Bois." *Public Culture: Bulletin of the Project for Transnational Cultural Studies* 17: 75–100.

Briggs, Laura. 2016. "Central American Child Migration: Militarization and Tourism." *American Quarterly* 68(3): 573–582.

Brown, Vincent. 2009. "Social Death and Political Life in the Study of Slavery." *American Historical Review* 114(5): 1231–1249.

Bucknor, Michael A. 2012. "Dangerous Crossings: Caribbean Masculinities and the Politics of Challenging Gendered Borderlines." *Journal of West Indian Literature* 21(1/2): vii–xxx.

Butler, Judith. 1997. *The Psychic Life of Power*. Stanford, CA: Stanford University Press.

Campbell, Howard. 1994. *Zapotec Renaissance: Ethnic Politics and Cultural Revivalism in Southern Mexico*. Albuquerque: University of New Mexico Press.

Campbell, Howard, Leigh Binford, Miguel Bartolome, and Alícia Barabas. 1993. *Zapotec Struggles: History, Politics, and Representations from Juchitán, Oaxaca*. Washington: Smithsonian Institution Press.

Carroll, Patrick J. 1991. *Blacks in Colonial Veracruz: Race, Ethnicity, and Regional Development*. Austin: University of Texas Press.

Castañeda, Angela N. 2012. "Performing the African Diaspora in Mexico." In *Comparative Perspectives on Afro-Latin America*, edited by Kwame Dixon and John Burdick, 93–113. Gainesville: University Press of Florida.

Censo de Población y Vivienda. 2020. *Instituto Nacional de Estadística y Geografía*. México: INEGI. https://www.inegi.org.mx/programas/ccpv/2020/

Cerón-Anaya, Hugo. 2019. *Privilege at Play: Class, Race, Gender, and Golf in Mexico*. New York: Oxford University Press.

Césaire, Aimé. 1972. "Discourse on Colonialism." *Monthly Review Press*, 1–24.

Chassen-López, Francie R. 1998. "Maderismo or Mixtec Empire. Class and Ethnicity in the Mexican Revolution, Costa Chica of Oaxaca 1911." *The Americas* 55(1): 91–127.

Chasteen, John C. 2011. *Born in Blood and Fire: A Concise History of Latin America*. New York: W. W. Norton and Company.

Chibnik, Michael. 2003. *Crafting Tradition: The Making and Marketing of Oaxacan Wood Carvings*. Austin: University of Texas Press.

Comaroff, Jean. 2006. "The End of History Again? Pursuing the Past in the Postcolony." In *Postcolonial Studies and Beyond*, edited by Ania Loomba, Suvir Kaul, Matti Bunzl, Antoinette Burton, and Jed Esty, 125–144. Durham, NC: Duke University Press.

Comaroff, John L., and Jean Comaroff. 2009. Ethnicity, Inc. Chicago: University of Chicago Press.

Cotton, Nichole Marie, and Anthony R. Jerry. 2013. "Drawing the Lines: Racial/Ethnic Landscapes and Sustainable Development in the Costa Chica." *Journal of Pan African Studies* 6(1): 210–226.

Cox, Aimee Meredith. 2015. *Shapeshifters: Black Girls and the Choreography of Citizenship*. Durham, NC: Duke University Press.

Cummings, R. 2010. "(Tans)Nationalisms, Marronage, and Queer Caribbean Subjectivities." *Transforming Anthropology* 18(2): 169–180.

Cunin, Elisabeth, and Odile Hoffman. 2014. "Introduction to Blackness and Mestizaje in Mexico and Central America." In *Blackness and Mestizaje in Mexico and Central America*, edited by Elisabeth Cunin and Odile Hoffman, xi–xix. Trenton, NJ: Africa World Press.

Das, Veena. 2004. "The Signature of the State: The Paradox of Illegibility." In *Anthropology in the Margins of the State: Comparative Ethnographies*, edited by Veena Das and Deborah D. Poole, 225–252. Santa Fe: School of American Research Press.

Das, Veena, and Deborah D. Poole. 2004. *Anthropology in the Margins of the State*. Santa Fe: School of American Research Press.

Dawson, Allan Charles. 2014. *In Light of Africa: Globalizing Africa in North East Brazil*. Toronto: University of Toronto Press.

Dávila, Julia Isabel Flores. 2007. *Afrodescendientes en México; Reconomcimiento y Propuestas Antidiscriminación*. México City, D.F.: Consejo Nacional para Prevenir la Discriminación.

Dávila, Julia Flores, and Florence Lézé. 2007. *Procesos de construcción de identidad, condiciones de vida y discriminación: Un estudio comparativo de comunidades de los afrodescendientes en México*. XXVI Congreso de la Asociación Latinoamericana de Sociología. Asociación Latinoamericana de Sociología, Guadalajara.

De la Cadena, M. 2000. *Indigenous Mestizos*. Durham, NC: Duke University Press.

De la Fuente, Alejandro, and George Reid Andrews. 2018. "The Making of a Field: Afro-Latin American Studies." In *Afro-Latin American Studies: An Introduction*, edited by Alejandro de la Fuente and George Reid Andrews, 1–26. Cambridge: Cambridge University Press.

Derby, Lauren. 2003. "National Identity and the Idea of Value in the Dominican Republic." In *Blacks, Coloureds and National Identity in Nineteenth-Century Latin America*, edited by Nancy Priscilla Naro, 5–37. London: Institute of Latin American Studies.

Diaz Pérez, Maria Christina. 1995. *Descripcion Etnografica de las Relaciones de Parentesco en Tres Comunidades Afromestizas de la Costa Chica de Guerrero*. México, D.F.: Escuala Nacional de Antropologia e Historia.

Dixon, Kwame, and John Burdick. 2012. "Introduction." In *Comparative Perspectives on Afro-Latin America*, edited by Kwame Dixon and John Burdick, 1–20. Gainesville: University Press of Florida.

Du Bois, W.E.B. 1968. *Dusk of Dawn: An Essay Toward an Autobiography of a Race Concept*. New York: Schocken Books.

Du Bois, W.E.B. 2007. *The Souls of Black Folk*. Oxford: Oxford University Press.

Du Bois, W.E.B. 2014. *The Word and Africa and Color and Democracy*. Oxford: Oxford University Press.

Duran de Huerta, Marta. 2000. "An Interview with Subcomandante Insurgente Marcos, Spokesperson and Military Commander of the Zapatista National Liberation Army (EZLN)." *International Affairs* 75(2): 269–279.

Edwards, Brent H. 2003. *The Practice of Diaspora: Literature, Translation, and the Rise of Black Internationalism*. Cambridge, MA: Harvard University Press.

Eisenstadt, Todd A. 2006. "Indigenous Attitudes and Ethnic Identity Construction in Mexico." *Mexican Studies/Estudios Mexicanos* 22(1): 107–130.

Elyachar, Julia. 2005. *Markets of Dispossession: NGOs, Economic Development, and the State in Cairo*. Durham, NC: Duke University Press.

Encuesta Intercensal 2015. 2017. *Perfil Sociodemográfico de la Población Afrodescendiente en México / Instituto Nacional de Estadística y Geografía*. México: INEGI.

Escobar, Arturo. 2008. *Territories of Difference: Place, Movements, Life, Redes*. Durham, NC: Duke University Press.

Espeland, Wendy Nelson, Stevens L. Mitchell. 1998. "Commensuration as a Social Process." *Annual Review of Sociology* 24: 313–343.

Falola, Toyin, and Matt D. Childs. 2004. *The Yoruba Diaspora in the Atlantic World*. Bloomington: Indiana University Press.

Fanon, Frantz. 2008. *Black Skin, White Masks*. New York: Grove Press.

Feldman, Heidi Carolyn. 2012. "Strategies of the Black Pacific: Music and Diasporic Identity in Peru." In *Comparative Perspectives on Afro-Latin America*, edited by Kwame Dixon and John Burdick, 42–71. Gainesville: University Press of Florida.

Ferguson, Roderick. A. 2003. *Aberrations in Black: Toward a Queer of Color Critique.* Minneapolis: University of Minnesota Press.

Fields, Barabara J. 1990. "Slavery, Race, and Ideology in the United States of America." *New Left Review* 0(181): 95–118.

Fields, Barabara J. 2003. "Of Rogues and Geldings." *American Historical Review* 108(5): 1397–1405. https://doi.org/10.1086/ahr/108.5.1397

Flathman, Richard E. 1995. "Citizenship and Authority: A Chastened View of Citizenship." In *Theorizing Citizenship*, edited by Ronald Beiner, 105–152. Albany: State University of New York Press.

Gamio, Manuel. August 1929. "Observations on Mexican Immigration into the United States." *Pacific Affairs* 2(8): 463–469.

García Orozco, Merced Dalia. 2010. *Collantes, una Localidad de la Costa Chica del Estado de Oaxaca, y de la Evocación Afromestiza en el arte de Cocinar.* México: Escuela Nacional de Antropología e Historia.

Gillingham, Paul. 2011. *Cuauhtémoc's Bones: Forging National Identity in Modern Mexico.* Albuquerque: University of New Mexico Press.

Gilroy, Paul. 1993. *The Black Atlantic: Modernity and Double Consciousness.* Cambridge, MA: Harvard University Press.

Godreau, I. 2002. "Changing Space, Making Race: Distance, Nostalgia, and the Folklorization of Blackness in Puerto Rico." *Identities* 9(3), 281–304.

Godreau, Isar P. 2006. "'Folkloric Others': Blanqueamiento and the Celebration of Blackness as an Exception in Puerto Rico." In *Globalization and Race: Transformation in the Cultural Production of Blackness*, edited by Kamari Maxine Clarke and Deborah A. Thomas, 171–187. Durham, NC: Duke University Press.

Godreau, Isar P., Mariolga Reyes Cruz, Mariluz Franco Ortiz, and Sherry Cuadrado. 2008. "The Lessons of Slavery: Discourses of Slavery, Mestizaje, and Blanqueamiento in an Elementary School in Puerto Rico." *American Ethnologist* 35(1): 115–135.

Goett, Jennifer. 2011. "Citizens or Anti-Citizens? Afro-Descendants and Counter Narcotics Policing in Multicultural Nicaragua." *Journal of Latin American and Caribbean Anthropology* 16(2): 354–379.

Gohar, Saddik. M. 2008. "The Dialectics of Homeland and Identity: Reconstructing Africa in the Poetry of Langston Hughes and Mohamed Al-Fayturi." *Tydskrif vir Letterkunde* 45(1): 42–74.

Goldberg, David Theo. 2002. *The Racial State.* Malden, MA: Blackwell Publishers.

Gomez, Michael A. 1998. *Exchanging Our Country Marks: The Transformation of African Identities in the Colonial and Antebellum South.* Chapel Hill: University of North Carolina Press.

Gordon, Edmund T. 1998. *Disparate Diasporas: Identity and Politics in an African Nicaraguan Community.* Austin: University of Texas Press, Austin, Institute of Latin American Studies.

Gordon, Edmund T., and Mark Anderson. 1999. "The African Diaspora: Toward an Ethnography of Diasporic Identification." *Journal of American Folklore* 112(445): 282–296.

Graeber, David. 2001. *Toward an Anthropological Theory of Value: The False Coin of Our Own Dreams*. New York: Palgrave.

Greene, Shane. 2007. "Introduction: On Race, Roots/Routes, and Sovereignty in Latin America's Afro-Indigenous Multiculturalisms." *Journal of Latin American and Caribbean Anthropology* 12(2): 329–355.

Greene, Shane. 2012. "Todos Somos Iguales, Todos Somos Incas: Dilemmas of Afro-Peruvian Citizenship and Inca Whiteness in Peru." In *Comparative Perspectives on Afro-Latin America*, edited by Kwame Dixon and John Burdick, 282–304. Gainesville: University Press of Florida.

Grieves, Maggie, Marina Adler, and Robin King. 2014. "To Preserve the Mountains and the Community: Indigenous Ecotourism as a Sustainable Development Strategy." *Social Thought and Research* 33: 83–11.

Guardino, Peter F. 1996. *Peasants, Politics, and the Formation of Mexico's National State: Guerrero, 1800–1857*. Stanford, CA: Stanford University Press.

Gupta, Akhil. 1995. "Blurred Boundaries: The Discourse of Corruption, the Culture of Politics, and the Imagined State." *American Ethnologist* 22(2): 375–402.

Gwynne, Robert N., and Cristobal Kay. 2000. "Views from the Periphery: Futures of Neoliberalism in Latin America." *Third World Quarterly* 21(1): 141–156.

Hale, Charles R. 1997. "Cultural Politics of Identity in Latin America." *Annual Review of Anthropology* 26: 567–590.

Hale, Charles R. 2002. "Does Multiculturalism Menace?: Governance, Cultural Rights, and the Politics of Identity in Guatemala." *Journal of Latin American Studies* 343: 485–524.

Hale, Charles R. 2005. "Neoliberal Multiculturalism: The Remaking of Cultural Rights and Racial Dominance in Central America." *PoLAR* 28(1): 10–28.

Hall, Stuart. 1980. "Race, Articulation, and Societies Structured in Dominance." In *Sociological Theories: Race and Colonialism*, edited by UNESCO, 305–345. Paris: UNESCO.

Hall, Stuart. 1994. "Cultural Identity and Diaspora." In *Colonial Discourse and Post-Colonial Theory: A Reader*, edited by Patrick Williams and Laura Chrisman, 222–237. New York: Columbia University Press.

Hall, Stuart. 2001. "Constituting an Archive." *Third Text* 15(54): 89–92. DOI: 10.1080/09528820108576903

Hanchard, Michael. G. 1994. *Orpheus and Power: The Movimento Negro of Rio de Janeiro and Sao Paulo, Brazil, 1945–1988*. Princeton, NJ: Princeton University Press.

Hanchard, Michael G. 1999. "Afro-Modernity: Temporality, Politics, and the African Diaspora." *Public Culture* 11(1): 245–268.

Handler, Richard. 1988. *Nationalism and the Politics of Culture in Quebec*. Madison: University of Wisconsin Press.

Harris, Cheryl I. 1993. "Whiteness as Property." *Harvard Law Review* 106(8): 1707–1791.

Harris, Leonard. 2009. "Cosmopolitanism and the African Renaissance: Pixley I. Seme and Alain L. Locke." *International Journal of African Renaissance Studies: Multi-, Inter- and Transdisciplinarity* 4(2): 181–192.

Harrison, Faye V. 1995. "The Persistent Power of 'Race' in the Cultural and Political Economy of Racism." *Annual Review of Anthropology* 24: 47–74.

Hartman, Saidiya. 1997. *Scenes of Subjection: Terror, Slavery, and Self-Making in Nineteenth-Century America*. New York: Oxford University Press.

Hébert, Martin and Michael Gabriel Rosen. 2007. "Forestry and the Paradoxes of Citizenship in Mexico: The Cases of Oaxaca and Guerrero." *Canadian Journal of Latin American and Caribbean Studies* 32(63): 9–43.

Hernández Cuevas, Marco Polo. 2004. *African Mexicans and the Discourse on Modern Nation*. Lanham, MD: University Press of America.

Herskovits, Melville. J. 1958. *The Myth of the Negro Past*. Boston: Beacon Press.

Heuman, Gad. 2014. *The Caribbean: A Brief History*. London: Bloomsbury.

Hobsbawm, Eric, and Terrance Ranger. 1983. *The Invention of Tradition*. Cambridge: Cambridge University Press.

Hoffman, Odile. 2006. "Negros y Afromestizos en México: Viejas y Nuevas Lecturas de un Mundo Olvidado" [Blacks and Afromestizos in Mexico: New and old readings of a forgotten world]. *Revista Mexicana De Sociología* 68(1): 103–135.

Hoffman, Odile. 2007. "De las 'Tres Razas' Razas al Mestizaje: Diversidad de las Reprentaciones Colectivas Acerca de lo 'Negro' en Mexico (Veracruz y Costa Chica)." *Diario de Campo, Suplemento* 42: 98–107.

Hoffman, Odile. 2014. "The Renaissance of Afro-Mexican Studies." In *Blackness and Mestizaje in Mexico and Central America*, edited by Elisabeth Cunin and Odile Hoffman, 81–116. Trenton, NJ: Africa World Press.

Hoffman, Odile, and Christian Rinaudo. 2014. "The Issue of Blackness and Mestizaje in Two Distinct Mexican Contexts: Veracruz and Costa Chica." *Latin American and Caribbean Ethnic Studies* 9(2): 138–155.

Hook, Derek. 2004. "Fanon and the Psychoanalysis of Racism" [online]. London: LSE Research Online. http://eprints.lse.ac.uk/2567.

Hooker, Juliet. 2005. "Indigenous Inclusion/Black Exclusion: Race, Ethnicity and Multicultural Citizenship in Latin America." *Journal of Latin American Studies* 372: 285–310.

Hooker, Juliet. 2009. *Race and the Politics of Solidarity*. Oxford: Oxford University Press.

Howe, Stephen. 1998. *Afrocentrism: Mythical Pasts and Imagined Homes*. London; New York: Verso.

Huerta, Itza Amanda Varela. 2019. "Nunca Más un México Sin Nosotros: Femenismo y Mujeres Afromexicanas." *Política y Cultura* 51: 105–124.

Huerta, Itza Amanda Varela. 2021. "Mujeres negras-afromexicanas en el movimiento político afrodescendiente: una genealogía." *A Contra Corriente* 19(1): 190–208.

Huet, Nahayelli Juárez. 2014. "The Transnational Networks and re-Africanization of the Santería in Mexico City." In *Blackness and Mestizaje in Mexico and Central America*, edited by Elisabeth Cunin and Odile Hoffman, 165–190. Trenton, NJ: Africa World Press.

Ignatieff, Michael. 1995. "The Myth of Citizenship." In *Theorizing Citizenship*, edited by Ronald Beiner, 53–78. Albany: State University of New York Press.

Israel, Jonathan Irvine. 1975. *Race, Class and Politics in Colonial Mexico, 1610–1670*. Oxford: Oxford University Press.

James, C.L.R. 1989. *The Black Jacobins: Toussaint L'Ouverture and the San Domingo Revolution*. New York. Vintage Books.

James, C.L.R. 2009. *You Don't Play with Revolution: The Montréal Lectures of C.L.R. James.* Edinburgh: AK Press.

Jeganathan, Pradeep. 2004. "Checkpoint: Anthropology, Identity, and the State." In *Anthropology in the Margins of the State,* edited by Veena Das and Deborah Poole, 67–80. Santa Fe: School of American Research Press, 67–80.

Jerry, Anthony Russell. 2018. "'The First Time I Heard the Word': The 'N-Word' as a Present and Persistent Racial Epithet." *Transforming Anthropology* 26(1): 36–49.

Jerry, Anthony Russell. 2021. "From Colonial Subjects to Post-Colonial Citizens? Considerations for a Contemporary Study of Black México." *Third World Quarterly.* DOI: 10.1080/01436597.2021.1951606.

Jones, Jennifer A. 2018. "Afro-Latinos: Speaking through Silences and Rethinking the Geographies of Blackness." In *Afro-Latin American Studies: An Introduction,* edited by Alejandro de la Fuente and George Reid Andrews, 569–614. Cambridge: Cambridge University Press.

Jones, Jennifer Anne Meri. 2013. "'Mexicans Will Take the Jobs That Even Blacks Won't Do': An Analysis of Blackness, Regionalism and Invisibility in Contemporary Mexico." *Ethnic and Racial Studies* 36(10): 1564–1581.

Joseph, Gilbert M., and Jürgen Buchenau. 2013. *Mexico's Once and Future Revolution: Social Upheaval and the Challenge of Rule Since the Late Nineteenth Century.* Durham, NC: Duke University Press.

Kallhoff, A. 2013. "Consumer Citizenship: A Self-Contradictory Concept." In *The Ethics of Consumption: The Citizen, the Market and the Law,* edited by Per Sandin and H. Helen Röcklinsberg, 177–182. Wageningen: Wageningen Academic Publishers 2013.

Kazanjian, David. 2003. *The Colonizing Trick: National Culture and Imperial Citizenship in Early America.* Minneapolis: University of Minnesota Press.

Kearney, Michael. 2000. "Transnational Oaxacan Indigenous Identity: The Case of Mixtecs and Zapotecs." *Identities Global Studies in Culture and Power* 7(2): 173–195. DOI: 10.1080/1070289X.2000.9962664

Knight, Alan. 1990. "Racism, Revolution, and Indigenismo: Mexico, 1910–1940." In *The Idea of Race in Latin America,* edited by Richard Graham, Thomas E. Skidmore, and Aline Helg, 73–94. Austin: University of Texas Press.

Lara, Gloria. 2014. "An Ethno-Political Trend on the Costa Chica, Mexico (1980–2000)." In *Blackness and Mestizaje in Mexico and Central America,* edited by Elisabeth Cunin and Odile Hoffman, 117–138. Trenton, NJ: Africa World Press.

Larson, Brokke. 2004. *Trials of Nation Making: Liberalism, Race, and Ethnicity in the Andes, 1810–1910.* Cambridge: Cambridge University Press.

Lewis, Laura A. 2000. "Blacks, Black Indians, Afromexicans: The Dynamics of Race, Nation and Identity in a Mexican Moreno Community (Guerrero)." *American Ethnologist: The Journal of the American Ethnological Society* 27(4): 898–926.

Lewis, Laura A. 2001. "Of Ships and Saints: History, Memory, and Place in the Making of Moreno Mexican Identity." *Cultural Anthropology* 16(1): 62–82.

Lewis, Laura A. 2003. *Hall of Mirrors: Power, Witchcraft, and Caste in Colonial Mexico.* Durham, NC: Duke University Press.

Lewis, Laura A. 2006. "Home Is Where the Heart Is: Afro-Latino Migration and Cinder-Block Homes on Mexico's Costa Chica." *South Atlantic Quarterly* 105(4): 801.

Lewis, Laura A. 2012. *Chocolate and Corn Flour: History, Race, and Place in the Making of "Black" Mexico*. Durham, NC: Duke University Press.

Lipsitz, George. 2006. *The Possessive Investment in Whiteness: How White People Profit from Identity Politics*. Philadelphia: Temple University Press.

Lomnitz, Claudio. 1999. "Modes of Citizenship in Mexico." *Public Culture: Bulletin of the Project for Transnational Cultural Studies* 11(1): 269.

Lomnitz, Claudio. 2001. *Deep Mexico, Silent Mexico: An Anthropology of Nationalism*. Minneapolis: University of Minnesota Press.

Lomnitz, Claudio. 2007. "Foundations of the Latin American Left." *Public Culture: Bulletin of the Project for Transnational Cultural Studies* 19(1): 23–28.

Lomnitz, Claudio. 2008. "Narrating the Neoliberal Moment: History, Journalism, Historicity." *Public Culture: Bulletin of the Project for Transnational Cultural Studies* 20(1): 39–56.

Lomnitz-Adler, Claudio. 1992. *Exits from the Labyrinth: Culture and Ideology in the Mexican National Space*. Berkeley: University of California Press.

Lucero, Jose Antonio. 2006. "Representing 'Real Indians': The Challenges of Indigenous Authenticity and Strategic Constructivism in Ecuador and Bolivia." *Latin American Research Review*, 41(2): 31–56.

Lucero, José Antonio. 2008. *Struggles of Voice: The Politics of Indigenous Representation in the Andes*. Pittsburgh: University of Pittsburgh Press.

Lugo, Alejandro. 2000. "Theorizing Border Inspections." *Cultural Dynamics* 12(3): 353–373.

Lugo, Alejandro. 2008. *Fragmented Lives, Assembled Parts: Culture, Capitalism, and Conquest at the U.S.-Mexico Border*. Austin: University of Texas Press.

Macpherson, C. B. 1978. "The Meaning of Property." In *Property: Mainstream and Critical Positions*, edited by C. B. Macpherson. Toronto: University of Toronto Press.

Mallon, Florencia E. 1994. "The Promise and Dilemma of Subaltern Studies: Perspectives from Latin American History." *American Historical Review* 99(5): 1491–1515.

Mallon, Florencia E. 1995. *Peasant and Nation: The Making of Postcolonial Mexico and Peru*. Berkeley: University of California Press.

Mallon, Florencia. 2011. "Indigenous Peoples and Nation States in Latin America." *In Oxford Handbook of Latin American History*, edited by Jose C. Moya, 282–308. New York: Oxford University Press.

Martínez-Echazábal, L. 1998. "'Mestizaje' and the Discourse of National/Cultural Identity in Latin America, 1845–1959." *Latin American Perspectives: A Journal of Capitalism and Socialism* 25(3): 21–42.

McGraw, Jason. (2014). *The Work of Recognition: Caribbean Colombia and the Postemancipation Struggle for Citizenship*. Chapel Hill: University of North Carolina Press.

McKittrick, Katherine. 2006. *Demonic Grounds: Black Women and the Cartographies of Struggle*. Minneapolis: University of Minnesota Press.

Melucci, A. 1985. "The Symbolic Challenge of Contemporary Movements." *Social Research* 52(4): 789–816.

Menchaca, Martha. 2001. *Recovering History, Reconstructing Race: The Indian, Black, and White Roots of Mexican Americans*. Austin: University of Texas Press.

Menjívar, Cecilia, and Leisy Abrego. 2012. "Legal Violence: Immigration Law and the

Lives of Central American Immigrants." *American Journal of Sociology* 117(5): 1380–1421. doi:10.1086/663575

Michaels, Walter Ben. 1992. "Race into Culture: A Critical Genealogy of Cultural Identity." *Critical Inquiry* 18(4): 655–685.

Mills, Charles W. 2014. "White Time: The Chronic Injustice of Ideal Theory." *Du Bois Review* 11(1): 27–42.

Mirmotahari, E. 2012. "Mapping Race: The Discourse of Blackness in Rudolph Fisher's Walls of Jericho." *Journal of African American Studies* 16(3): 574–587.

Molina, Natalia. 2010. "The Power of Racial Scripts: What the History of Mexican Immigration to the United States Teaches Us about Relational Notions of Race." *Latino Studies* 8(2): 156–175. DOI:10.1057/lst.2010.20

Moreno Figueroa, Mónica G. 2010. "Distributed Intensities: Whiteness, Mestizaje and the Logics of Mexican Racism." *Ethnicities* 10(3): 387–401.

Moreno Figueroa, Mónica G. 2020. "De qué sirve el asco? Racismo Anti-Negro en México." *Revista de la Universidad de México, Septiembre*: 63–67.

Moreno Figueroa, Mónica G., and Emiko Saldívar Tanaka. 2016. "'We Are Not Racists, We Are Mexican': Privilege, Nationalism and Post-Race Ideology in Mexico." *Critical Sociology* 42(4–5): 515–533.

Moten, Fred. 2003. *In the Break: The Aesthetics of the Black Radical Tradition*. Minneapolis: University of Minnesota Press.

Mullen, Harryette. 1994. "Optic White: Blackness and the Production of Whiteness." *Diacritics* 24(2/3): 71–89.

Napolitano, Valentina. 2002. *Migration, Mujercitas, and Medicine Men: Living in Urban Mexico*. Berkeley: University of California Press.

Nash, June. 2003. "Indigenous Development Alternatives." *Urban Anthropology and Studies of Cultural Systems and World Economic Development* 32(1): 57–98.

Neyazi, Taberez Ahmed. 2010. "Cultural Imperialism or Vernacular Modernity? Hindi Newspapers in a Globalizing India." *Media, Culture, and Society* 32(6): 907–924.

Ng'weno, Bettina. 2007. "Can Ethnicity Replace Race? Afro-Colombians, Indigeneity and the Colombian Multicultural State." *Journal of Latin American and Caribbean Anthropology* 12(2): 414–440.

Ng'weno, Bettina. 2012. "Beyond Citizenship as We Know It: Race and Ethnicity in Afro-Colombian Struggles for Citizenship Equality." In *Comparative Perspectives on Afro-Latin America*, edited by Kwame Dixon and John Burdick, 156–175. Gainesville: University Press of Florida.

Nixon, Rob. 2005. "Environmentalism and Postcolonialism." In *Postcolonial Studies and Beyond*, edited by Ania Loomba, Suvir Kaul, Matti Bunzl, Antoinette Burton, and Jed Esty, 233–251. Durham, NC: Duke University Press.

Oliver, Kelly. 2004. *The Colonization of Psychic Space: A Psychoanalytic Social Theory of Oppression*. Minneapolis: University of Minnesota Press.

Omi, M., and H. Winant. 1994. *Racial Formation in the United States: From the 1960s to the 1990s*. New York: Routledge.

Palmié, Stephan, and Charles Stewart. 2016. "Introduction: For an Anthropology of History." *Journal of Ethnographic Theory* 6(1): 207–236.

Paschel, Tianna S. 2016. *Becoming Black Political Subjects: Movements and Ethno-Racial Rights in Colombia and Brazil.* Princeton, NJ: Princeton University Press.

Patterson, Orlando. 1982. *Slavery and Social Death: A Comparative Study.* Cambridge, MA: Harvard University Press.

Poole, Deborah. 2004. "Between Threat and Guarantee: Justice and Community in the Margins of the Peruvian State." In *Anthropology in the Margins of the State*, edited by Veena Das and Deborah Poole, 35–66. Santa Fe: School of American Research Press.

Postero, Nancy Grey. 2007. *Now We Are Citizens: Indigenous Politics in Postmulticultural Bolivia.* Stanford, CA: Stanford University Press.

Pratt, Mary Louise. 1992. *Imperial Eyes: Travel Writing and Transculturation.* London: Routledge.

Ramirez Rios, Bernardo. 2019. *Transnational Sport in the American West: Oaxaca California Basketball.* Washington: Lexington Books.

Ramirez Rios, Bernardo, and Anthony Russell Jerry. 2020. "Transnational Migration, Racial Economies, and the Limitations to Membership." In *Handbook of Culture and Migration*, edited by Jeffery H. Cohen and Ibrahim Sirkeci, 219–223. Cheltenham: Edgar Elgar Publishing.

Ramsay, Paulette A. 2016. *Afro-Mexican Constructions of Diaspora, Gender, Identity, and Nation.* Kingston: University of the West Indies Press.

Rand McNally and Company. 1929. *Rand McNally World Atlas.* New York: Rand McNally.

Ranger, Terrence. 1983. "The Invention of Tradition in Colonial Africa." In *The Invention of Tradition*, edited by Eric Hobsbawm and Terrence Ranger, 211–262. Cambridge: Cambridge University Press.

Restall, Matthew. 2000. "Black Conquistadors: Armed Africans in Early Spanish America." *The Americas* 57(2): 171–205.

Restall, Matthew, and Ben Vinson III. 2009. *Black Mexico: Race and Society from Colonial to Modern Times.* Albuquerque: University of New Mexico Press.

Restrepo, Eduardo. 2002. "Políticas de la Alteridad: Etnización de 'Comunidad Negra' en el Pacífico sur Colombiano." *Journal of Latin American Anthropology* 7(2): 34–58.

Rinaudo, Christian. 2014. "Mestizaje and Ethnicity in the City of Veracruz, Mexico." In *Blackness and Mestizaje in Mexico and Central America*, edited by Elisabeth Cunin and Odile Hoffman, 139–164. Trenton, NJ: Africa World Press.

Ritter, Jonathan. 2011. "Chocolate, Coconut, and Honey: Race, Music, and the Politics of Hybridity in the Ecuadorian Black Pacific." *Popular Music and Society* 34(5): 571–592.

Robinson, Cedric J. 1983. *Black Marxism.* Chapel Hill: University of North Carolina Press.

Robinson, Cedric J. 2007. *Forgeries of Memory and Meaning: Blacks and the Regimes of Race in American Theater and Film before World War II.* Chapel Hill: University of North Carolina Press.

Robinson, Cedric J. 2019. *Cedric J. Robinson: On Racial Capitalism, Black Internationalism, and Cultures of Resistance*, edited by H.L.T. Quan. London: Pluto Press.

Rodríguez Lopez, A. 2009. "Inside My Head." California African American Museum, May 7–September 27.

Roque Ramirez, Horacio. N. 2003. "'That's My Place!': Negotiating Racial, Sexual, and

Gender Politics in San Francisco's Gay Latino Alliance, 1975–1983." *Journal of the History of Sexuality* 12(2): 224–258.

Roque Ramirez, Horacio N. 2005. "A Living Archive of Desire: Teresita La Campesina and the Embodiment of Queer Latino Community Histories." In *Archive Stories: Facts, Fictions, and the Writing of History*, edited by Antoinette Burton, 111–135. Durham, NC: Duke University Press.

Roque Ramirez, Horacio. N. 2007. "'Mira, Yo Soy Boricua y Estoy Aqui': Rafa Negra's Pan Dulce and the Queer Sonic Latinaje of San Francisco." *CENTRO Journal* XIX(1): 274–317.

Rosaldo, Michelle Zimbalist. 1980. "The Use and Abuse of Anthropology: Reflections on Feminism and Cross-Cultural Understanding." *Signs* 5(3): 389–417.

Rosaldo, Michelle Zimbalist, and Louise Lamphere. 1974. *Woman, Culture, and Society*. Stanford, CA: Stanford University Press.

Rosaldo, Renato. 1989. *Culture and Truth: The Remaking of Social Analysis*. Boston: Beacon Press Books.

Safa, Helen I. 1998. "Introduction." *Latin American Perspectives* 25(3): 3–20.

Safa, Helen I. 2005. "Challenging Mestizaje." *Critique of Anthropology* 25(3): 307–330.

Sahlins, Marshall. 1985. *Islands of History*. Chicago: University of Chicago Press.

Sahlins, Marshall. 1993. "Goodby to Tristes Tropes: Ethnography in the Context of Modern World History." *Journal of Modern History* 65(1): 1–25.

Saldaña-Portillo, María Josefina. 2003. *The Revolutionary Imagination in the Americas and the Age of Development*. Durham, NC: Duke University Press.

Saldívar, Emiko. 2014. "'It's Not Race, It's Culture': Untangling Racial Politics in Mexico." *Latin American and Caribbean Ethnic Studies* 9(1): 89–108.

Saldívar, Emiko, and Casey Walsh. 2014. "Racial and Ethnic Identities in Mexican Statistics." *Journal of Iberian and Latin American Research* 20(3): 455–475.

Secretaria de Asuntos Indigenas. 1998. "Ley de derechos de los pueblos y comunidades indigenas del estado de Oaxaca." Oaxaca: Gobierno del Estado de Oaxaca.

Sewell Jr., William H. 2005. *Logics of History: Social Theory and Social Transformation*. Chicago: University of Chicago Press.

Shachar, Ayalet, and Ran Hirschl. 2007. "Citizenship as Inherited Property." *Political Theory* 35(3): 253–287.

Shavit, Yaacov. 2001. History in Black: African-Americans in Search of an Ancient Past. London: Frank Cass.

Shay, Anthony. 2002. *Choreographic Politics: State Folk Dance Companies, Representation, and Power*. Middletown, CT: Wesleyan University Press.

Smith, Adam, and Edwin Cannan. 2000. *The Wealth of Nations*. New York: Modern Library.

Speed, Shannon. 2005. "Dangerous Discourses: Human Rights and Multiculturalism in Neoliberal Mexico." *Political and Legal Anthropology Review* 28(1): 29–51.

Stephen, Lynn. 2007. *Transborder Lives: Indigenous Oaxacans in Mexico, California, and Oregon*. Durham, NC: Duke University Press.

Stoler, Ann Laura. 2008. "Imperial Debris: Reflections on Ruins and Ruination." *Cultural Anthropology* 23(2): 191–219.

Sue, Christina A. 2010. "Racial Ideologies, Racial-Group Boundaries, and Racial Identity in Veracruz, Mexico." *Latin American and Caribbean Ethnic Studies* 5(3): 273–299.

Sue, Christina A. 2013. *Land of the Cosmic Race: Race Mixture, Racism, and Blackness in Mexico*. New York: Oxford University Press.

Taussig, Michael. 1987. *Shamanism, Colonialism and the Wild Man: A Study in Terror and Healing*. Chicago: University of Chicago Press.

Taussig, Michael. 1993. *Mimesis and Alterity: A Particular History of the Senses*. London: Routledge.

Taylor, Charles. 1994. "The Politics of Recognition." In *Multiculturalism: Examining the Politics of Recognition*, edited by Amy Gutmann and Charles Taylor, 25–74. Princeton, NJ: Princeton University Press.

Telles, Edward E. 2004. *Race in Another America: The Significance of Skin Color in Brazil*. Princeton, NJ: Princeton University Press.

Telles, Edward, and Denia Garcia. 2013. "'Mestizaje' and Public Opinion in Latin America." *Latin American Research Review* 48(3): 130–152.

Telles, Edward, and the Project on Ethnicity and Race in Latin America (PERLA). 2014. *Pigmentocracies: Ethnicity, Race, and Color in Latin America*. Chapel Hill: University of North Carolina Press.

Troike, Nancy P. 1978. "Fundamental Changes in the Interpretations of the Mixtec Codices." *American Antiquity* 43(4): 553–568.

Trouillot, Michel-Rolph. 1984. "Caribbean Peasantries and World Capitalism: An Approach to Micro-Level Studies." *New West Indian Guide* 58(1/2): 37–59.

Trouillot, Michel-Rolph. 1992. "The Caribbean Region: An Open Frontier in Anthropological Theory." *Annual Review of Anthropology* 21: 19–42.

Trouillot, Michel-Rolph. 1995. *Silencing the Past: Power and the Production of History*. Boston: Beacon Press.

Turner, Bryan S., and Peter Hamilton. 1994. *Citizenship: Critical Concepts*. London: Routledge.

Tutino, John. 1993. "Ethnic Resistance: Juchitán in Mexican History." In *Zapotec Struggles: Histories, Politics, and Representations from Juchitán, Oaxaca*, edited by Howard Campbell, Leigh Binford, Miguel Bartolome, and Alícia Barabas, 41–61. Washington: Smithsonian Institution Press.

UNESCO. 2014. "The Slave Route, 1994–2014: The Road Travelled. Paris: UNESCO. https://unesdoc.unesco.org/ark:/48223/pf0000228475

Vasconcelos, Jose. 1997. *The Cosmic Race: A Bilingual Edition*. Baltimore: Johns Hopkins University Press.

Vasquez, Irene A. 2010. "The Long Durée of Africans in Mexico: The Historiography of Racialization, Acculturation, and Afro-Mexican Subjectivity." *Journal of African American History* 95(2): 183–201.

Vaughn, Bobby. 2001. "Race and Nation: A Study of Blackness in Mexico." PhD dissertation. Stanford, CA: Stanford University Press.

Vaughn, Bobby. 2005a. "The African Diaspora through Ojos Mexicanos: Blackness and Mexicanidad in Southern Mexico." *Review of Black Political Economy* 33(1): 49–57.

Vaughn, Bobby. 2005b. "Afro-Mexico: Blacks, Indigenas, Politics, and the Greater Diaspora." In *Neither Friends nor Enemies: Latinos, Blacks, Afro-Latinos*, edited by Anani Dzidzienyo and Suzanne Oboler, 117–136. New York: Palgrave Macmillan.

Villareal, Andrés. 2010. "Stratification by Skin Color in Contemporary Mexico." *American Sociological Review* 75(5): 652–678.

Vincent, Ted. 1994. "The Blacks Who Freed Mexico." *Journal of Negro History* 79(3): 257–276.

Vinson III, Ben. 2001. *Bearing Arms for His Majesty: The Free-Colored Militia in Colonial Mexico*. Stanford: Stanford University Press.

Vinson III, Ben. 2005a. "Afro-Mexican History: Trends and Directions in Scholarship." *History Compass* 3: 1–14.

Vinson III, Ben. 2005b. "Fading from Memory: Historigraphical Reflections on the Afro-Mexican Presence." *Review of Black Political Economy*, Summer: 59–72.

Vinson III, Ben, and Matthew Restall. 2009. *Black Mexico: Race and Society from Colonial to Modern Times*. Albuquerque: University of New Mexico Press.

Vinson III, Ben, and Bobby Vaughn. 2004. *Afroméxico*. Mexico: Fondo de Cultura Económica.

Von Germeten, Nicole. 2006. *Black Blood Brothers: Confraternities and Social Mobility for AfroMexicans*. Gainesville: University Press of Florida.

Wade, Peter. 1993. *Blackness and Race Mixture: The Dynamics of Racial Identity in Colombia*. Baltimore: Johns Hopkins University Press.

Wade, Peter. 2001. "Racial Identity and Nationalism: A Theoretical View from Latin America." *Ethnic and Racial Studies* 24(5): 845–865.

Wade, Peter. 2005. "Rethinking 'Mestizaje': Ideology and Lived Experience." *Journal of Latin American Studies* 37(2): 239–257.

Wade, Peter. 2010. *Race and Ethnicity in Latin America*. London: Pluto Press.

Wade, Peter, Michiel Baud, Arturo Escobar, Jean Muteba Rahier, Livio Sansone, Carlos Alberto Uribe, Fernando Urrea Giraldo, and Jim Weil. 1999. "Working Culture: Making Cultural Identities in Cali, Colombia." *Current Anthropology* 40(4): 449–471.

Walters, Ronald W. 1993. *Pan Africanism in the African Diaspora: An Analysis of Modern Afrocentric Political Movements*. Detroit: Wayne State University Press.

Ward, Henry George. 1829. *Mexico: His Majesty's Chargé D'Affaires in that Country During the Years 1825, 1826, and Part of 1827 with and Account of the Mining Companies and of the Political Events in that Republic, to the Present Day*. London: Henry Colburn, New Burlington Street.

Warren, Jonathan W. 2001. *Racial Revolutions: Antiracism and Indian Resurgence in Brazil*. Durham, NC: Duke University Press.

West, Cornel. 2002. "A Genealogy of Modern Racism." In *Critical Theories: Text and Context*, edited by Philomena Essed and David Theo Goldberg, 90–112. Malden: Blackwell Publishers.

Whitten, Norman E., and Arlene Torres 1992. "Blackness in the Americas." *Report on the Americas* 25(4): 16–46.

Whitten, Norman E., and Arlene Torres. 1998. *Blackness in Latin America and the Caribbean: Social Dynamics and Cultural Transformations*, Vol. 1. Bloomington: Indiana University Press.

Wianant, Howard. 1994. *Racial Conditions: Politics, Theory, Comparisons*. Minneapolis: University of Minnesota Press.

Wilderson III, Frank B. 2020. *Afropessimism*. New York: Liveright Publishing Corporation.

Williams, Brackette F. 1989. "A Class Act: Anthropology and the Race to Nation across Ethnic Terrain." *Annual Review of Anthropology* 18: 401–444.

Wilson, David. 2009. Introduction: Racialized Poverty in U.S. Cities: Toward a Refined Racial Economy Perspective. The Professional Geographer 61(2: 139–149.

Wolf, Eric R. 1982. *Europe and the People without History*. Berkeley: University of California Press.

Wynter, Sylvia. 1979. "Sambos and Minstrels." *Social Text* 1: 149–156.

Wynter, Sylvia. 1984. "The Ceremony Must Be Found: After Humanism." *boundary 2* 12(3): 19–70.

Wynter, Sylvia. 2003. "Unsettling the Coloniality of Being/Power/Truth/Freedom: Towards the Human, After Man, Its Overrepresentation–An Argument." *New Centennial Review* 3(3): 257–337.

Wynter, Sylvia. 2005. "On How We Mistook the Map for the Territory, and Reimprisoned Ourselves in Our Unbearable Wrongness of Being, of Desêtre: Black Studies Toward the Human Project." In *I Am Because We Are: Readings in Africana Philosophy*, edited by Fred Lee Hord, Mzee Lasana Okpara, and Jonathan Scott Lee, 267–280. Amherst: University of Massachusetts Press.

Yashar, Deborah J. 2005. *Contesting Citizenship in Latin America: The Rise of Indigenous Movements and the Post-liberal Challenge*. Cambridge: Cambridge University Press.

Index

Anthony Russell Jerry is assistant professor at the University of California, Riverside. He is the author of "'The First Time I Heard the Word': The 'N-Word' as a Present and Persistent Racial Epithet," in *Transforming Anthropology*, and "From Colonial Subjects to Postcolonial Citizens? Considerations for a Contemporary Study of Black México," in *Third World Quarterly*.

NEW WORLD DIASPORAS

Edited by Kevin A. Yelvington

This series seeks to stimulate critical perspectives on diaspora processes in the New World. Representations of race and ethnicity, the origins and consequences of nationalism, migratory streams and the advent of transnationalism, the dialectics of homelands and diasporas, trade networks, gender relations in immigrant communities, the politics of displacement and exile, and the utilization of the past to serve the present are among the phenomena addressed by original, provocative research in disciplines such as anthropology, history, political science, and sociology.

More Than Black: Afro-Cubans in Tampa, by Susan D. Greenbaum (2002)
Carnival and the Formation of a Caribbean Transnation, by Philip W. Scher (2003)
Dominican Migration: Transnational Perspectives, edited by Ernesto Sagás and Sintia E. Molina (2004)
Salvadoran Migration to Southern California: Redefining El Hermano Lejano, by Beth Baker-Cristales (2004)
The Chrysanthemum and the Song: Music, Memory, and Identity in the South American Japanese Diaspora, by Dale A. Olsen (2004)
Andean Diaspora: The Tiwanaku Colonies and the Origins of South American Empire, by Paul S. Goldstein (2005)
Migration and Vodou, by Karen E. Richman (2005; first paperback edition, 2008; second paperback edition, 2018)
True-Born Maroons, by Kenneth M. Bilby (2005)
The Tears of Hispaniola: Haitian and Dominican Diaspora Memory, by Lucía M. Suárez (2006)
Dominican-Americans and the Politics of Empowerment, by Ana Aparicio (2006)
Nuer-American Passages: Globalizing Sudanese Migration, by Dianna J. Shandy (2006)
Religion and the Politics of Ethnic Identity in Bahia, Brazil, by Stephen Selka (2007)
Reconstructing Racial Identity and the African Past in the Dominican Republic, by Kimberly Eison Simmons (2009)
Haiti and the Haitian Diaspora in the Wider Caribbean, edited by Philippe Zacaïr (2010)
From Douglass to Duvalier: U.S. African Americans, Haiti, and Pan Americanism, 1870–1964, by Millery Polyné (2010)
New Immigrants, New Land: A Study of Brazilians in Massachusetts, by Ana Cristina Braga Martes (2010)
Yo Soy Negro: Blackness in Peru, by Tanya Maria Golash-Boza (2011; first paperback edition, 2012)

Trance and Modernity in the Southern Caribbean: African and Hindu Popular Religions in Trinidad and Tobago, by Keith E. McNeal (2011; first paperback edition, 2015)

Kosher Feijoada and Other Paradoxes of Jewish Life in São Paulo, by Misha Klein (2012; first paperback edition, 2016)

African-Brazilian Culture and Regional Identity in Bahia, Brazil, by Scott Ickes (2013; first paperback edition, 2015)

Islam and the Americas, edited by Aisha Khan (2015; first paperback edition, 2017)

Building a Nation: Caribbean Federation in the Black Diaspora, by Eric D. Duke (2016; first paperback edition, 2018)

Tampa: Impressions of an Emigrant, by Wenceslao Gálvez y Delmonte, Translation by Noel M. Smith, Introduction and Notes by Noel M. Smith and Andrew T. Huse (2020)

Blackness in Mexico: Afro-Mexican Recognition and the Production of Citizenship in the Costa Chica, by Anthony Russell Jerry (2023)